DRUGS, MONEY, AND SECRET HANDSHAKES

In the warped world of prescription drug pricing, generic drugs can cost more than branded ones, old drugs can be relaunched at astronomical prices, and low-cost options are shut out of the market. In *Drugs, Money and Secret Handshakes*, Robin Feldman shines a light into the dark corners of the pharmaceutical industry to expose a web of shadowy deals in which higher-priced drugs receive favorable treatment and patients are channeled toward the most expensive medicines. At the center of this web are the highly secretive middle players who establish coverage levels for patients and negotiate with drug companies. By offering lucrative payments to these middle players (as well as to doctors and hospitals), drug companies ensure that inexpensive drugs never gain traction. This system of perverse incentives has delivered the kind of exorbitant drug prices - and profits - that everyone loves except for those who pay the bills.

ROBIN FELDMAN is the Arthur J. Goldberg Distinguished Professor of Law at the University of California Hastings. She is an award-winning scholar whose work has been called 'absolutely remarkable' and a 'must read'. Feldman has published four books and more than fifty articles, and she has been cited by the White House and members of Congress. In 2017, she participated in the GAO's report to Congress on Artificial Intelligence and in an Army Cyber Institute threatcasting exercise on weaponization of data.

D0075446

Drugs, Money, and Secret Handshakes

THE UNSTOPPABLE GROWTH OF PRESCRIPTION DRUG PRICES

Robin Feldman
University of California Hastings College of the Law

CAMBRIDGE
UNIVERSITY PRESS

CAMBRIDGE
UNIVERSITY PRESS

University Printing House, Cambridge CB2 8BS, United Kingdom

One Liberty Plaza, 20th Floor, New York, NY 10006, USA

477 Williamstown Road, Port Melbourne, VIC 3207, Australia

314–321, 3rd Floor, Plot 3, Splendor Forum, Jasola District Centre, New Delhi – 110025, India

79 Anson Road, #06–04/06, Singapore 079906

Cambridge University Press is part of the University of Cambridge.

It furthers the University's mission by disseminating knowledge in the pursuit of education, learning, and research at the highest international levels of excellence.

www.cambridge.org
Information on this title: www.cambridge.org/9781108482455
DOI: 10.1017/9781108687676

© Robin Feldman 2019

This publication is in copyright. Subject to statutory exception and to the provisions of relevant collective licensing agreements, no reproduction of any part may take place without the written permission of Cambridge University Press.

First published 2019

Printed in the United Kingdom by TJ International Ltd. Padstow Cornwall

A catalogue record for this publication is available from the British Library.

ISBN 978-1-108-48245-5 Hardback

Cambridge University Press has no responsibility for the persistence or accuracy of URLs for external or third-party internet websites referred to in this publication and does not guarantee that any content on such websites is, or will remain, accurate or appropriate.

To my husband Boris, with whom I have shared 32 wonderful years, and to the children we have been blessed to receive, Natalie, Talya, Eli, Sam, and Adam.

TABLE OF CONTENTS

FIGURES

TABLES

ACKNOWLEDGMENTS

I am deeply grateful to those who were willing to answer endless queries and provide comments on prior drafts, including Gretchen Cappio, Juliette Cubanski, Leemore Dafney, Richard Evans, Matt Gallaway, Jeremy Goldhaber-Fiebert, Jack Hoadley, Jane Horvath, Elizabeth Jex, Cheryl Johnson, Kurt Karst, Kristie LaSalle, Mark Lemley, Gretchen Obrist, Vanessa Plaister, David Rousseau, Lynn Sarko, and Henry Su. Any errors are entirely my own. I am indebted to Nanette McGuinness for incomparable proofreading. I also wish to thank Ehrik Aldana, Giora Ashkenazi, John Gray, Nicholas Massoni, Prianka Misra, Rabiah Oral, Sophia Tao, Nick Thieme, and Jennifer Wong for invaluable research assistance. Finally, I wish to express my deep gratitude to Connie Wang for her extraordinary contributions to research design and implementation. Without Connie, Chapter 5 would not have been possible.

Research for this piece was funded in part by a generous grant from the Laura and John Arnold Foundation. Portions of this work were adopted from two works, Perverse Incentives: Why Everyone Prefers High Drug Prices – Except for Those Who Pay the Bills (*Harvard Journal on Legislation* 2019) and May Your Drug Price Be Ever Green (*Journal of Law and the Biosciences* 2018) (peer-reviewed), and are included here with the permission of those journals.

In accordance with the protocols outlined in the *Harvard Journal of Law & Technology Open Letter on Ethical Norms*, all of the data from Chapter 5 is publicly available for future use by other academics through the Inter-University Consortium for Political and Social Research (ICPSR), www.icpsr.umich.edu/icpsrweb/; *see* Robin

Feldman, Mark A. Lemley, Jonathan S. Masur & Arti K. Rai, Open Letter on Ethical Norms in Intellectual Property Scholarship, 29 *Harvard J.L. & Tech.* 339, 350–52 (2016) (signed by dozens of professors). In further accordance with these protocols, funding information for the UC Hastings Institute for Innovation Law can be found at http://innovation.uchastings.edu/about/funding/.

1   INTRODUCTION

Everyone has a limit. Every budget has an end point. Although sellers would love to raise prices continually, it doesn't take fancy economics to know that, at some point, the money runs out. Why isn't that basic principle working as expected in the pharmaceutical industry? Instead, drug prices are rising continually and reaching astronomical levels, with no end in sight. In May 2018, analysts reported that a company is contemplating a US$1.5 million price tag for its new hemophilia cure.[1] (The current hemophilia therapies already cost an astounding $580,000–800,000 per year.[2]) Along the same lines, Spark Therapeutics' cure for a rare form of blindness will cost $850,000,[3] rivaling Novartis' planned $475,000 price tag for its Car-T drug Kymriah.[4]

Even outside the eye-popping headlines, prescription drug prices across the board have risen to an alarming and puzzling level. A government inspector general's report found that the high cost of brand medications for common conditions (diabetes, high cholesterol, and asthma) were the true problem for patients on Medicare.[5] In fact, pharmaceutical companies have raised the prices most sharply for commonly used medications such as these.[6] Similarly, an analyst report concluded that in 2016, the average price for a set of specialty drugs known as "orphan drugs" was $140,000 a year and the average price of ordinary drugs was almost $28,000 a year.[7]

The list price of drugs tells only part of the story, given the many rebate and discount processes that exist within the industry.[8] Nevertheless, real spending for drugs is rising as well. According to the Health and Human Services Inspector General's report, even after accounting for rebates, Medicare spending for branded drugs still rose 62 percent between 2011 and 2015.[9] Worse yet, the department responsible for Medicare and Medicaid projects that the increase in national prescription drug spending will more than double in 2018 from the prior year's significant rise.[10] In 2017, this increase in spending outpaced increased healthcare spending as a whole and the 2017–18 consumer price index (CPI).[11] All of this, despite the fact that roughly 80 percent of the prescriptions in this country are filled using generic drugs.[12]

No one would ever suggest that spending within the healthcare system follows an ordinary, rational model. The patient as consumer does not absorb the full costs of health care, given the effects of private insurance and government programs.[13] Nor does the consumer possess full information about the products purchased or the cost of choices, and even physicians may experience information gaps. Most important, the value consumers place on their own lives creates distortions that differ from buying choices in ordinary markets. Nevertheless, dollars are finite, and some limits must exist.

One can see the mounting pressure in government budgets, which are struggling to cover the cost of new, expensive medicines. If the Defense Department had treated all Veterans Administration (VA) patients infected with hepatitis C in 2015 using the breakthrough cure Sovaldi, the $12 billion cost would have accounted for 20 percent of the department's annual medical budget – just for treating a single disease.[14] With budgets in the home, patients report rationing or forgoing medications for lack of funding.[15] This is precisely the type of boundary point that should create pressure to reduce prices. And yet the rise persists.

This book analyzes and explains the phenomenon, which has puzzled modern commentators and policymakers alike. Why do drug prices stubbornly continue to rise, despite the promise of competition from generic drugs? Quite simply, the phenomenon occurs because internal incentives push every market participant toward behaviors that increase prices, knocking out the normal checks that should operate as brake-points on the market.

At the center of the system lies the highly secretive and highly concentrated industry known as "pharmacy benefit managers" (PBMs). These middle players negotiate prices between branded drug companies and those who pay the bills, arranging for rebates from various drug companies. They also establish the formularies, which are the schedules that set the terms on which patients can access particular drugs and the reimbursement rates patients will get. The PBM middle players are supposed to act to ensure good bargains for patients and health insurers, but the reality is far from that ideal. Moreover, the system is deeply hidden. The contracts between drug companies and the PBMs are a closely guarded secret, with the details known only to the drug companies and the PBMs themselves. Government entities and the private insurers who pay the bills are not permitted to see the full terms of the contracts. Even their auditors generally are not permitted full access to the contract terms.[16] Those who pay are given periodic rebates without full information regarding the actual net pricing for any particular drugs. Markets thrive on information, and, from the standpoint of competition, such an industry design is problematic.

Despite the extreme secrecy, details have begun to seep out – through case documents (including recent contract disputes among parties), government reports, reports to shareholders, state Medicaid actions, and industry insider reports. Piecing together information from these original sources, this book presents – for the first time – a full picture of the perverse profit-taking incentive structures in the industry. The book demonstrates the way in which encouraging consumers to use drugs with higher prices operates in the interests of so many players – including doctors, clinics, hospitals, PBMs, brand drug companies, health plans, patient assistance programs, and patient advocacy groups. Payment flows are structured so that higher prices benefit the intermediaries who should be the watchdogs for the patients. Given these incentive structures, higher-priced drugs receive more favorable reimbursement treatment, and patients are channeled toward more expensive drugs.

The system also operates to support competition-free zones for pharmaceutical companies. The perverse incentive structures allow pharmaceutical companies to share monopoly profits with parties at each level of the market, maintaining their position at the top and ensuring that lower-priced competitors cannot knock them off their perch. In exchange for financial payoffs, structured in different ways to appeal to different groups, drug companies can ensure that, as lower-priced substitutes enter the market, those firms cannot gain a foothold.

The system fits within a larger framework in which drug companies block competitors – even paying them to stay off the market for periods of time. It is a win–win for everyone – except, of course, for consumers, taxpayers, and society in general.

Thus, this book describes the way in which the system creates incentives for prices to rise unchecked and for consumers and taxpayers to experience harm. The book also proposes approaches to better align incentives and analyzes the flaws in some popular proposals. Specifically, Chapter 2 of the book describes the extent of the rising prices and economic effects. Chapter 3 describes how incentive structures in place for PBM middle players and insurance companies drive prices higher. Chapter 4 explains how incentive structures in place for pharmacies, doctors, and patient groups drive prices higher. Chapter 5 explains the broader framework within which drug companies keep lower-priced competitors out, demonstrating that, in the process, companies are largely recycling and repurposing old drugs, rather than creating new ones. Chapter 6 suggests how to begin realigning the industry's incentives with society's interests. Each chapter begins with a short summary, for those who like to skip around.

2 THE LANDSCAPE

2.1 BRANDED PRESCRIPTION DRUGS

Research and development in the pharmaceutical industry is a long and arduous affair. Scholars disagree over the full extent of the cost to bring a drug to market. Nevertheless, no matter how one slices the numbers, it takes many years, and the cost is substantial, with estimates ranging from US$161 million to $2.5 billion for a single drug to get to market.[1]

The pharmaceutical industry in the United States has introduced extraordinary advances in health care. One cannot overemphasize the major life improvements over the last century that flow from innovation in prescription medications, including new life-saving antibiotics, treatments for pain, psychopharmacological treatments, and cancer drugs. As one physician pointed out to me, former US President Jimmy Carter is now approaching three years since his diagnosis with metastatic cancer, thanks to a drug that did not exist a decade ago. Pharmaceuticals also constitute a major export for the United States, with domestic companies accounting for 45 percent of the global market.[2]

To incentivize this substantial and uncertain investment, new drugs are generally protected by a patent, which prevents others from copying the drug and competing in the market. Other regulatory awards, for activities such as engaging in new studies or pediatric analyses, can extend that protection for limited periods of time.[3] When the various patent and regulatory protections that allow a period of time for recoupment of investment have expired, the Hatch-Waxman system for approval of generic drugs steps in to expedite the entry of generic competitors.[4]

Not all patent-protected drugs represent major healthcare innovations. Some are merely combinations of existing medications that can be purchased for less individually, such as Treximet, a migraine medicine that combines an old migraine medicine and naproxen.[5] Others are tweaks of existing medicines, with dosage or delivery system altered in an effort to obtain additional protection.[6] As detailed in Chapter 5, the patent and exclusivity system, unfortunately, incentivizes this type of behavior.

The price of a generic drug averages 75–90 percent below the cost of the original branded drug.[7] This price reduction tends to happen across time, with the largest reduction occurring as more generic drugs become available on the market.[8] This, of course, is when the generic market is working at its best, which is not always the case. Some scholars have observed generic drugs experiencing high prices or sharp price increases.[9]

During the period of protection for a branded drug, however, monopoly pricing reigns. There may be drugs within the same general class of medications that can serve as therapeutic alternatives, but most branded drug companies enjoy considerable freedom in setting the price in the United States. With any commodity in a monopoly price setting, of course, the upper bounds of pricing are set by the limits of the budgetary capacity of those consuming the product.[10] No budget is endless, and all goods must compete to some extent with other items in the consumer's basket. After all, I will pay only what I am willing to pay – I want to provide for my family and go to the movies once in a while – and what I can afford to pay – I have to eat, keep a roof over my head, and buy a coat so I can survive in the winter.

Health, however, is no ordinary expenditure, and the healthcare industry is an odd market.[11] Although patients are the ultimate consumers of prescription drugs, they lack full information and may be insulated from the full costs in a variety of ways.[12] For example, employer-provided health insurance is subsidized by federal and state governments, in the form of tax advantages for the employers and employees.[13] Insurance itself can insulate users from the full costs of their care, spreading the cost across a pool of other workers and across time. For many of those without a connection to employment, Medicare, Medicaid, government health plans, and other government programs absorb much or all of the cost.

The patient also suffers from an information disadvantage in health care, relying on the expertise of healthcare professionals. With prescription medication in particular, consumers are not able to make the purchasing choice; rather, the physician makes the ultimate decision regarding what to prescribe. And, as will be described in detail below, the purchasing preference for both doctor and patient may be influenced by the insurer's willingness to reimburse for the medication, as well as by less savory aspects, including direct-to-consumer advertising[14] and drug companies courting physicians.[15] Accurate information on both the price and quality of healthcare services can benefit consumers, both by helping them to become better shoppers and also by spurring competition among providers along both price and quality dimensions.[16] However, delivering that information in an easily understandable format – and one that is not drowned out by other messages such as advertising – can be challenging.[17]

Most important, buying decisions for health care do not follow ordinary economic logic, stretching the boundaries of rationality.[18] My own life may be of incalculable value to me – well beyond what my budget or society's budget can rationally afford. That may be true even when the likelihood of successful treatment is low or the additional lifespan provided is no more than weeks or months.[19] And when someone else is paying the bill, the value to me, measured by my willingness to consume the good, could become infinite. Of course, not all prescription drug buying decisions are a matter of life and death, but the general irrationality of health decisions can distort ordinary purchase choices in a society whose citizens generally exist well beyond the subsistence level. All of this suggests that the normal budgetary limitations that a monopolist might face have less force in the healthcare system.

Even within the distorted world of health care, however, prescription drug prices stand out, rising faster than any other form of healthcare spending, including hospitalization and nursing home care.[20] In a 2017 report to Congress, the Medicare Payment Advisory Commission (MedPac), a nonpartisan legislative branch agency, reported that, between 2006 and 2014, drug prices in Medicare Part D rose by an average of 57 percent cumulatively, with dramatic increases in 2013–14 in particular.[21] One industry report for 2016 projected that prescription drug prices would rise 11.6 percent for Americans younger than 65 and 9.9 percent for older adults, compared to wage increases projected for that year of 2.5 percent.[22]

Some price rises stand out in particular. A report from the U.S. Government Accountability Office estimated that, between 2000 and 2008 alone, 416 branded products displayed extraordinary price increases.[23] Those increases mostly ranged from 100 percent to 499 percent.[24]

Such price increases are driven by rising prices in branded medications. According to the generic pharmaceutical industry group, although branded drugs account for only 11 percent of prescription volume in the country, they account for 74 percent of the spending.[25] Thus, although the pharmaceutical industry correctly points out that generic medications represent most of the prescription volume in this country, and the U.S. Food and Drug Administration (FDA) approves a vast number of new generics every year,[26] the year-to-year increases in the prices of branded drugs, along with higher prices for new branded drugs, are swamping the savings from generic competition.[27]

Consider, first, list prices. The list prices for branded medications continue to rise sharply. The list prices for branded drugs rose 12.4 percent in 2015 and increased 10 percent or more annually for each of the prior three years.[28] Although there may be some moderation in pricing as a result of public pressure, the general trend of increasing prices appears likely to hold for the foreseeable future. For example, Eli Lilly's transparency report noted that the company raised list prices 14 percent on average in 2016;[29] Allergan increased its list prices for 18 medications by 9.5 percent.[30]

These price increases have played a significant role in drug company profits in recent years. For example, the *Wall Street Journal* reported in 2015 that 80 percent of the growth in profits for the 20 largest drug companies were the result of increasing prices on existing drugs, not of new drugs or increased drug sales.[31]

In general, the price rises are most dramatic in a category called "specialty drugs." Neither the industry nor the federal government's Centers for Medicare and Medicaid Services (CMS) has a consistent definition of "specialty drug," but the category tends to include drugs that are used to treat a rare condition, require special handling, use a limited distribution network, or require ongoing clinical assessment.[32] Some drugs are categorized as "specialty," however, simply because their cost exceeds $10,000 a year.[33] The National Academy of Sciences (NAS) reports that, over the last five years, spending on specialty medicines has nearly doubled, outpacing the consumer price index (CPI) from 2011 and 2013, and composing more than two-thirds of growth in drug spending between 2010 and 2015.[34] The 2016 annual report from Express Scripts PBM projects that 1 percent of all drugs will account for 50 percent of the drug spend because of higher-cost specialty medicines.[35] In other words, more of the drug spend is flowing into the specialty drug category.

List prices, of course, are only the beginning of the story. Drug companies enter into a variety of contracts that provide for rebates from the list price. Although these price concessions are a closely guarded secret, and it is difficult to tease out the actual net price that different entities pay along the drug chain,[36] the net price paid to the drug company is substantially less than the list price.[37] For example, in defending against complaints about rising drug prices, industry group PhRMA reported at a Federal Trade Commission (FTC) roundtable that, after accounting for rebates and discounts, prices grew only 3.5 percent in 2016.[38] Similarly, a leading analysis group estimates that, although list prices increased 13.5 percent in 2014, the net price increase was only 5.5 percent.[39] Even these net price increases, how-ever, outstrip the inflation rate over the last five years, which has ranged from a low of less than 1 percent in 2014 and 2015 to a high of 2 percent for 2016 and 2017, with the same projected for 2018.[40] In other words, even assuming that everyone pays discounted prices, rather than full list prices, the discounted prices are still rising far more rapidly than inflation.

Many people, however, *do* pay the full list price. Private insurance plans often require that patients contribute an amount based on a percentage of the full list price of the drug.[41] Other plans require that patients pay the total price of medications at the list price until patients meet an individual or family deductible.[42] Specifically, nearly 30 per-cent of those enrolled in employer-sponsored healthcare plans have high-deductible plans in which patients pay 100 percent of their

healthcare costs up to a defined amount.[43] Other plans require substantial deductibles or co-pays, with studies showing dramatic reductions in coverage and increased cost-sharing burdens for higher-priced
drugs across time.[44] Even when full Medicare coverage is in place,
patients must pay part of the cost of medications, with gaps occurring
that can force patients to pay the majority of costs.[45] These amounts
are largely based on the list price and not the net price of the medication, thus depriving consumers of the benefit of the rebate price
concessions.

In addition, although the number of people with health insurance
increased substantially after passage of the Affordable Care Act of
2010,[46] 10 percent of those under the age of 65 in the United States
still had no insurance in 2017, and not all of those who had health
insurance enjoyed prescription drug coverage.[47] Even with Medicare,
12 percent of beneficiaries are neither enrolled in prescription drug
coverage nor covered by another prescription plan such as veteran's
benefits.[48] Thus cash-paying consumers who lack sufficient drug
benefits also pay the exaggerated list price. And, of course, when
prices rise year after year, rebates have less meaning in real dollar
terms. A 10 percent rebate on a price that has risen 20 percent in
recent years is not much of a bargain. As a result, the total out-of-
pocket amount that US consumers are spending on medication continues to rise sharply.[49]

Against this backdrop, drug companies have retained a healthy
profit margin. Gross profits on brand drugs are roughly 76 percent.[50]
In addition, despite the costs of research and development, drug
company profits are rising overall. Eli Lilly, for example, saw a 6 percent increase in revenue and a 14 percent increase in net income
between 2015 and 2016.[51]

The pharmacy benefit manager (PBM) industry also enjoys a
healthy and rapidly expanding balance sheet. For example, Express
Scripts, one of the three major PBMs, reports a steady increase in its
net income, climbing from $1,898 million in 2013 to $3,404 million in
2016 – an increase of 79.3 percent.[52] Diluted earnings per share more
than doubled over the same period, increasing from $2.31 to $5.39.[53]
Similarly, OptumRx reported operating profits of $2.7 billion in 2016,
up from $1.7 billion the prior year.[54]

2.2 THE BYZANTINE WORLD OF DRUG SALES

Health insurance plays a key role in paying for prescription drugs, with most people in the United States having some form of plan that covers medicine. Such health insurance flows from both public and private plans, including:

- employer-sponsored health insurance and individually purchased plans, such as those offered by Cigna, Anthem, Blue Cross, or Kaiser Permanente;
- Medicare for those over the age of 65;
- Medicaid for those below a certain level of income;
- government employee plans, including Veterans Administration (VA) benefits, as well as plans for federal, state, and local workers;
- government insurance that provides health care to prisoners; and
- state health insurance sold in exchanges established under the Affordable Care Act.

State Medicare and Medicaid plans are funded by the federal government but are administered by each individual state, generally through health insurance companies.[55] In addition, state and federal employee plans are generally operated by insurance companies, such as Cigna, Anthem, Blue Cross, Kaiser Permanente, etc. Employer plans may operate through private health insurance companies, through what are known as "self-insured plans," or a combination of a private plan and self-insurance – a route taken by some prominent companies such as Google and Walmart.[56]

2.2.1 What Is a Pharmacy Benefit Manager?

With each of the forms of insurance, there is a significant middle player who negotiates between drug companies and those who pay the bills, whether the payors are insurance companies, self-funding employers, or Medicare/Medicaid systems. The middle players are known as "pharmacy benefit managers" (PBMs).[57] (If you are hoping for simple, intuitive names to help you to figure out "Who's on first,"[58] the healthcare industry will always disappoint you.)

Pharmacy benefit managers negotiate drug prices on behalf of their health plan clients. The PBMs leverage the volume of demand from patients within an insurance plan to negotiate price concessions from a drug company. In other words, the PBM says to the drug company, "I will deliver a large volume of patients to you under this health insurance plan, if you will give a large rebate."[59] In Chapter 2 and throughout the book, the term "drug companies" refers to drug manufacturers – that is, the companies that make the medicines – as opposed to wholesalers.

In theory, PBMs use their negotiating leverage, along with their knowledge of things such as the post-rebate prices on similar drugs that drug companies have offered to their various clients in the past, to negotiate the lowest possible prices for their clients. As benchmarks for these negotiations, the parties generally use the national average wholesale price (AWP),[60] which refers to the average price a company charged for its drug at the wholesale level. Drug companies report the information to commercial third-party data companies.[61] These AWPs are published by these third parties and are commonly called "list prices."

Some refer to AWP as "Ain't What's Paid," because the figure does not include reductions for rebates or discounts. What's more, the figure is neither verified nor regulated, and the U.S. Department of Health and Human Services has noted disparities among these related indexes.[62] In addition, lawsuits have alleged collusion between the commercial publishers of AWP information and wholesalers to artificially inflate those numbers, increasing the markup spreads for the wholesalers.[63]

The constantly shifting – and unverified – price lists used by PBMs contribute to the opacity of the system, masking the nature of the transactions occurring. For example, a recently unsealed complaint in a whistleblower case provides a fascinating glimpse of possible price list manipulations at the PBM Caremark.[64] In simplified form, the complaint alleges that Caremark repeatedly adjusted the lists used to establish the reference prices for drugs, making it appear that patients always received precisely the discount that had been promised.[65] The scheme allegedly allowed the PBM to defraud Medicare and to pocket a greater return.[66]

A PBM's contract with a drug company can include complicated calculations of concessions and volume-based rebates. These will be measured periodically by reference to items such as the total volume of drugs purchased, the number of product prescriptions filled, or maintaining or exceeding the prior year's percentage of an insurer's patients who filled their prescriptions in that drug class with that drug.[67] In other words, deliver more heads (or "lives," in healthcare lingo), and drug companies will offer more attractive terms to the PBM.

The PBMs also manage each health plan client's drug reimbursement claims and help each client to establish formularies. Formularies are the lists of drugs for which a health plan will reimburse patients. An insurer typically is required to cover at least one drug in each class of medications, but it is not required to include all drugs within a class.[68] Exceptions exist in the Medicare system, for which insurance plans are required to cover all drugs within the protected classes of antiretrovirals, antidepressants, antipsychotics, anticonvulsants, immunosuppressants, and antineoplastics.[69]

Insurance plans also require different levels of patient cost sharing for different drugs, managing these through what are known as "formulary tiers."[70] In one of the most significant aspects of the system, the PBM, together with the insurance plan, decides which drugs to include on which tier of the insurer's formulary. This includes establishing the incentives (and barriers to utilization) that will drive patients toward particular drug options.[71] Historically, healthcare economists and policymakers presumed that formularies would drive patients toward generic drugs and lower-cost options. Recent evidence suggests that is not the case.

2.2.2 What Insurers Don't Know

As strange as it may seem, the insurance companies – which are the payors in this system – generally do not know the actual net price paid for individual drugs.[72] How is it possible that insurers such as Blue Cross and companies such as Walmart never know the net prices of the drugs they are paying for? Quite simply, that information is a fiercely guarded secret. The contracts between PBMs and drug manufacturers are claimed as trade secrets and staunchly protected, even from a

PBM's own health insurance client.[73] In some cases, the contract between the health insurance plan and the PBM offers minimal audit rights. When audit rights are granted and the plan exercises those rights, the plan's auditors are likely to be denied full access to the PBM's drug company contracts, even for the limited purpose of confirming that the plan's own contracts are being carried out as negotiated.[74] One insurance industry consultant describes the situation as "buying blind."[75]

In addition, as Chapter 3 describes in detail, health plans have difficulty ferreting out the per-unit price they are paying for a particular drug across all purchases, let alone on a particular purchase. That information is tucked within the folds of complex data and contractual calculations, including rebates that may flow – in whole or in part – to the health plan later in the year.[76] Here is how it works: The health plan knows how much it pays to the pharmacy at the moment the patient buys the drug,[77] but that payment reflects the list price. The PBM will send a rebate check to the plan later in the year – a check that may represent many drugs and many transactions. Thus, the actual price of a particular drug transaction is buried within payments that the health plan receives in large chunks some time later. The plan never knows the net price that the drug company receives from the PBM.

2.2.3 Concentration in the PBM Industry

The PBM industry is highly concentrated. Three PBMs – Express Scripts, CVS Health, and OptumRX – dominate 85 percent of the commercial insurance market.[78] In an indication of the power of the big three outside that market, the three major PBMs reportedly also handled 50 percent of the prescription drug benefits for the Medicaid managed-care population in 2015.[79] Further exacerbating the problem of concentration is the use of a small group of PBM consultants, who offer advice to the PBM clients on going rates, based on databases of prices and formulary costs. These consultants provide a potential source of collusion, in which the PBM competitors do not need to speak to each other, but can nevertheless converge on similar prices and terms.

A number of PBMs also have acquired their own pharmacies. Patients may be offered preferred deals at those pharmacies or, in some cases, required to purchase certain types of drug from the PBM's own pharmacies. In the 1990s, some drug companies acquired PBMs, although the FTC eventually required the drug companies to effectively unwind some aspects of those acquisitions, citing competition concerns.[80] Of even greater concern would be a drug company purchasing a health insurer or forming some form of joint venture. The industry flirted with that type of arrangement in the 1990s.[81] Nothing came to fruition, however, perhaps as a result of FTC scrutiny of competition in the industry.[82]

Consider the following competition risk of a drug company alliance with a health insurer. DrugCo, with a 30 percent market share in a drug, offers to underwrite capitation for a health insurer. In other words, DrugCo agrees to take on the burden of paying a group of doctors or healthcare providers a certain amount per enrolled patient, regardless of whether or how much the enrolled patient seeks care. Many health maintenance organizations (HMOs) are structured on a capitation basis, for example.[83] In exchange, the health insurer would agree to give DrugCo a 40 percent market share. In this manner, DrugCo could purchase a greater market share.

2.2.4 How the Money Flows

Pharmacy benefit managers are paid by their insurance company clients, with contracts that have their own complex calculation categories. In addition to those payments, PBMs may keep all or part of the rebate money that drug makers send. Finally, PBMs may receive administrative, software, or data fees from pharmaceutical companies, as well as fees for other services rendered to the pharmaceutical companies.[84]

Pharmacies themselves operate as an additional middle layer within the drug supply chain. Pharmacists are on the front lines of filling prescriptions and providing information for customers. They mark up the price of the drug by a dispensing fee amount, collecting that total from a combination of payments from the patient (reflecting co-pay or co-insurance amounts)[85] and payments from the insurance

U.S. Distribution and Reimbursement System: Patient-Administered, Outpatient Drugs

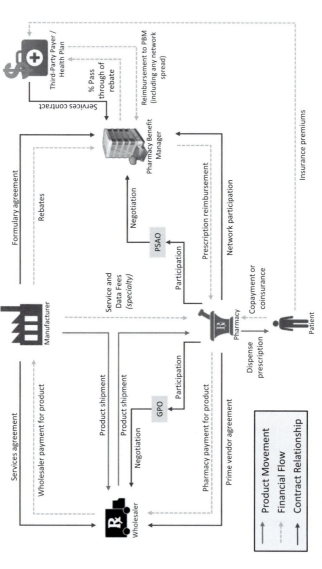

GPO = Group Purchasing Organization; PSAO = Pharmacy Services Administrative Organization
Source. Fein, Adam J., *The 2018 Economic Report on U.S. Pharmacies and Pharmacy Benefit Managers*, Drug Channels Institute, 2018. Chart illustrates flows for Patient-Administered, Outpatient Drugs. Please note that this chart is illustrative. It is not intended to be a complete representation of every type of product movement, financial flow, or contractual relationship in the marketplace.

Figure 2.1 Flow of payments through the pharmaceutical supply chain[89]

plan.[86] State substitution laws govern the circumstances in which a pharmacist may substitute a generic version of the brand product, when the prescription is written for the brand.[87] The pharmacist, however, cannot substitute a drug that is not the approved generic for that brand, even if a therapeutically similar drug is less expensive.[88]

Figure 2.1 illustrates the flow of payments throughout the drug supply chain, including pharmaceutical companies, wholesalers, PBMs, patients, and third-party insurance payors.

2.2.5 All in the Public's Best Interest

In theory, the system is designed so that, at numerous points throughout the drug distribution system, the incentives align in favor of obtaining the lowest-cost drug for the patient. The job of the PBM, historically, has been to provide valuable services to the health insurance plans by providing the lowest-cost and highest-quality drug benefit for each plan – whether public or private. Insurers should be able to use their volume-buying power to obtain rebates that individual patients could never obtain on their own. Insurers also should be motivated to obtain good pricing structures and lower premiums, in order to compete in the market for patient enrollees. Pharmacists, who know the prices of the drugs in their stock and see the patient's cost-sharing amounts at the cash register, should be able to give patients information on how to find the best deal and should be motivated to provide those deals so that patients can afford their medicines.

In addition, the norms of the medical profession obligate doctors to make decisions in the best interests of the patient,[90] while public interest groups should be motivated to step in and nudge the system in healthier directions. Finally, all of this occurs against the backdrop of a national policy to expedite and encourage vigorous competition through the rapid entry of generic drugs as soon as patents expire.[91]

Something, however, is not working in the system.

3 PHARMACY BENEFIT MANAGERS AND INSURERS

As described in Chapter 2, in a competitive market, the incentive structures should operate to create competition and keep prices in check. The reality in modern pharmaceutical markets is quite different. At numerous levels, the incentives operate to drive prices higher and reduce competition among therapeutically similar products – or what economists might call "substitute products." This includes incentives for pharmacy benefit managers (PBMs), incentives for insurers (including insurers for Medicare and other government plans), incentives for some pharmacists, doctors, and patient advocacy groups, and, of course, incentives for the drug companies themselves. Together, this alignment of incentives operates so that higher prices are a win–win for everyone – except for those who pay the bill.

3.1 WHY PBMS MAY PREFER HIGHER PRICES

The core of the incentive problem lies with the PBM system. These middle players, which establish the drug formularies and negotiate between drug companies and the insurance plans, have evolved in a manner that creates upward pressure on prices.[1] The PBMs are uniquely situated, with the bargaining power, drug information, and data to negotiate the most aggressive price concessions from drug companies. Unfortunately, PBM behavior has been distorted by reimbursement schemes that reward the PBMs most significantly when drug prices and drug spending increases. These shiny baubles distract PBMs from their original path of pursuing lower drug prices.

The problem starts with a payment structure that, on the surface, would appear to be procompetitive, but which, in reality, minimizes the pressure to reduce prices.[2] Here is how it works: Insurers pay their PBMs based on the extent of the *discount* that a PBM can negotiate with individual drug companies.[3] In other words, the greater the distance between the list price and the final price, the more money a PBM makes.[4] In theory, this might encourage PBMs to drive prices down, given that their pay is directly tied to the level of discounts and rebates.[5] In reality, the incentives are operating to drive prices higher. Drug companies have developed a pretty simple trick: Instead of giving a greater discount, the drug company raises the prices.

Think of the following analogy. Suppose you are a broker, and a customer says to you, "Go negotiate a cheap price on a new Mercedes for me. I'll let you keep half of the discount."

Then imagine that when you go in to negotiate, the car dealer says to you, "Hey, I'll just raise all my prices. So when your customer pays the old price, it counts as a *big* discount, and you get to keep a nice chunk of change. Sounds pretty good, no?"

It is a little like a department store that raises prices right before the sale, so that the sale discount looks more appealing.

In this manner, the drug company can offer a sweeter deal to a PBM, without absorbing the full cost of that sweetener. Moreover, the contract between the PBM and the insurance plan is based on the rebate level the parties think the PBM will be able to negotiate, while the insurance plan is never permitted to know the actual level of that rebate. If the rebate is more than the companies anticipated, the PBM pockets that difference as well.

Contracts with PBMs have been reported to last as long as seven years, while drug companies change their prices at least annually and sometimes more frequently.[6] On the one hand, this shifts risk to the PBM to ensure that it can constantly deliver at least the rebate for which it has contracted with its insurance client; on the other hand, drug companies and PBMs together use the system to increase revenue to the drug firm and income to the PBM by raising list prices.

One need not ascribe any sinister motive to drug companies: Drug companies have simply found a way of operating within the system to their own greatest advantage. Can we really expect anything different from profit-making enterprises?

In addition to rebates, drug companies offer payments to PBMs in the form of administrative fees or data-managing fees.[7] These administrative fees do not have to be reported to the health insurance plans or included in any type of payments that flow through to the plan or to the patient. Increasingly, drug companies are offering creative fees for "services," such as providing research and information to the drug company.[8] These fees have the advantage of being invisible to the insurers in certain circumstances. Even when a drug company pays for services from a PBM, if the value of the service is substantially less than the payment made, the transaction is simply an indirect price concession. Once again, raising list prices can leave room for the drug company to offer these goodies without reducing the drug company's net income from sales of the drug. And, of course, many people will be forced to pay the higher list prices.[9]

As a transfer of money from the drug company to the PBM, these payments reduce the drug company's net income from sales of the drug and increase the PBM revenue related to a specific drug. In this manner, the drug company shares some of its monopoly rent with the PBM. Together, the rebates and other transfers of value can be called "persuasion payments."

So what does a drug company get in return? As an outcome of this complex process of payments and inducements, the drug company's product may be placed in an advantageous position on the PBM formulary,[10] or the PBM may even entirely exclude a competing drug in the same class from being reimbursed at all.[11] Consider documents recently submitted to the U.S. Senate Committee on Finance. These show that, in 2014, PBM Express Scripts negotiated a significant rebate from AbbVie on its hepatitis C drug in exchange for giving that drug an exclusive position on its formulary.[12] Thus, the PBM agreed to completely exclude the two competing drugs. The Senate documents also note that some states followed suit, awarding AbbVie's drug a preferred position on their formulary in light of the fact that "AbbVie submitted more aggressive rebates."[13]

If the rebates were operating to reduce prices, resulting in the plan choosing the lowest price drug, one might have reason to celebrate. However, the aggressive rebates may simply contribute to a greater profit for the middle players, while real prices remain at the same level or higher. Worse yet, as detailed below, lower-priced competitors may be blocked out. In those circumstances – hold the champagne.

In these deals between the drug company and the PBM, the rebate, or the size of the rebate, may be conditioned on the PBM's client purchasing a certain volume of the drug. All of the various payments can be structured as volume discounts, loyalty discounts, or market penetration rebates.

When a drug company has a portfolio of drugs to offer, the opportunities for blocking competition increase. Consider a drug company that has three drugs, and imagine that two of the drugs are strongly buttressed against competition, perhaps protected by strong patents or regulatory exclusivities or perhaps because there is no competitor on the horizon. The company's third drug is vulnerable to competition, either because its patents and exclusivities have expired or because the remaining patents are weak, secondary ones.[14] The company can bargain so that the weaker drug receives an exclusive or preferred position on the formulary.

For example, in 2015, AstraZeneca entered into a small settlement with the U.S. Department of Justice regarding its drug Nexium.[15] The case alleged that AstraZeneca provided rebates to a PBM in exchange for giving Nexium sole and exclusive status on formularies.[16] The case also alleged that, as part of the deal, the drug company gave price concessions on other drugs, including Prilosec.[17] At the time, the drug company was already engaged in shifting the market away from Prilosec to Nexium. Thus, the drug company was giving price concessions on a drug that it was intending to drive patients away from, in exchange for exclusive status on the drug that it was driving patients toward. In the end, the price concessions for Prilosec would not hurt the company and would provide little benefit to the PBM's insurance client.[18] The price concessions would, however, provide a tidy profit for the PBM. And, of course, the entire deal would keep the market clear of any lower-priced competitors.

In a well-functioning market, companies engage in price competition. With pharmaceuticals, however, the incentives are turned entirely upside down: Companies compete not by lowering their prices, but by raising their prices.

3.1.1 The Power of Volume

The name of the game in this bargaining is volume. Volume rebates provide a significant advantage to entrenched market participants at the expense of lower-priced entrants. The more volume rebates a drug firm can offer the PBM, the better the deal it can command to exclude its rivals. It is a little like Budweiser approaching a bar owner, saying: "Okay, at the end of the year, I'll pay you 50 cents a bottle if you've sold 40,000 bottles of Bud. Better yet, I'll make it $1 a bottle if you don't put any of that microbrewery's beer on the menu."

If the microbrewery sells a limited number of bottles, how could it ever compete? The microbrewery could never offer enough off the price of its few beers to compensate for the tens of thousands of dollars the bar owner would forgo by rejecting Budweiser's offer. The point is simply the following: The greater a drug's volume, the more the drug company can spread out a persuasion payment across each unit of the drug sold.[19]

These rebate schemes do not necessarily aim for exclusivity in the market or even for massive increases in the market. If a drug company has a 50 percent market share, it may be irrationally expensive (or legally impossible) to extract too much additional market share. For example, if the competing drug is not a perfect substitute, some patients simply will refuse to switch, supported by laws that require a plan to continue coverage for patients who remain with their original drug under certain circumstances.[20]

Other patients may choose to pay for their original drug out of pocket, which could prevent the PBM from reaching the volume required for the best rebate payments. In those circumstances, the drug company would have to spread its persuasion payments across fewer units, thereby increasing the cost per unit of such payments.

At the end of the day, the cost of moving to complete market dominance simply may be too high. Recall that the PBM is paid by the health plan based on the amount of discount. If low-priced generics have gained a significant foothold – perhaps the branded drug now has only 50 percent of the market, rather than 80 percent of the market – the drug company that wants to knock out those generics will have to pay a fortune to compensate the PBM for the income it will lose by walking away from the cheaper drug.

With each of these circumstances – imperfect substitutes, coverage continuation laws, patients paying out of pocket, and lower market share – or a combination of these circumstances, a company could simply aim to increase its market share by 10 or 15 percent. This type of behavior may be more difficult to measure in traditional federal antitrust terms. In the tying context, for example, federal antitrust law tends to categorize behavior as inappropriate only when it rises to the level of attempts at market dominance, rather than smaller increases in market share.[21] Unfortunately, consumers, not to mention competition, may be suffering at an earlier point.

The volume rebate barriers are particularly problematic in combination with gaming of the patent system and other aspects of the drug approval process – behaviors that can create barriers to entry.[22] When a drug's patent or other regulatory exclusivities expire, lower-priced generic competitors should be able to enter the market quickly and drive prices down.[23] The brand-name company, however, is likely to have enjoyed unfettered access to markets, so that, when the patent expires, the company holds a majority of market share, if not total market dominance.[24] Given the advantages of volume in the PBM system, competitors may be unable to break through and gain more than limited market shares, despite their vastly lower prices. In short, when downstream players can receive persuasion payments per item sold, the patent and exclusivity system ensures that a new entrant that wants to drive prices down faces an existing market player whose position in the market speaks volumes.

In other words, a patent grant has a long tail. Although Hatch-Waxman was intended to help generics to overcome obstacles for getting to market, we have yet to address the forces pushing against gaining traction in that market.

Other terms in the contracts between drug companies and PBMs can further entrench a market leader. An incumbent drug company with a PBM contract may be given the right of first refusal. This would allow the drug company to match any lower price that another company may bid when requests for new bids go out.

On the flip side, the drug company could pledge its undying loyalty to the PBM: The drug company could promise that it will not offer its drug at a lower price to any other PBM or buying group.[25] Sometimes called "most-favored-nation (MFN) clauses," these agreements not only deter price competition among PBMs, but also may have the effect of setting uniform prices for drugs across the industry.

Specifically, to the extent that state or federal reimbursements are based on the lowest prices available or the average sales price of a particular drug, loyalty promises could help drug companies to maintain price levels.

The power of volume can easily get lost in translation, as policy-makers take aim at rising drug prices, and pharmaceutical companies scramble to defend themselves. For example, in March 2018, the *Wall Street Journal* published a piece on pharmaceutical company Johnson & Johnson in which the company touted declining prices for its medicines, which it attributed to "the level of competition that exists in the U.S. market."[26] The company provided aggregate pricing data to demonstrate that, while it raised list prices for its medicine by an average of 8.1 percent, the average net price fell by 4.6 percent as a result of discounts and rebates.[27] Tucked into the various statistics, however, was the fact that Johnson & Johnson's overall sales did well that year, rising 6.7 percent to $21.5 billion, which the company attributed to higher volume.[28] At the end of the day, that higher volume may be far more significant, in terms of blocking competition, than any reduction in net pricing.

Think of it from the following perspective: If the increased volume indicates an increased market share, the price concessions may simply be a vehicle for blocking out competitors who would otherwise bring the prices down to truly competitive levels. Thus we could end up celebrating a minor reduction in an astronomical price when, in the long run, we are allowing behavior that prevents competitors from bringing prices down to earth. And, of course, Johnson & Johnson's bottom line improved nicely as well, demonstrating that increasing list prices while providing rebates can be a profitable strategy.

If one magnifies that volume power across multiple drugs, a large pharmaceutical company can obtain an even greater advantage, particularly against a competitor that makes fewer drugs. The strategy employed is known as "packaged," "bundled," or "loyalty" rebates.[29] A drug company tells a PBM that, to get the best rebate, the PBM's client must accumulate a certain volume not across only one drug, but across all of the drugs. It is not enough to buy the full volume of one drug; the purchases must range across all, or several, of a drug company's drugs.

Under those terms, a competitor with only one drug may be wholly unable to offer a comparable deal. The competitor's payments to the PBM, which would be based on the price of the single drug, would have to be large enough to account for the drug payments to the PBM, based on the prices across a drug company's full stable of drugs.

Think back to the bar owner and Budweiser's offer of a better volume discount to block out the microbrewery. Imagine if Budweiser also owned the top-selling vodka and whisky: The little microbrewery could never discount enough across its limited sales to make up for the discounts across all of the beer, vodka, and whisky drinks.

The strategy may be particularly powerful when one or some of the drugs that are part of the bundle enjoy significant market share. For example, health plans are required to offer at least one drug in each class.[30] Thus, if there is only one drug in a class, insurers must offer that drug. This could happen when a drug is protected by the original patent or by strong secondary patents, which are keeping any competing drug out of the market. In that circumstance, a brand-name company could offer a break on the price of the patented product – for which there is strong protection against competition – in exchange for a preferred position for drugs that are facing competition. The competitor would not be in a position to offer a comparable deal. For example, if the government dictates that vodka must be sold and allows only one brand of vodka, and if the established company can use its vodka volume to provide a deal on its beer brand, a new beer competitor is in a tough position.

Recent examples exist in the real world of drug companies, not only the world of craft beer.[31] For example, in October 2017, Shire Pharmaceuticals sued Allergan Pharmaceuticals, alleging that Allergan used bundled rebates to block competition and preserve its dominant market share in blockbuster dry-eye medication Restasis.[32] According to the complaint, the brand drug enjoyed a complete monopoly on the preferred tier of Medicare formularies from 2002 until the U.S. Food and Drug Administration (FDA) approved the competing brand drug Xiidra. Allergan then developed this scheme to shore up its monopoly position as the competing drug emerged.[33] The complaint alleges further that the scheme has made it impossible for the new drug to gain reasonable formulary access. According to one Medicare plan administrator, given Allergan's bundling scheme, Shire could give the new drug away for free, and the numbers still wouldn't work.[34]

In a similar vein, a case filed in late 2017 alleges that Johnson & Johnson attempted to suppress competition following expiration of the patent protection on its inflammation drug Remicade.[35] Johnson & Johnson's drug dominated the market from 1998 through 2016, when Pfizer introduced the biosimilar version, Inflectra.[36] According to the complaint, just weeks after Inflectra's introduction, Johnson & Johnson began its "Biosimilar Readiness Plan," which included anticompetitive bundling, coercive rebates, and exclusionary contracts.[37] The complaint contends that Johnson & Johnson induced insurers to enter into contracts that required an explicit commitment to exclude the biosimilar completely from formularies or to provide reimbursement only in the rarest of circumstances.[38]

Tactics cited in the complaint include threatening to withhold rebates on Remicade prescriptions – from both existing and new patients – unless insurers agreed to exclusivity[39] and bundling the rebates across multiple products, so that any insurers refusing to grant Remicade exclusivity would suffer rebate losses across their drug portfolio.[40] The deals applied not only to insurers, but also to providers such as hospitals, which purportedly declined to stock the biosimilar, even though it was covered by government programs. This effectively forced the government to continue reimbursing providers for the more expensive Remicade.[41]

In the vaccine market, as opposed to medications, Sanofi paid to settle an antitrust bundling suit.[42] The suit alleged that, when a competing company planned to enter the market to compete against Sanofi's pediatric meningitis vaccine Menactra, Sanofi charged prices up to 34.5 percent higher for the vaccine unless buyers agreed to purchase all of Sanofi's vaccines exclusively.[43] Sanofi paid $61.5 million in October 2017 to settle the case, which was pending in a federal district court in New Jersey.[44]

3.1.2 Bundling Drugs – A Tried and True Idea

The idea of bundled rebates is not new: I wrote about this approach almost 20 years ago, detailing a saga that occurred in the market for a particular class of antibiotics.[45] In the 1970s, a dispute between competing pharmaceutical companies SmithKline and Eli Lilly exposed a monopolistic rebate scheme involving cephalosporin antibiotics.[46] Lilly had held a monopoly over the cephalosporin market for almost a decade when SmithKline introduced two new types of cephalosporin not covered by Lilly's patents.[47] Lilly responded by producing its own version of the new cephalosporins, along with a revised rebate plan providing optimal prices only when hospitals purchased a certain amount of at least three of Lilly's five cephalosporin options.[48] The sales representatives specifically emphasized that the rebate was an incentive to purchase Lilly drugs instead of the newer drugs and offered promotional materials showing the steep rebate that the new competitor would need to offer to match Lilly's deal.[49]

SmithKline brought an antitrust action against Eli Lilly, alleging that Lilly's marketing scheme constituted an unlawful tying device and that Lilly had committed unlawful monopolization.[50] The district court found no illegal tying arrangement. The court ruled that the competitor would have to prove that Lilly completely refused to sell the two desired drugs unless the hospital purchased the undesired third. In this case, however, buyers certainly could choose to buy the products individually and forgo the rebate.[51]

The definition of "choice" embodied in the court's analysis leaves much to be desired. At some point, the notion of what constitutes a choice is so extreme as to become absurd. For example, suppose I say, "I'm not forcing you to buy both products. You could certainly buy them separately. I will just take your first-born child as payment, if you do." Would we really say this is a choice?

And when it comes to profits – the beloved child of free enterprise – is it really a choice when the economic effects are so drastic?

Despite failing to find tying, the court did find that Lilly had monopolized the market and that the rebate scheme constituted "willful maintenance of monopolistic power."[52] In particular, the court noted that it is impermissible to use a pricing scheme linking monopolistic products with another competitive product to deter entry or effective competition in the market.[53] On appeal, the Third Circuit agreed with the district court's characterization.[54]

The case demonstrates how pharmaceutical manufacturers manage to use rebates, along with market power, to engage in monopolization even where there is no patent exclusivity.[55] In short, bundling pharmaceutical rebates is an anticompetitive strategy that has worked in the past. Today, however, it is being deployed on a vastly more sophisticated and powerful scale, given the incentive structures and information asymmetries in the PBM market.

Loyalty discounts and volume discounts are not unique to the pharmaceutical industry.[56] A manufacturer of computer chips, for example, may offer Apple a volume discount to entice Apple to choose its chips as a component. Similarly, such suppliers may offer a "meet-the-competition" enticement, designed to keep a customer from moving to a competitor.

Context, however, is always the key. The branded drug company holds a high-volume, monopoly position in the market based on the government-granted benefit of a patent. When that benefit ends, we want consumers to move to the generic drug or cheaper alternative, and we want the branded drug to come down to a competitive price. If the branded drug company can prevent its nascent competitor from gaining traction in the market, prices will not come down to a competitive level. And the government-granted monopoly – one that should have passed out of existence – is the driver.

Moreover, the notion of purchaser choice becomes attenuated in the PBM context particularly if one thinks of the consumer as a purchaser. The chip manufacturer is trying to help Apple to sell its computers to customers, and the customers have free choice. If the consumer wants a Dell computer, instead, the consumer can walk into a store and buy a Dell.

With drugs, however, that is not the case. When the PBM and the drug company agree on a loyalty price, the PBM then goes on to write the health plan's formulary. If the competitor's drug is not covered on the formulary, the consumer effectively has no choice. Few of us could manage to pay the full list price for a drug permanently, even if we were forced to pay the list price partially or part of the year. If the drug isn't covered on the formulary at all, the "Ain't What's Paid" price becomes our price day in and day out.[57] To get a sense of this – if you are fortunate enough to have health insurance for prescription drugs – try asking your pharmacist what the uncovered costs would be for various drugs for your family. (Just don't do it unless your blood pressure medication is handy.[58]) The point is simply that, with PBMs writing the formularies, the supposed choice offered to patients is truly absurd.

Now, patients *could* always choose to enroll in another health plan. Those choices may be limited, however, to what is offered by the employer or within the region. Most important, patients must factor in numerous issues when choosing a health plan – and many of those issues are extraordinarily complex. An individual drug company can take comfort in the likelihood that a patient's frustration over formulary placement for a single drug may get lost in the noise.

The PBMs and drug companies might argue that bundled behavior is not possible, asserting that PBMs negotiate rebates with a drug company on a drug-by-drug basis. Even to the extent that this is accurate, however, other fees flowing from drug companies to PBMs need not be based on a single drug. Moreover, the complexity of the contracts can camouflage the bundling aspects. For example, a drug company's bid on insulin can stipulate that if the plan provides a favored position for another one of the company's drugs, then the rebate on insulin will increase by an additional amount. In that way, the drug company can reference other drugs in its bid for a single drug.

Finally, PBMs also may favor dealing with fewer manufacturers, to reduce transactions costs. Once again, this favors the company with more drugs in a way that can provide more room for bundling effects.

3.1.3 Odd Results of Formulary Games

The PBM system certainly provides strange results, some of which are beginning to leak into public view. For example, a 2017 article in the *New York Times* reported on insurance plans that punished patients for filling prescriptions with the generic version, rather than the brand.[59] One patient learned that using the generic version of Adderall would cost her family $50 more per month; another found that his plan would not cover the generic version of Adderall at all, with the result that he had to pay $90 a month in co-payments, when he would normally pay $10 or less a month for his generic medications. Tactics such as these have helped Adderall to keep 29 percent of the market share, when the average market share for brands after one year of generic competition is far less.[60] Similarly, pharmacists were informed at the end of 2017 that some Medicare prescription drug plans (with formularies designed by the PBM CVS Caremark) would cover only brand-name versions of 12 drugs, some of which have generic competitors on the market.[61] These reimbursement decisions led one physician to describe the pattern as "Alice-in-Wonderland time in the drug world."[62]

Similarly, a pair of class-action lawsuits filed in 2017 against Walgreens and CVS allege that the pharmacies charged patients more for purchasing certain generic drugs than they would have had to pay without insurance or if paying cash.[63] The cases allege violations of the Racketeering Influence and Corrupt Organizations Act of 1970 (RICO), fraud, violations of state unfair competition and consumer protection laws, breach of fiduciary duty, and violation of provisions of the patients' healthcare plans.[64]

One former analyst for a Wall Street hedge fund described the power that rebates had in relation to Horizon Pharmaceutical's drug Duexis, which treats aspects of rheumatoid arthritis.[65] Duexis is essentially two over-the-counter medications combined, Advil and Pepcid.[66] Nevertheless, Horizon Pharmaceuticals was able to get the more expensive combination onto drug formularies by offering steep and attractive rebates to the PBMs.[67]

Brand-name drugs are not the only ones involved in results that frustrate policymakers and the public. Pharmaceutical company Valeant drew public fury when it raised the price of its branded drug Syprine from $652 in 2010 to $21,267 in 2015.[68] Coming to the rescue in February 2018, Teva Pharmaceuticals announced that it would sell a generic version of the drug.[69] Joy and optimism were dampened, however, when the price for the generic emerged: At $18,375 for a bottle of 100 pills, the generic version is hardly a bargain – and certainly not for a drug that cost $652 in 2010.[70] As the Syprine example shows, the systemic structures that push *brand* prices higher can create opportunities for soaring *generic* prices as well. The system creates an umbrella effect, sheltering the generics from having to reduce prices too quickly or too steeply.

Some insurers have begun to require that the PBMs pass through part of all of the rebates they receive from drug companies.[71] While a noble effort, rebate pass-through provisions have limited power when insurers do not have the right to see the contracts between the drug companies and PBMs. Most importantly, rebate pass-through attempts miss the point. The term "rebate" is a slippery one that is easily manipulated. As one industry consultant notes, even when PBM contracts specify that all or most of rebates must be passed through to the health insurer, the language defines the term "rebate" as amounts attributable to utilization of pharmaceuticals by the health plan.[72] This is normally interpreted as excluding price concessions paid on mail-order and specialty pharmacies, bundled rebates or loyalty payments, and fees not designated as rebates.[73] Similarly, another commentator has pointed out that the Express Scripts template excludes "inflation payments" from its definition of rebates.[74] Drug companies pay inflation payments to PBMs to cover annual increases in list prices[75] – a payment that looks remarkably like a rebate. In short, drug companies can simply shift that money to other types of side payment that the PBM can hold on to. The incentives continue unabated.[76]

A similar problem could hinder other valiant attempts to attack the PBM system. For example, the U.S. Department of Health and Human Services is exploring a new regulation that would have the effect of characterizing rebates as illegal kickbacks. Entitled "Removal of Safe Harbor Protection for Rebates to Plans or PBMs Involving Prescription Pharmaceuticals and Creation of New Safe Harbor Protection,"[77] the rule has been touted as having the potential to make the PBM's business model "evaporate."[78] The details, as always, will be key: If the rule applies only to rebates, much of the money flow could simply shift to other types of payment.

In short, one can think of the role of the PBM as analogous to that of a travel agent. In theory, both of them ought to be looking for the best price for the customer – but a travel agent, who may be paid by the airline and hotel based on the cost of the vacation, has the incentive to sell you a nice Caribbean cruise, rather than a trip to a cheap motel at the beach town nearby. As long as the travel agent can get the trip for you at a price cheaper than other agents will charge, or cheaper than you could get on your own, the travel agent is in a good position.

And if there are only three travel agents in the country, that's even better.

3.2 WHERE ARE THE INSURERS?

Why would a health insurer acquiesce to all of this? If rising costs impact a health insurer's premiums so that patients flee, the health insurer suffers as well.[79] Isn't it in the health insurer's interests to ensure competition among drug companies and to control costs? Can't health insurers – at least ones with considerable market presence – bargain for better terms? Surely, there are health insurers that are sophisticated profit-making enterprises. These are not hapless waifs.

Well, yes – and no. The answer can be found in a combination of market characteristics and plain old self-interest. Various factors include information asymmetries, the bargaining power of the players, the ability to shift costs, and the allure of short-term benefits over long-term uncertainties.

As described in Chapter 2, information asymmetries are a problem. The health insurance plan does not have access to the contracts between the PBMs and the drug companies. In addition, the health insurance company may not know the dollar amount it actually paid for a particular drug or a particular prescription – at least not on a granular, per-unit level. Although the health insurer sees what it pays for a particular claim at the point of sale, the rebates come in later and cover large numbers of claims or even multiple drugs. Thus, the health insurer does not receive a clear view of either side of the equation.

But why not bargain for a better deal – one that provides an accurate line of sight?

3.2.1 Disincentives for Insurers – The Big Players

Consider a highly sophisticated and economically powerful private health insurer or self-insured employer. A player with that level of sophistication and buying power, in theory, could demand a different deal from its PBM (although, of course, that weight is difficult to leverage within a highly concentrated PBM market). Nevertheless, in theory, the sophisticated plan could require that its PBM pass through all rebates (and, in theory, the plan could even require pass-through of other types of payment from the drug companies). Now, the PBM may require a higher fee in return, but the plan could negotiate such an arrangement. The sophisticated player also could negotiate that the PBM provide comprehensive data files on all claims along with the rebate checks. Moreover, the sophisticated insurer may have the knowledge to require delivery of the proper data, as well as the knowledge to audit or interpret that deluge of data. Thus, such a player could theoretically negotiate and pay for the data that grants it a reasonably complete view of the health plan's cost for each prescription.

However, it may *not* be in the health plan's immediate economic interests to bargain for that degree of information. The route without full pass-through or without complete data and claims access may be a more appealing deal. For example, PBMs charge the health insurer more if the insurer demands a pass-through of rebates, as can be seen in recent exchanges between the PBM Express Scripts and the U.S. Securities and Exchange Commission (SEC). In the process of defending its accounting procedure, Express Scripts explained that:

> [O]ne client may prefer to keep a greater percentage of rebates and compensate us for our services through greater administrative fees, while another client may prefer to keep a smaller percentage of rebates in exchange for reduced administrative fees.[80]

In other words, "if you ask us for rebate pass-through, we will certainly charge you more."

Most important, one cannot overestimate the data analysis challenges and the enormous time and resources necessary for health insurers to fully interpret what is happening – even on their own side of the equation. A full, claims, data transfer can be akin to giving people the alphabet and assuring them that they can write Shakespeare. Yes, in theory, in time, they could – but it's not an appealing approach.

Information costs and asymmetries, however, are not the only reason why health insurers may lack the motivation to push back on PBMs. The real problem is that the insurer's economic interests simply may not align with those of society. The health plan's short-term goal is to keep this year's payments to the PBM – and through the PBM to the drug companies – as low as possible. Remember, volume agreements can work so that those who are already in the market and have a high volume can offer deals that cheaper entrants cannot match (see section

3.1.1 on the power of volume). Thus, to the PBM and to the plan, the price *is* cheaper.

Finally, PBMs are already well ahead of the game when it comes to offering attractive deals to health insurance plans. A more recent innovation in PBM contracting does not involve rebates at all. Known as "price protection," this approach completely obscures payments from drug companies to the PBM. If a large plan with some level of market clout asks for access to contract terms and claims information, a PBM can offer, as an alternative, that the price won't rise more than 2–4 percent, for example. Why engage in all that grubby, expensive detail when what you care about is the bottom line? This type of approach may have a rational appeal to health insurers, particularly on a short-term basis.

Even if the health insurer had sufficient size and economic power to exert its muscle, it still might be entirely rational to go with the flow. Any individual insurer that tried to buck the system would bear all the burdens of trying to ensure competition in the drug industry, meaning that no one would be willing to move alone. As economists ask, why would any single player choose to incur the full costs of a policy that would benefit everyone?[81] Although coordination among the health plans would allow the group to share the burdens and spread the benefits, such collective action is the province of government. Collective action by commercial parties is known as "collusion," and it runs afoul of antitrust laws. If health insurance plans were to coordinate efforts to push back against the drug companies, it would likely be considered collusion by competitors against an upstream supplier.

One might think that Medicare, a massive federal government health insurance program, would be able to bridge the divide. After all, Medicare commands a large share of customers, while enjoying the protection of government action. Medicare certainly does have considerable ability to influence the course of the industry. Nevertheless, the system is not quite so simple. Medicare is a federal program, administered by the states. The government enters into contracts with private health insurers to operate Medicare plans, and Medicare patients choose from among those private plans to decide where to enroll. Thus the private health insurance plans are generally the relevant actors, not the government.[82]

Moreover, long-term competition is a speculative affair. A health plan cannot control when and whether successful generics will choose to enter nor can a health plan control whether changes in laws or regulations may eliminate the potential for additional competition in the pharmaceutical market.[83] Companies could rationally conclude that responding to the clear short-term benefit is a better choice.

Finally, people have an unfortunate tendency to overvalue short-term benefits and to undervalue long-term costs.[84] These long-term versus short-term problems are magnified by the pressures public companies face of satisfying the annual and quarterly expectations of shareholders and market analysts. In particular, for both public and private companies, year-end or quarterly bonuses, designed to incentivize performance, may create pressure on contracting departments and company executives to favor short-term over long-term interests, to secure their bonus payments.[85] Next year or next quarter, someone else could have replaced them in the job, or the bonus structure could have changed, so the value of collecting a bonus today increases. In sum, any long-term benefit is difficult to perceive, measure, and respond to in the short term.

This is not to suggest that individuals enter into some complex calculation of long-term versus short-term interests. It is simply that the pressures of the short-term horizon, combined with the diffusion of the long-term benefits, drown out any long-term considerations. As described throughout this chapter, it is simply a matter of the way in which the incentive structures are operating.

A recent news report has suggested an additional way in which incentives can drive insurers toward higher costs – similar to the incentive structure driving PBMs. Premiums are the fees that patients pay to enroll in a health insurance plan. The Affordable Care Act of 2010 mandates that health insurance companies must spend at least 80 percent of premium dollars on paying medical claims.[86] Profits and administrative costs are confined to the remainder. Known as the "80/20 rule," the mandate is designed to help to keep costs down.[87] After all, limiting profits for health insurance companies should help to keep a lid on overall costs.

Unfortunately, the incentives do not necessarily fall in favor of cost reduction. Quite simply, health insurance companies can sometimes increase their profits when the cost of medicine increases.

Consider a simplified example: Under the 80/20 rule, if the cost of medical inputs (including drugs) is $80, a health insurance company can take home profits of $20 and charge patients $100 to enroll in the plan. This meets the 80/20 rule. If the cost of medical inputs (including drugs) rises to $800, the health insurance company gets to take home the higher amount of profit of $200 and charge patients $1,000 to enroll in the plan.

In other words, when the allowable profit is measured as a percentage of total cost, the health insurance company does better when the cost of inputs rises. As one commentator noted, "[I]f a mom told her son he could have 3 percent of a bowl of ice cream[, a] clever child would say, 'Make it a bigger bowl.'"[88]

Premiums, of course, are not unbounded. Competitive pressures and simple budget constraints operate to limit a health plan's ability to raise premiums. As described in Chapter 2, however, oddities of the healthcare system make those costs less responsive to budgetary pressures than many other types of spending.[89] At the end of day, health insurance companies have less of an incentive to push against the rising cost of medication when those increased costs can lead to increased profits.

Much of the discussion of health insurers so far has assumed that they have sufficient power and information to strike different bargains with the PBMs. The reality, however, is quite different for many. Concentration in the PBM market also makes it difficult for insurance companies to push back. When the big three PBMs offer some of the same key terms – including refusing to give auditors access to the drug company contracts – a health insurance company's options are limited.

3.2.2 Disincentives for Insurers – The Smaller Players

Many insurance plans are not sufficiently large or sophisticated to find their way through the complexities or to bargain for better information, let alone a better deal. First, the health insurance plan could be a small regional plan, small state or local government, or an employer that has decided to "self-insure." The plan may not be sufficiently sophisticated or have the necessary time and personnel to sort all of that information. After all, the health plan hired the PBM, in part, to handle all of that data flow.

The information asymmetries are enhanced by the complexity of the contracts and the volume of claims-based data that would have to be analyzed to understand the nuances. The contracts between PBMs and insurers are devilishly complex, using techniques that can camouflage the impact of particular provisions. For example, a PBM can tell the health insurance plan with angelic sincerity that it has successfully obtained a variety of specific rebates from a particular drug company. That information may be 100 percent accurate – and completely useless. It may be that the plan's utilizations operate in such a way that those rebates are unlikely to come to fruition. For example, the plan's population may be unlikely to use that class of drug or that particular drug very much, or may be unlikely to achieve sufficient market penetration to trigger the rebates.[90] Such facts will be far easier for the PBM to determine than the health plan. Only the PBM sees the full drug company contract, along with all of the claims and utilization information for a particular plan. Secrecy and information asymmetries magnify the complexity problems, making it difficult for health insurers – particularly smaller plans – to see and learn from their mistakes.

Finally, information asymmetries are significant beyond the information involved for a particular health plan. If true net pricing is hidden, the only players who see the net prices throughout the market are the large middle players (such as PBMs), who see the full picture across a range of drugs and a range of deals.[91] Such asymmetries create disadvantages not only for the insurers,[92] but also for smaller PBMs that try to break into the PBM market but struggle to compete against the big three.

3.2.3 Stampedes at Dusk

Timing plays a role as well. The timing of certain contracting circumstances may align incentives in favor of higher prices. When a drug company is the only game in town, it is difficult for PBMs to gain an advantage in the price negotiations. Thus, a drug company can increase pricing just before the drug goes off patent. Health insurance plans also may be motivated to move as many of their patients as possible onto the branded drug whose patent is about to expire, so that it will be easier to get the patients onto the substitutable generic when the generic gets to market.

That extra pricing bump serves to enhance the volume effects across the stable of the company's drugs, magnifying the value of the side payments that the drug company can offer to entice a PBM not to shift to new entrants into the market. Although the higher price certainly allows generics and new entrants to offer attractive rebates from the inflated prices that exist when they enter the market, the volume advantages described above can offset that effect.[93] In other words, you raise prices at the tail end of a monopoly period, so that you can lower them in a way that provides a bargaining tool that entrants will be unable to match.

This type of practice differs from what economists call "predatory pricing" – that is, where a company lowers prices with the intent of raising them when competitors have been driven out of the market.[94] In contrast, this behavior is more akin to pay-for-delay strategies, in which a company spends a part of its monopoly rents to build a stronger bulwark against future entrants.[95] It is also somewhat similar to the notion of "raising rivals' costs," a strategy that raises costs for competitors without incurring any concomitant costs for the company itself.[96] To the extent that raising list prices, combined with rebate strategies, can produce greater payments to PBMs without any cost to the drug company,[97] the drug company has succeeded in raising the cost to incoming rivals without incurring any costs itself.

That timing may also create a mismatch of incentives. The PBM may be more inclined to yield on contracts late in the patent term, based on the expectation that new market entrants will arrive shortly to change the competitive landscape. A similar timing could affect negotiations near the end of a drug company's contract with a PBM. Recall that drug companies raise prices frequently, while PBM contracts are negotiated infrequently. Near the end of the contract, the PBM may be less inclined to push back on a drug company's pricing strategies, knowing that the contract will end soon and that negotiations will begin anew. Once again, the opportunity for extra price increases, prior to PBM negotiations with competitors, provides an additional cushion that will disadvantage the competitor.

Why don't the PBMs themselves see the long-term effects of the timing problem and resist those last-minute price efforts by the drug companies? Part of the answer lies in the tension between long-term and short-term interests. More importantly, however, rising prices simply are in the interests of PBMs. These rising prices provide opportunities for side payments and rebates that go directly into the PBMs' pockets.

In short, given the realities on the ground, most insurers will not have a full picture of the per-unit price on their side of the equation, let alone the net price paid to the drug company. Thus, although we might hope that the insurer would push back on behavior that entrenches higher-priced drugs, the incentives are misaligned, and the information that might drive them in that direction is incomplete.

3.2.4 Burden Shifting

An additional incentive problem may cause the health insurance plans to go with the flow. Quite simply, the payment system may insulate insurers from the effects of high prices or, in some cases, may even provide incentives for insurers to gravitate toward higher pricing. Consider the strange case of the Medicare system. Medicare health insurance plans may create incentives in certain circumstances for higher drug prices. This occurs for two reasons, both stemming from provisions in the Affordable Care Act.[98] First, once a Medicare patient reaches the out-of-pocket threshold, the government picks up 80 percent of the cost through what is known as "reinsurance."[99] Thus higher drug prices push Medicare patients more quickly into the territory in which the government picks up a greater portion of the tab, and the health insurance company pays less.

Second, Medicare makes the health insurance company allocate the rebate dollars it receives from pharmaceutical companies back to the government's reinsurance plan. However, the formulas operate in a way that allows the health plan to keep more of the rebate when most of those rebates are for higher-priced drugs. When most of the rebates are for higher-priced drugs, the health insurer actually pays less, the government's reinsurance obligations rise, and the patient pays more.[100] As one government report noted, a Medicare health insurance plan's decision to place higher-priced drugs on its formulary rather than lower-priced ones "may be a rational response to the incentives they face."[101]

In short, patients will be able to move past the uncovered gap more quickly, and the health insurance plan will have more dollars that could be spent on controlling premium growth for all patients, when the Medicare patient utilizes a higher-priced, nongeneric drug. That has indeed happened in recent years. According to government reports, the fact that the rebate system pushes Medicare patients more quickly into catastrophic coverage levels explains why Medicare premiums have experienced only modest growth in comparison to the more dramatic rise in the price of drugs.[102]

But slowing the rise of Medicare premiums for patients is not cost-free. Someone must shoulder those costs that the health plan is avoiding. As an initial matter, that "someone" is the federal government. During the period in which rebates have increased sharply, Medicare costs per patient have also risen sharply, which the government attributes in part to the increase in costs that the government must absorb in the catastrophic phase.[103] Further, although premiums may have risen modestly, Medicare patients pay more for their medication. A Medicare patient's cost-sharing obligation is generally based on the list price, not the final price after rebate. Thus, patients pay more when they purchase the medication. Finally, all of society loses in the long run, given the risk to competition. If the PBMs and the insurance plans do better with higher-cost medicines, generic companies are out of luck. As with other incentive structures discussed throughout this chapter, this is not what society might hope for.

Other avenues may exist for shifting burdens as well. A recently unsealed complaint in a whistleblower case against the PBM Caremark alleges that Caremark engaged in schemes to defraud Medicare through rebate and reporting manipulations. Among the allegations, the complaint alleges that the PBM negotiated a swapping arrangement in which pharmacies would receive higher payments for Medicare-covered drugs in exchange for lower payments for drugs covered by commercial plans.[104] In other words, the complaint suggests that, by tricking the government into paying more for drugs, the PBM could give lower prices to commercial plans.

Additional details of the whistleblower complaint suggest other burden-shifting approaches. In particular, the complaint argues that, by falsely reporting higher drug-pricing information to Medicare, the Caremark PBM: (a) lined its own pockets;[105] (b) made patients pay higher co-pays and deductibles;[106] and (c) hid true costs in a way that allowed the company's health plan arm to show lower premiums for its Medicare drug coverage bids.[107] The last point is particularly striking. It suggests that, where competition does exist, the ability to camouflage various payments can not only shift costs, but also improve a company's competitive position when it comes to health insurance plan premiums.

Beyond odd twists and turns in the Medicare system, health insurers always are able to shift costs to patients across the board by increasing co-pays and co-insurance, as well as premiums. That has indeed happened in recent years.[108] Particularly in markets in which there is more limited competition among health insurance plans, patients will have little choice.

Burden-shifting capacity may be different for different types of payor. Ordinary insurers, such as Anthem or Kaiser, may pass on the increased costs directly to the patient through increased annual payments and lower coverage. For employers who self-insure, however, they are carrying the risk themselves and may feel the risk most directly, because the self-insured employer has to pay the employer's side of the premium. Moreover, labor markets are certainly more competitive than either the PBM market or the insurance market. Losing qualified and experienced workers is a real threat to employers, which makes cost-shifting more challenging.

Oddly, however, when employers decided to "self-insure" for health care, the system may make the related health insurance company less likely to push for controlling drug costs. When an employer, such as Walmart, self-insures, the company generally takes on the financial risk, while contracting out to an ordinary health insurance company, such as Aetna, to manage the claims flow.[109]

In that circumstance, although the health insurance company is the one to see the individual claims and raise questions about costs, it is the employer who actually pays the bill. Once again, the health insurance company has less of an incentive to push for cost control. And, of course, health insurance companies are not immune from the pressures that encourage executives to focus on short-term, profit-maximizing concerns rather than long-term interests.[110]

In sum, although one might hope that health insurers would apply the brakes to runaway prices, the market structure makes that unlikely. For those who might have the power to push back, it simply is not in their economic interests to incur the costs of such a battle. And, for many health insurers, information asymmetries and lack of bargaining power ensure that they will be unable to play a constructive role. Finally, for all health insurers, the ability to shift costs in some circumstances and the appeal of short-term benefits over long-term uncertainties seals the deal. Although health insurers may rail against PBMs,[111] they lack sufficient power or incentive to resist the forces driving the system toward higher prices and less competition.

3.3 THE PBM INCENTIVE STRUCTURE – WHO PAYS THE BILLS?

We return now to the PBM and drug company side of the equation. As the foregoing discussion demonstrates, rising prices are largely cost-free to the drug company.[112] The drug company can return the extra amount collected with the price increase to the PBMs in the form of side payments and rebates, while maintaining or increasing the same drug sales revenue.[113] As my mother always told me, however, if it looks too good to be true, it *is* too good to be true. Thus, if price increases are cost-free for a drug company, who is paying the bill?

At the head of the line are the employers. Insurance companies pass on the increased price of medications to the employers in the form of more expensive health insurance.

Next in line is the individual patient. As described in Chapter 2,[114] many people pay the full list price at some point, and some patients pay the full list price all of the time. Individual patients also pay in the form of higher rates for purchasing the insurance in the first place, as portions of the increased costs are passed down to them.

Government programs, and the citizens whose taxes provide the funding for those programs, also pay in terms of the need to provide social and charitable programs when individuals become impoverished by medical costs. Society's greatest cost, however, is the reduction of competition among drug substitutes. Rising prices help drug companies to secure advantageous positions on the formularies, blocking lower-priced entrants from gaining much of a foothold. The system also reinforces the dominant position of larger drug companies and larger PBMs. The overall reduction in competition redounds to the great detriment of a society that depends on open and vigorous competition.

In short, it is the perfect lose–lose for patients. Manufacturers raise the price, the consumer pays the higher price, the extra goes to the PBM, and, in exchange, the PBM creates competition-free zones for the drug company's drug.[115] In the short term, the patient pays more in the form of higher prices; in the long term, the patient pays more in the form of fewer competitors to offer lower-priced drugs. Today and tomorrow, society pays and pays again.

4   PHARMACIES, DOCTORS, AND PATIENT GROUPS

4.1 WHY PHARMACIES MAY PREFER HIGHER PRICES

Pharmacies also play a key role in the drug supply chain, as the point of sale contact for patients. The pharmacist collects the insurance reimbursement payment from the plan, along with the co-pay or co-insurance amount from the patient,[1] and this may be the first time patients see how much they must contribute to a particular drug's cost.

4.1.1 Silencing the Pharmacist

In theory, pharmacists should inform patients about lower-priced alternatives. This is particularly important when the calculations for co-insurance or co-payments are complex, and a patient might be better off paying for the drug on a cash basis, rather than paying a high co-pay out of pocket. Unfortunately, both contract law and state dispensing laws get in the way of providing information to the patient. Some contracts between pharmacy benefit managers (PBMs) and pharmacies contain gag rules that prevent pharmacists from volunteering or even providing the cash price to the patient.[2] In October 2018, Congress passed an anti-gag clause that at least will remove the gag for pharmacists. However, pharmacists still can provide information only if they have it and if they are motivated to share it with the patient.

In addition, many dispensing laws allow pharmacists to substitute the precise generic for the brand, but they do not allow substitution within the same class of drugs – that is, the laws do not allow substitution among drugs that treat the same disease and provide similar results, but are not specified as the generic approved by the U.S. Food and Drug Administration (FDA) for that precise version of the brand[3] – nor do they allow pharmacists to substitute a generic unless that generic is rated to the brand drug for which the prescription is written.[4] Thus, drug companies can develop a new version of the drug, with a different timing, dosage, or delivery system. The new version will be protected by new patents, such that the generic may have to wait more than a decade before offering its version. In that case, the pharmacist cannot suggest that the patient go with the older generic version, even though the price may be much lower for something that is essentially the same.[5]

4.1.2 Financial Incentives for Pharmacies

Large pharmacies such as substantial retail pharmacy chains also may receive side payments from drug companies. These can include payments for monitoring data or providing other information. If those payments are based on a percentage of total revenue or unit volume flow of the drug for the pharmacy's customers, these, again, can provide incentives for the pharmacy to prefer a drug company with greater market share or with the most expensive drug. To the extent that any of these payments are ever based on the price of the drug, this can also create a bias toward higher prices.

In addition, higher-volume drug companies that sell to more patients drive more patients into a pharmacy – and those patients may buy nonprescription items offered at the pharmacy.[6] Once again, the pharmacy's interests may lie in arrangements favorable to the large-volume drug companies that hold greater market share, and unfavorable to newer players, such as generics entering the market.

Specialty pharmacies generally are those that deal only with costly or complex treatments.[7] For specialty pharmacies, the incentives for higher prices may be even stronger. Some specialty pharmacies handle only a single drug. In that case, the pharmacists would never have the incentive, or even the opportunity, to substitute a generic version.[8] Specialty pharmacies also have been used by drug companies as part of strategies to prevent generic hopefuls from getting the samples necessary to gain FDA approval. In this strategy, the brand-name company supplies its drug only through specialty pharmacies and declines permission to sell samples to potential generic competitors, preventing the generics from completing their FDA approval applications.[9]

Finally, specialty pharmacies can provide easy opportunities for drug companies to offer side payments, in a manner that helps to buttress the drug's market position. For example, in 2015, Novartis paid US$390 million to settle a case with the U.S. Attorney in the Southern District of New York that involved drugs related to side effects from blood transfusions and organ transplants.[10] The case alleged that Novartis gave rebate deals to specialty pharmacies in return for recommending the two drugs, as well as created incentives and put pressure on doctors to prescribe the drug related to transfusions.[11]

Other opportunities exist for drug companies to provide payments directly to specialty pharmacies, and some of those opportunities flow from FDA drug approval regulations. In particular, the FDA is increasingly approving drugs on condition that the company provide additional information about their safety and efficacy across time, for example with Alzheimer's medications.[12] These approvals are in response to pressure on the FDA to move drugs to market more quickly. The FDA requirements mean that the drug company has an incentive to track its drugs closely, which provides an avenue to confer tracking payments to any type of pharmacy. It may also allow drug companies to limit the distribution networks to particular specialty pharmacies, even when such limited distribution is not required by the FDA. To the extent that those payments are volume-based, as well as if the payments are out of proportion to the costs of the service the pharmacy provides to the drug company, this structure again reinforces market position and erects barriers against new entry.

4.1.3 When PBMs and Pharmacies Merge

The greatest concerns, however, exist when PBMs purchase or run their own pharmacies, which magnifies the anticompetitive opportunities. First, a PBM has much greater power to direct patient buying practices than a pharmacy, given that the PBM designs the formulary, which dictates how much a patient will have to pay for a given drug. The PBM's power to direct patients can combine with incentive distortions in the pharmacy space. These distortions are especially problematic when the PBM also owns a specialty pharmacy that shares monopoly rents with a drug company, particularly a current market leader or large-volume drug company.[13]

In addition, when formularies require that patients purchase their specialty medicines from the PBM's own pharmacy, the PBM's incentives and control systems are perfectly aligned in favor of the drug company that is able to offer the highest level of persuasion payments. One interest group report asserted that certain PBMs write their contracts to mandate that specialty drugs must be filled at their own pharmacies and then reclassify various drugs as falling within the specialty category to drive traffic to their own pharmacies.[14] Given the lack of a consistent definition of "specialty drugs," such a tactic certainly would be possible.

Consider the May 2016 class action filed in the wake of a contract dispute between health insurance company Anthem and PBM Express Scripts. In 2009, Express Scripts purchased a smaller PBM that was owned by Anthem. Details of the complex deal, which involved a ten-year agreement for the PBM to administer Anthem's prescriptions, emerged when the parties entered litigation over the terms of the contract.[15] Poring over that litigation, the class action alleges that the companies breached their fiduciary duties to patients by negotiating that Express Scripts would pay more to purchase the smaller PBM company in exchange for the ability to charge patients above competitive market price for prescription drugs.[16] In other words, Anthem got more money out of the sale in exchange for patients paying more over time.

The PBM also could give preference to its own retail pharmacy, restricting patients' access to drugs and preventing independent drugstores from competing for new customers. One Caremark plan, for example, restricts patients from getting 90-day supplies of a drug from any pharmacy other than Caremark's own CVS pharmacies.[17]

If a PBM uses its formulary power to drive patients toward its own retail pharmacies, the combined entity again benefits, in the form of the ancillary purchases, such as tissues, soap, or over-the-counter medications, which the patient may make once in the store.[18] As one commentator noted, regardless of whether the dominant company in the combined pair is the PBM or the pharmacy, the combination provides incentives for the PBM to steer patients to its own pharmacies, rather than to contract with as many pharmacies as possible to provide maximum location, convenience, and care for its patients, tying its products together to some degree.[19]

4.1.4 The Power of Information When PBMs Combine with Pharmacies

Finally, the information that a PBM can gain from owning a general or specialty pharmacy – particularly about patient usage and patient behaviors – increases the information asymmetries that put its insurance clients at a disadvantage.[20] To the extent that ethical walls might be built between the two sides of the business, those walls could be paper-thin. In short, when PBMs own pharmacies, the originally intended structure, in which the PBM is responsible for negotiating the best bargain on drug prices, becomes so tilted that patients' interests are bound to suffer.

Consider the drug Zyprexa, which is prescribed for psychiatric conditions including schizophrenia and bipolar disorder. Documents unsealed in a lawsuit filed by health insurance plans show that CVS Caremark, a combined PBM and pharmacy, offered to send a letter to 120,000 relevant doctors touting the benefits of Zyprexa.[21] One might imagine that the claims information would allow the PBM to target physicians who had prescribed Zyprexa and possibly to target doctors who had prescribed competing drugs.[22] The text of the proposed letter appears in court documents, along with internal documents from the maker of Zyprexa, noting "the first wave of results from the most recent [PBM] physician mailings."[23]

The letter has the feel of being designed to dance right up to the edge of legality without stepping over it, although the complaint suggests that Caremark may have tripped past the line anyway. The language is carefully worded to appear to be simply a health plan intermediary providing useful information, noting that "Caremark manages the prescription drug benefit plan for one or more of your patients," "we are pleased to provide you the enclosed information ... to review at your convenience," and "[w]e hope you find this information useful in your practice."[24] The letter goes on to tout the benefits of Zyprexa and to downplay recent reports of side effects, by pointing physicians to reports of similar side effects with other drugs and placebos.[25]

The tone of the letter is to approach physicians oh-so-gently with the sense of "don't mind us – we just thought you might like to have some useful information."[26] At the end of the day, however, the PBM's combination with one of the largest pharmacies in the country gave it the ability to mine data to push a particular drug over that of its competitor.[27] The potential power of such arrangements give drug companies the opportunities to advance their sales agendas in a manner that will appeal to the PBM's incentive structures and harm competition. Such arrangements also highlight the dangers of PBM mergers with pharmaceutical companies, particularly in highly concentrated PBM and pharmacy markets.[28]

4.1.5 Clawbacks – How PBMs Squeeze Independent Pharmacies

The PBMs also pocket another aspect of the payments that may be helping to drive prices higher: Independent pharmacists have complained that PBMs are charging the payors more than they are paying the pharmacists. In other words, the PBM charges the health plan $10, but pays the pharmacy only $5 when the prescription is filled.[29] The two sets of payments are based on different and constantly shifting lists – lists that the PBMs control.[30] The pharmacist does not even know what the payments will be until the moment of ringing up the sale. Such lists feed into what the PBMs call their "brand/generic algorithm," which leads to a reimbursement amount that no one can know until the pharmacist rings up the sale.[31]

Not only do the extra payments threaten to drive costs higher, but also they may end up squeezing the pharmacist. Independent pharmacists have complained that the PBMs are reimbursing them less than the wholesale cost of purchasing the drug, while charging the health plan a higher amount.[32] In other words, the pharmacist has the choice of losing money on the transaction or turning the patient away at the last second.[33]

The problem is particularly troubling when independent pharmacies must compete with PBMs that own their own pharmacies. In the case of a combined PBM and pharmacy, what goes from one pocket to the next may simply even out. In contrast, an independent pharmacist must swallow a loss on a drug sale as a result of a PBM squeeze, and the money does not flow back in any conceivable way.

In 2005, shortly after the rise of the PBM industry, Congress directed the Federal Trade Commission (FTC) to investigate whether conflicts of interest or "self-dealing" might arise if PBMs were to own mail-order pharmacies. Concerns included that such integration might lead to a failure to substitute and dispense generics, or to the possibility of replacing generics with more expensive drugs.[34] The FTC's report examining the potential anticompetitive effects of PBM's owning mail-order pharmacies, however, concluded that these allegations were without merit.[35] Despite the report's conclusions, the increased vertical and horizontal concentration in the PBM industry over the last 15 years, as well as anecdotal evidence, suggest that an updated analysis of this and other aspects of the industry would be warranted.

4.2 DOCTORS, HOSPITALS, AND OTHER MEDICAL PRACTITIONERS

For some doctors, hospitals, and other medical practitioners, the incentive structures may be similar to those for PBMs. Medical practitioners or entities such as outpatient centers, which provide medicines directly to patients, may be open to a variation of the persuasion payments given to PBMs. For example, doctors may be offered payments in the form of what are called "key opinion leader" payments, along with lesser forms of benefits that flow when drug sales representatives wine and dine doctors.[36]

For example, California's Health Insurance Commission filed a suit against AbbVie in September 2018, alleging that the company engaged in illegal practices to promote Humira, its blockbuster drug for treating rheumatoid arthritis.[37] The lawsuit alleges that AbbVie provided kickbacks to doctors and nurses in the form of cash, meals drinks, gifts, trips, and patient referrals to inappropriately induce them to use its drug.[38] More troublingly, the lawsuit alleges that the company employed a network of nurse "ambassadors," who were ostensibly visiting patients at home to help to administer the drug, but in reality were deployed to push patients to continue using Humira, and to provide free insurance processing and prior authorization services.[39] AbbVie is not the only company to come under fire for deploying nurses to promote its drugs in schemes that may be skirting too close to the line of kickbacks.[40]

Moreover, with hospitals and doctors who directly provide medications, drug companies can offer rebates.[41] Such rebate opportunities can occur when hospitals and medical practitioners provide in-house infusions or other treatments, such as for certain forms of cancer, as well as for medications during surgery or hospitalization. Doctors may also have a financial interest in the surgical center for outpatient procedures. Although regulations may require physicians to disclose that they have a financial interest in the surgical facility, patients might easily believe that they are in better hands in a facility familiar to the physician, without understanding the long- and short-term financial implications. In addition, when the procedure is covered by insurance, the same issues arise as with PBMs, including that the deals may be hidden from the insurers, and patients may be caught paying higher co-pays and co-insurance as health insurers try to shift rising costs.[42]

In return for the rebate, the doctor or treatment facility charges patients the list price, or even some rebate off the list price, and pockets the spread. In this way, drug companies can raise the list price of the drug and offer a larger rebate, thereby both maintaining revenue and offering enticing payments. As with PBMs, the drug company may condition rebates on volume or exclusivity. The hospital may even believe it is getting a good deal for its patients, obtaining a rebate for them by guaranteeing volume across the full patient load. As described in Chapters 2 and 3,[43] however, the patient pays in the form of reduced competition in the long run, as well as higher prices if the facility does not pass the rebate through in full.

Courts have not been sympathetic to competitors complaining about these types of activity under antitrust law. In 2016, the Third Circuit confirmed its dismissal of a case against Sanofi, regarding rebates to hospitals for its anticoagulant drug Lovenox.[44] The plaintiff alleged that the threat of not obtaining these rebates effectively "handcuffed" hospitals, forcing them to choose Lovenox over the competitor's product, which had different, but overlapping, indications.[45] The circuit court, however, saw only a reasonable marketing effort and ruled that, "to the extent that Sanofi's conduct caused damage to its competitors, that is not a harm for which Congress has prescribed a remedy." And, ultimately, the court found that there was "no evidence that Sanofi's actions caused broad harm to the competitive nature" of the market.[46]

4.2.1 Section 340B and the Problem of Nonprofit Hospitals

A particularly troubling issue arises with what are known as "340B hospitals." Section 340B of the federal Public Health Service Act of 1944 provides that certain nonprofit hospitals that serve the nation's most vulnerable patients receive large rebates on drugs used in outpatient treatment, which is thought to be used for indigent care.[47] Drug companies provide these rebates up front, as steep discounts off the list price – discounts that may amount to as much as 50 percent.[48] Medicare then reimburses these drugs at a much higher rate: 6 percent above the average list prices. The relevant hospitals receive these rebates even for patients who have private insurance. Private plans generally reimburse for the drugs at rates even higher than Medicare, further increasing the spread.

In theory, the discounts are intended to help these hospitals in their work for low-income or vulnerable patients, but the law does not require the hospitals to show that the funds are actually used in that manner. Some government sources and commentators have questioned whether the spread simply increases a hospital's bottom line and market share.[49] More than 42,000 entities participate in the 340B program.[50] Whenever spreads exist, the economics create incentives for rising prices and agreements that entrench large drug companies and disfavor lower-cost or newer entrants.

Similar criticisms have arisen with Medicare reimbursements to doctors for drugs administered even outside of the 340B hospital program. Under Medicare, drugs administered by a doctor are handled differently from drugs that a patient buys from the pharmacy.[51] For drugs administered by a doctor, such as injectable or infused cancer or rheumatology drugs, Medicare will reimburse the doctor at a rate of the average selling price *plus* 4.3 percent.[52] Remember the child who is offered a percentage of a bowl of ice cream?[53] The analogy works here, as well. Doctors will receive more money from the government for using a higher-priced drug in comparison to a lower-priced drug, which creates an incentive to use the higher-priced drug. As one commentator noted, "4.3% of a $100 drug is only $4.30, but 4.3% of a $10,000 drug is $430."[54] The financial incentive combines with the unconscious bias that higher-priced items may be of higher value,[55] particularly if the higher-priced item is accompanied by extensive advertising, to push doctors toward more expensive treatments.

4.3 PATIENTS AND PATIENT ADVOCACY GROUPS

Perhaps the most vulnerable and easily misled populations are patients and so-called patient advocacy groups. These groups can be seduced into actions that harm their interests in the long run, not to mention the interests of society at large.

4.3.1 The Problem with Patient Coupons

Looking first at patients, drug manufacturers increasingly provide coupons or coupon cards to patients, to encourage them to purchase what might otherwise be an expensive drug. In this manner, drug companies can appeal directly to the patient's wallet. With a coupon or coupon card, the brand-name company agrees to pay all or a significant portion of the patient's out-of-pocket costs.

Warning signs that the payments may be problematic include that the co-payment offsets are almost always offered by branded drugs – primarily when competition exists from generics or other brands – and that the benefits are normally directed at patients who have prescription drug insurance plans.[56] In other words, this is not an example of drug company largesse toward the poor and downtrodden.

The dangers range beyond blocking lower-cost competition – although that is certainly of great concern. The economic effects are distorted, as well. For example, the cost of reimbursing the patient's co-pay is much less than the full cost difference between the branded drug and the generic. Thus, although the patient pays little, the insurance company bears a far higher cost.[57] In addition, when the patient's cost goes to zero, drug companies can encourage overconsumption of the drug.[58] Overconsumption can occur when patients stockpile drugs they do not need, allow automatic refills of drugs they may not be using, or have less incentive to ask doctors if the drugs are still necessary.

Although the goal, in many circumstances, is to find the least costly alternative for the patient, strategies like coupons can encourage the highest-priced drug, driving demand away from lower-cost substitutes. In the process, companies can purchase brand loyalty, once again along with the volume that provides a platform for the PBM strategies described in Chapters 2 and 3.

Coupons increasingly are found as a common feature of the drug landscape. Between 2007 and 2010, spending on branded drugs that offer coupons grew from 30 percent to more than 50 percent as a percentage of spending on all branded drugs.[59]

The strategy seems to have conferred considerable benefit on drug companies. Studies suggest that co-pay coupons increase brand drug sales by 60 percent, mostly by reducing sales to generic competitors, as well as by increasing drug costs for all enrollees in prescription drug plans.[60] The blockbuster arena of cholesterol-lowering drugs provides an example of the coupon practice. In 2012, only three medications made up more than 75 percent of the statin market, with the two brand drug companies widely distributing co-pay coupons.[61] When the first generic competitor entered the market, the maker of brand drug Lipitor engaged in an aggressive coupon strategy to maintain market share, until additional generics were finally able to enter the market.[62] Presumably, the strategy helped to preserve market share and revenue as long as possible, until the presence of multiple generics made the strategy too expensive and difficult to maintain. One commentator has suggested that coupon plans constitute unregulated insurance, in which the drug company handing out the coupon indemnifies the patient for any higher cost-sharing that may result from using the branded drug.[63]

4.3.2 Meals, Gifts, and Other Inducements

In other cases, drug companies have provided meals, gifts, or other payments to patients, so that the patients will advocate for the use of a particular branded drug. For example, the *New York Times* reported that hemophilia drug manufacturers and specialty pharmacies, whose products cost between $30,000 and hundreds of thousands of dollars annually, have taken to courting patients and their relatives by offering free meals and hiring opportunities. These behaviors have blurred the lines between patient and sales representative, creating ethical dilemmas in the community.[64]

From coupons to gifts, approaches to patients have a happy side effect: If certain patients begin to complain too loudly, a drug company can pay them off in a manner that reduces public relations friction, while shifting the costs to insurers.[65] But, as always, the long-term burdens fall on society, in the form of reduced competition and higher healthcare costs overall.

4.3.3 Patient Advocacy Groups

Patient advocacy groups are another way in which drug companies can influence market behavior. Ostensibly, these groups are formed by patients who have a particular disease in order to advocate for policies and practices in the interests of others who have the same disease. These organizations are not required to disclose their funding sources, however, and research shows that the majority of patient advocacy groups receive significant support from drug and device companies.[66] One analysis concluded that in 2015, 14 drug companies donated $116 million to patient advocacy groups, far exceeding the $63 million that those companies spent in lobbying activities.[67]

To maintain their funding levels, patient advocacy groups may directly or indirectly advocate for policies that push drug prices higher, and the opioid crisis offers an example of the role of patient advocacy groups. According to a report by Senator McCaskill of Missouri, patient advocacy groups amplified industry messages and lobbied for policies that the industry favored, while receiving more than $9 million in donations from opioid makers.[68]

4.3.4 Ah, the Joys of Tax Benefits!

Funding patient assistance programs and patient advocacy groups has additional financial advantages for the drug company, including tax credits. In particular, drug companies can donate drugs to their own foundation or to independent charitable organizations that support the purchase of the company's drugs, earning charitable deductions in the process.[69] In fact, such patient assistance programs represented 10 of the largest 15 charitable foundations in the United States as at 2014.[70]

Why is this activity so popular? Because donations such as these are particularly valuable. Under a tax code provision, the company gets to deduct an amount that is greater than the cost of the drug. Specifically, branded drugs are relatively inexpensive to make, with the bulk of expenditures coming from research and development, as well as the approval processes.[71] A special enhanced-deduction provision allows drug companies to deduct not only the cost basis of the inventory they donate, but also the basis *plus* half the difference between that and the fair market value, up to twice the basis.[72] In other words, the provision gives the company an enhanced deduction for the appreciation in the value of the product. This tax provision makes the donations unusually valuable, and the higher the list price, the greater the benefit to the company – at least until the company reaches the cap.

And, finally, if all of the other incentives pushing toward higher prices are not bad enough, our own psychology may trick us as well. A recent study published in the *Journal of American Medical Association* gave volunteers a placebo pain pill before administering a mild shock. Some volunteers were told that the pill cost $2.50; others were told that the pill had been discounted to 10 cents per pill. Between the groups, 85 percent of those who were told the price of $2.50 reported less pain afterward, while only 61 percent of those who took the cheaper pill reported feeling less pain.[73]

We may simply be conditioned to believe that miracles cost money and that Cadillac prices deliver better cures.

4.4 THE FULL LANDSCAPE OF THE PERVERSE INCENTIVES

In short, despite a healthcare system that relies on competition to reduce prices, the system, in fact, contains precisely the opposite incentives. Nearly all of the parties along the drug supply chain – including PBMs, as well as certain types of pharmacies, insurers, doctors, hospital, and patient advocacy groups – do better when prices rise.[74] In particular, woven throughout all of these chapters have been the incentives for the drug companies themselves. The system allows drug companies to use some of their monopoly rents to entrench their market shares and to share those rents with each segment along the drug distribution continuum.

With consumer spending on the rise and frustration mounting, everyone is pointing fingers at others in the system.[75] As one commentator noted dryly, however, insurers, drug companies, and PBMs would do better for investors if they "just kept quiet to preserve their very profitable relationship."[76]

To some extent, all of those pointing their fingers are correct, although greater blame may lie with some players than others. In particular, although much anger is focused on PBMs, PBMs are merely responding to the rent-sharing opportunities placed in front of them. The core problem lies instead with the distorted incentive structures – and if society fails to fix this, we can add ourselves to the list of those to blame.

4.5 BUT DON'T WE WANT TO INCENTIVIZE INNOVATION?

Patients throughout the country – and throughout the world – are benefiting from the advances in medical treatment that flow from the US pharmaceutical industry. Shouldn't we be willing to pay the price? Isn't that consistent with the goal of patents and exclusivities, which is to create the incentives that will encourage drug companies to engage in the costly and lengthy drug research and development process?[77]

After all, the intellectual property rights system has a simple and intuitive design at its core: From the store of activities that should be free to all people, we remove some, for a limited time and a limited purpose, in the hopes that the pause will redound to the benefit of all of society.[78] This conceptualization echoes basic Lockean theories on the formation of government, in which individuals emerge from perfect freedom in the state of nature, choosing to relinquish certain liberties (and only certain liberties) for these individuals' mutual benefit.[79] In short, the basic concept of the US intellectual property rights system is

quite simple: Give inventors the possibility of garnering a return from
their innovations, and they will invest in creating those innovations and
in sharing the fruits of their labors with society.[80]

At first glance, one might think the intellectual property rights
system simply disavows competition. The system is designed to grant
benefits that block competitors, giving the rights holder free rein in the
market – a result that is decidedly noncompetitive.[81] That perspective,
however, only skims the surface of the theoretical bases of intellectual
property. The reality is far more nuanced and layered when one
plunges the depths of the system's design.

At a fundamental level, the intellectual property rights system
exudes a deep faith in the power of competition. Competition may be
held in abeyance, but those who receive the benefit of a patent or
exclusivity must pay for that privilege by disclosing sufficient information that competitors will be able to step into the market. And, as the
protection clock winds down, other inventors can use that disclosure,
making preparations to enter the competitive field or to jump ahead to
the next generation.[82]

Nowhere does this concept apply more fully than in the context of
pharmaceutical development. As noted in Chapter 2,[83] the processes
of developing new drugs, conducting the clinical trials, obtaining FDA
approval, and bringing the drugs to market are extraordinarily expensive. Academics and commentators disagree over the magnitude of the
cost,[84] but no matter how one measures it, big is big. The prospect that
a second entrant to the market could simply copy the drug after all of
that effort would deter even the heartiest of souls, and thus the intellectual property rights system provides the opportunity to secure a
return. In idealized form, a company invests in developing a drug:
When the company succeeds, it obtains market exclusivity for a period
of time; and when the exclusivity expires, generic companies step in to
create a vigorous competitive environment.

Whether society grants intellectual property rights in the form of a
patent or a regulatory exclusivity, the systems are designed such that,
after a period of time, competitors are encouraged to enter. Information revealed in the patent allows others to create a competing drug
(rather than to repeat the research themselves).[85] Data used in clinical
trials for the drug are available, after a period of exclusivity, so that

follow-on generics need only prove that their drug is the same, rather than repeat the original company's safety and efficacy trials.[86] Thus, when the benefit expires, competitors should step in, and competition should drive prices down to competitive levels – at least in theory. The system's incentives should then encourage the brand-name company to go back to the bench and invent something new. In short, the intellectual property rights system should be priming the pump for innovation, followed by competition, followed by exciting new innovation, followed by more competition. And if that were happening, we could all celebrate.

That is not, however, what is happening on the ground. When there is a highly concentrated market (such as the PBM market) situated downstream from a monopoly market (that is, drug companies with patents or exclusivities) in which the monopolists have mechanisms to maintain their power, the results are unlikely to be pretty. This is not a path to innovation; rather, it leads to the entrenchment of current players and the blocking of new innovation.

The empirical research laid out in Chapter 5 offers stark evidence of how that is happening on the ground right now. As it will demonstrate, 78 percent of the drugs associated with new patents are not new drugs, but existing ones. Thus, society is not getting the full innovation return on its patent investment, but only a recycling and repurposing of what already exists.

Throw in a dash of the irrationality of healthcare markets, and the result is not a recipe for innovation; it is a recipe for disaster.

5 MAY YOUR DRUG PRICE BE EVER GREEN

No individual system of the body operates alone. So it is with the rebates and formulary games described in Chapters 3 and 4. The rebate disease – as devastating as it is – embodies only one symptom. To fully diagnose the problem, it must be understood in the context of the larger systemic disease, in which drug companies weaken and attack the Hatch-Waxman system for the rapid entry of generic drugs.

Although Hatch-Waxman encourages the rapid entry of generic drugs as soon as patents expire, drug companies have proven extraordinarily adept at holding onto their protections. Companies can move through a progression: first, extending patents and exclusivities to block generic approval; then (for some companies), paying generics to stay off the market when approval looms; and, finally, moving on to formulary games to keep generics from gaining traction in the market.

Thus, the rebates that drive up prices do more than feed the spread for intermediaries such as pharmacy benefit managers (PBMs); they also enhance a drug company's ability to continue extending protections of its drugs. This chapter provides a window into that broader behavior and examines just how pervasive the behavior has become.

In the past, anecdotal evidence has identified examples of "evergreening," which can be defined as artificially extending the life of a patent or other exclusivity by obtaining additional protections to extend the monopoly period.[1] Scholarly work, including my own, has documented these behaviors as examples have emerged in individual cases and in press reports.[2] Just how pervasive are such behaviors? Is it simply a matter of certain bad actors, to whom everyone points repeatedly, or is the problem endemic to the industry? Only by answering this question can we contemplate the extent to which strategic behaviors aiming to block generic competition may be contributing to rising drug prices. This chapter approaches that question by means of an empirical analysis.

Providing a robust empirical analysis was no easy task. Transparency is not in the industry's interests, and companies have been known to go to great lengths to camouflage strategic behavior.[3] After all, a pharmaceutical company would be loath to let regulators and legislators know what it is up to, let alone competitors, which might mimic the clever strategies. To accomplish our study, we turned to government sources, analyzing more than a decade of data published by the U.S. Food and Drug Administration (FDA). This involved extracting and analyzing detailed information on as many as 11 different aspects of roughly 1,800 drugs.

The task would have been sufficiently challenging if the information were readily available. It was not. The project required teasing information painstakingly out of each monthly and annual publication, many of which are no longer available from the government in any form. Moreover, the complexities of pharmaceutical regulation and approval require intricate analysis of the information disclosed by the government, when that information is disclosed at all. In all, our work required assembling and analyzing more than 160,000 individual cells of data, all entered by hand.

The results, however, are striking, and they show a startling departure from the classic conceptualization of intellectual property rights protection for pharmaceuticals. The data demonstrate that, throughout the industry, companies create serial barriers to hold off the type of competitive entry that is fundamental to our innovative system.

Key results include the following.

- Rather than creating new medicines, pharmaceutical companies are recycling and repurposing old ones. In fact, 78 percent of the drugs associated with new patents were not new drugs coming on the market, but existing drugs.
- Adding new patents and exclusivities to extend the "protection cliff" is particularly pronounced among blockbuster drugs. Of the roughly 100 bestselling drugs, more than 70 percent had their protection

extended at least once, with more than 50 percent having the protection cliff extended more than once.

- Looking at the full group, almost 40 percent of all drugs available on
  the market created additional market barriers by having patents or
  exclusivities added on to them.
- Once a company starts down this road, there is a tendency to keep
  returning to the well. Of those that added protections, 80 percent
  added more than one.
- Among those adding more than one barrier, some were serial offenders, with almost half adding four or more protections and some
  adding more than 20.
- The problem is growing across time. The number of drugs that had a
  patent added on to them almost doubled during the period of study.
  The addition of certain other types of barrier, such as "orphan drug"
  exclusivity, increased at an even greater rate – some even tripling.

These results may easily understate the landscape. In designing the
methodology, we repeatedly adopted a conservative approach,
following the path that would point away from suggesting a competitive barrier. In addition, the pharmaceutical industry has developed
techniques for erecting competitive barriers that do not involve
obtaining additional patents and exclusivities – techniques that would
not be captured by our analysis.[4] Finally, our analysis examined only
the patents listed at the FDA. A range of other patents exist that drug
companies do not need to file with the FDA.[5]

Thus, for the first time in the literature, this study definitively shows
that stifling competition is not limited to a few pharma bad apples;
rather, it is a common and pervasive problem endemic to the pharmaceutical industry. Although the end of life for a patent or exclusivity
may be a traumatic event in the life of a pharmaceutical enterprise,
companies increasingly decline to "go gentle into that good night."[6]

In short, this is not an image of innovation and competitive entry; it
is an image of a system that provides for repeated creation of
competition-free zones, pushing a competitive market further and
further out into the future. The problem is not only pervasive and
persistent; it is also growing across time. Against this backdrop, it is no
wonder that drug prices are skyrocketing.

5.1 A BRIEF TOUR OF THE MODERN DRUG APPROVAL PROCESS

The modern system for drug approval in the United States is a long and arduous process.[7] Companies wishing to bring an entirely new drug to market must develop the drug, determine how to manufacture it on a mass scale and in a way that is consistently stable, and prove to the FDA that the drug is safe and effective by means of rigorous clinical trials. Survivors of this marathon – at least those whose innovation is significant enough to earn a patent – are rewarded with the right to exclude others from making, using, or selling the drug.[8]

The cost of obtaining a patent is minuscule compared to the hundreds of millions of dollars necessary to take a drug through clinical safety and efficacy trials.[9] Moreover, companies try to plant their patent stake in the ground as soon as possible, to mark off their territory and keep others out. Given both of these realities, companies obtain many patents that never make it into viable products, including many patents that sit idly on the shelf.

With patenting occurring early in the drug development cycle, some of the patent term will have expired before the drug gets to market. Estimates suggest that the average remaining patent period for a new drug is 12 years. Although far less than a term of 20 years from the time of a patent application, 12 years of exclusivity is a considerable reward, particularly for a blockbuster drug that will garner many billions of dollars a year in revenue.

One should note that, even with patents outside the pharmaceutical space, companies will not necessarily enjoy a full 20 years of exclusivity on the market. It takes time to develop and market any product, as well as time to get through the Patent Office's approval process. In addition, many products contain numerous patents, along with trade secrets and other know-how, such that a single patent will not lead immediately to a marketable product.[10] Nevertheless, the lag time for drug development is likely to exceed the lag time for many other products, even if the difference is not a full eight years. Similarly, the lag time for copies of drugs also exceeds the lag time for copies of many other products. When patents on television parts expire, a generic television requires only mimicking and marketing. In contrast, a generic drug company must obtain FDA approval.

All good things must come to an end, however,[11] and the Hatch-Waxman system, along with the accompanying regulatory and judicial structure, provides the vehicle for rapid entry of generic drugs.[12] Under Hatch-Waxman, generic hopefuls can clear the legal and regulatory hurdles ahead of time in order to hit the ground running.

Given that a generic will have nothing new to patent, the generic company has no potential for monopoly returns from excluding others from the market. Thus, the financial incentive for engaging in lengthy and costly clinical trials is seriously limited for generic drugs nor would repeating those trials necessarily represent a good use of societal resources, considering that the brand-name company has already established the safety and efficacy of the chemical formula.[13] In light of these constraints, Hatch-Waxman allows generic companies to reference the safety and efficacy data from the brand-name company's original drug application, which is known as a "new drug application" (NDA).[14] The generic company need only demonstrate bioequivalence.[15] In other words, the generic company does not need to show that the formula is safe and effective, but only that its product is the same as that of the brand name.

As part of keeping prices low, generic companies generally do not engage in extensive advertising, either to providers or directly to consumers; rather, they depend on drug substitution laws that allow pharmacists to substitute a cheaper generic version when a physician prescribes a medication.

In creating the Hatch-Waxman system, Congress recognized that the U.S. Patent and Trademark Office (USPTO, or Patent Office) unfortunately grants many patents of dubious quality. The problem is not surprising, given that, on average, the Patent Office spends only 18 hours across a two-year period examining a patent application.[16] This is painfully little time for patents, particularly pharmaceutical patents, which may contain hundreds of claims. Although the number of patent examiners has doubled since 2005,[17] the number of patents approved each year has doubled as well, rising to more than 300,000 new patents in the fiscal year ending August 2017.

Patents of questionable validity can operate to improperly block competitors from entering the market. An additional problem can occur when a perfectly valid patent is applied inappropriately to a drug. For example, the FDA requires companies to submit any patents that relate to a drug within 30 days of the drug's approval or receipt of the patent. Under the Hatch-Waxman system for approval of generics, there are repercussions for brand-name companies that do not file within the proper time limits.[18] The FDA does not scrutinize the company's representations, however, but merely records what the company submits, publicizing the information in what is known as the "Orange Book." Thereafter, a competitor seeking approval of a generic version of the drug must battle every patent listed in the Orange Book in relation to the drug.[19] Thus simply listing a patent in the Orange Book can operate to block or delay competition even if that patent does not cover the drug.

To address the problem of invalid patents or patents invalidly applied, Hatch-Waxman provides an incentive for generics to engage in such battles with a brand-name company. Specifically, the first generic to successfully challenge a drug patent or to successfully challenge the application of that patent to its generic version will be the only generic allowed on the market for six months.[20] During this six-month period, a duopoly market will exist in which the only players are the brand-name company and the first generic.[21]

The introduction of generics is a shock to the system for a drug company. Prices can drop as much as 20 percent when the first generic enters the market; with multiple generics, the prices may eventually drop by 80–85 percent.[22] As a result, drug companies have a powerful incentive to delay competitive entry for as long as possible. Even small delays can have a big impact on a company's bottom line. A few months of delay can be worth hundreds of millions of dollars for blockbuster drugs, given that sales of blockbuster drugs reach billions of dollars a year.[23]

It should come as no surprise that drug companies do all they can to soften the blow of losing market monopoly. For example, companies have engaged in a strategy known as "pay for delay," which operates as follows. A generic company files for approval with the FDA, making a representation that the brand-name company's patents have expired or are invalid. This may occur when the main chemical patent on the drug has expired, and the only patents remaining are weak secondary patents that are likely to be invalidated. In fact, a government study concluded that, when generic companies challenge patents and the case goes to trial, the generic company wins three-quarters of the time.[24] With risks such as these hanging over their heads, some brand-name companies have entered into settlements with the generic company – settlements in which the brand-name company transfers value to the generic company and the generic agrees to stay off the market for a period of time. The payment could be a simple cash exchange or a complex series of value transfers that are difficult for authorities to trace and interpret.

Pay-for-delay settlements have been criticized on a number of grounds.[25] Some critics have pointed out that these settlements allow the brand-name company to share monopoly rents in a manner that delays competitive entry and maintains high prices. Others have argued that the lawsuits leading to the settlements are themselves a sham, using the drug approval system to browbeat competitors into submission. For example, a federal district court ruled, in June 2018, that AbbVie engaged in sham litigation against potential generic versions of its testosterone replacement drug AndroGel, eventually entering into a pay-for-delay settlement.[26] Despite criticism of pay-for-delay settlements, as well as increasing scrutiny of those settlements by courts and by state and federal competition authorities, the settlements persist.[27]

Other strategies involve what is known as "evergreening."[28] Although commentators use the term in slightly different contexts,[29] this chapter uses it in its broadest connotation of a company trying to refresh its monopoly protection on a drug. Simple evergreening techniques can involve obtaining new protections on existing drugs by filing for additional patents, sometimes based on methods of producing or manufacturing the drugs or on other aspects.

More complex evergreening strategies involve developing new formulations, dosage schedules, or combinations that can be used to obtain new patents. These can be combined with attempts to move the market toward the slightly altered product, by advertising extensively, by pressuring doctors to write prescriptions including terms such as "Dispense as Written" or "Brand Medically Necessary," or even by withdrawing the old product from the market entirely. Using these techniques, brand-name companies try to prevent pharmacists from being able to fill a prescription with a generic.[30] At the very least, the brand-name company might be able to bifurcate the market, with some patients moving to the new version for which no generic is available.

In an empirical study of secondary pharmaceutical patents between 1985 and 2005, one study found that secondary patents – covering ancillary elements of a drug such as formulation or method of use, as opposed to the primary chemical compound – were highly common.[31] These supplementary formulation patents added an average of 6.5 years of patent life, and supplementary method-of-use patents added an average of 7.4 years of patent life.[32] Other work has determined that secondary patents are likely to be overturned by generic challengers if the case is litigated to completion. For example, another study found that almost 90 percent of patents in pay-for-delay settlements are secondary patents.[33] Moreover, when the lawsuits were pursued to completion, rather than settled in that manner, the brand-name companies won only 32 percent of the time with secondary patents, as opposed to winning 92 percent of the time with active-ingredient patents.[34]

Many of these evergreening strategies involve applying for new patents. Even if the patents are of questionable validity, the process of challenging them through Hatch-Waxman litigation is expensive and lengthy for a generic, again allowing years of additional profits for the brand-name company.[35]

When companies are able to develop new formulations, dosage schedules, combinations, and the like, in a way that justifies obtaining new patents or exclusivity protections, these companies not only minimize damage from tumbling off the "protection cliff," but also may be able to delay going over the edge in the first place. Consider the dementia medication Namenda, a blockbuster drug that was scheduled to lose patent protection in 2015.[36] The company launched a longer-acting version of the original drug product and began encouraging patients and doctors to switch to the patent-protected, longer-acting version to undermine generic competition.[37] In our data set, we recorded a trail of patent extensions for the drug and its variants. For one version of Namenda, approved in October 2003, the protection cliff was extended once in 2009. For another version, approved in

April 2005, the protection cliff was extended twice: once until 2014 and once more until 2015. Finally, for Namenda XR, approved in 2010, the protection cliff was extended until 2029. Throughout this series of maneuvers, the drug company was able to extend its protection of Namenda by at least 24 years.

One cannot overstate the value to companies of engaging in evergreening strategies. Consider the simple approach of combining existing drugs into a single medication. Although patents on the individual components may have expired, companies can reclaim their market position by patenting a pill that combines the components. For example, a recent study in the highly respected *Journal of the American Medical Association* looked at Medicare spending on branded combination drugs, the individual components of which are available in generic form.[38] The study concluded that Medicare could have spent close to US$1 billion less if patients had simply bought the generic medications and taken them together.[39]

These are not the only strategies companies use to extend protection. As described earlier in the chapter, the FDA takes the company's word for whether a patent should be listed as applying to a particular drug. The same is true for the company's description of what uses of the drug are covered by the patent's claims. Specifically, the FDA requires the drug company to submit a short statement describing the approved uses claimed by the patent, which the FDA then assigns a number and lists in the Orange Book as a use code.[40] Scholars have demonstrated that brand-name companies often submit use codes that are overly broad or inaccurate in describing the actual content of the patent.[41]

Given that the FDA does not read or construe patent claims, generics have little recourse for correcting incorrect use codes.[42] In 2012, the Supreme Court ruled in *Caraco* that generic companies can file statutory counterclaims to seek correction of inaccurate use codes,[43] but the approach requires the generic to enter into the extensive legal dance of submitting a Hatch-Waxman certification, attracting a lawsuit from the brand-name company asserting infringement, and then successfully defending against that infringement suit.[44]

In response to continued concerns about use codes, new FDA regulations, which became effective at the end of 2016, have established the "Orange Book Patent Listing Dispute List."[45] To dispute the accuracy of a use code under this newly implemented system, one may submit a "statement of dispute" to the FDA, which the FDA will then send to the company whose use code is in dispute. The company must confirm the correctness of the use code, or else withdraw or amend the patent information, and must also include a description explaining how the existing or amended use code is accurate. It sounds great – but, unfortunately, the process has no teeth. The FDA will simply post information on these use code disputes online under the "Orange Book Patent Listing Dispute List."[46]

In addition, although there is some penalty for failing to list a patent in the Orange Book in a timely manner, even that penalty is lessened in the case of use codes.[47] Once a patent has been submitted, the company can determine at any point in the life of the patent that the patent covers a new use. In other words, let's say that the company holds a patent and has listed it in the Orange Book as relating to certain uses of a drug. At some point before the patent expires, the company can simply say, "Oh, my goodness! I see that my patent covers another use. Guess I'll just add that right in, now."

Obtaining new patents from the Patent Office and adding use codes to the Orange Book are not the only ways of extending one's protection on a drug. There are also more than ten different exclusivities that a company can obtain from the FDA, all of which can create competition-free zones for a specified period of time. Sometimes called "regulatory exclusivities," or "regulatory property,"[48] these programs were approved by Congress during the periods in which Congress passed legislation opposed by the pharmaceutical industry.[49] Drug companies can apply for the benefits for a variety of reasons, including performing pediatric testing, performing other new clinical studies, developing so-called orphan drugs, and developing drugs for tropical diseases.[50] These benefits can operate to extend protection by adding to the length of the patent term, creating a time period during which other companies are not permitted to receive approval to market the drug or to use existing safety and efficacy data, adding to the length of already existing nonpatent exclusivities, or providing for combinations of these benefits.[51]

Of course, attempts to block out competitors may not always be successful. Competitors may be able to overturn or avoid weak patents, challenging them as either invalid or not infringed. Other behaviors can be used to avoid the patent deluge in limited circumstances, such as producing a drug with a label designating a narrow use, while knowing that physicians are likely to suggest off-label use of the drug.[52] Even where such approaches are successful, however, the cost and waste of rent-seeking behavior, and behavior to counter such rent-seeking, do not constitute a model of an effectively functioning market.

In short, despite the quaint theory that competitors will enter after a pharmaceutical patent expires, the reality is quite different. Numerous strategies and opportunities exist that allow companies to extend their protection and prolong the period of market monopoly for their drugs. Such game playing involving patents and exclusivities has been explored primarily from a theoretical standpoint and by means of case studies, without comprehensive, quantitative examination of such strategies across the industry.

This study fills that gap.

5.2 METHODOLOGY[53]

To examine the landscape of evergreening behavior, we assembled a large volume of FDA data that would allow us to analyze the prevalence and specific contours of patent and exclusivity game-playing in an empirically rigorous manner. However, before diving deep into the analysis, we had to test whether or not a widespread pattern of adding patents and exclusivities would be detectable. To do this, we tested the hypothetical assertion of *no* widespread behavior beyond one or two additions. In testing this on our data, we found evidence that refutes the hypothesis. Therefore, we moved on to examine in depth the alternative hypothesis of widespread multiple additions.

To perform these analyses, we used data published in the FDA's "Orange Book."[54] Locating FDA data and converting it into a usable format was a formidable task. Although each monthly supplement and annual edition across time contains a wealth of information, only the most recent edition is available from the FDA.[55] We were fortunate to locate archived copies of the monthly and annual editions from another researcher. From that data, we extracted all of the patent and exclusivity information from the 11 years of Orange Books included in our study, examining each to determine detailed information on the nature of the addition or change. Enormous effort was required to gather the data set and render it usable for empirical analysis.

Consistent with a commitment to transparency and ethical standards in data-driven academics, the data set has been made publicly available.[56] Because pharmaceutical pricing is a key focus of public policy debates, we hope the data set will assist other researchers, regulators, and the general public in future investigations into the pharmaceutical industry

5.3 RESULTS

5.3.1 Overview

The results demonstrate definitively that the patent system is not functioning as a time-limited opportunity to garner a return, followed by open competition; rather, companies throughout the industry obtain repeated extensions of their competition-free zones. The behavior has steadily increased between 2005 and 2015, especially on the patent front and for certain highly valuable exclusivities. Most troublingly, the data suggest that the current state of affairs is harming innovation in tangible ways. Rather than creating new medicines – sallying forth into new frontiers for the benefit of society – drug companies are focusing their time and effort on extending the patent life of old products. This, of course, is not the innovation one would hope for, as the greatest creativity at pharmaceutical companies should be in the lab, not in the legal department.[57] The following sections of the chapter describe the study results in detail, but here are the key takeaways.

- Rather than creating new medicines, pharmaceutical companies are recycling and repurposing old ones. In fact, 78 percent of the drugs associated with new patents were not new drugs coming on the market, but existing drugs.
- Adding new patents and exclusivities to extend the protection cliff is particularly pronounced among blockbuster drugs. Of the roughly 100 bestselling drugs, more than 70 percent extended their

protection at least once, with more than 50 percent extending the protection cliff more than once.

- Looking at the full group, almost 40 percent of all drugs available on the market created additional market barriers by having patents or exclusivities added on to them.
- Once a company starts down this road, there is a tendency to keep returning to the well. Of those that added protections, 80 percent added more than one.
- Among those adding more than one barrier, many were serial offenders, with almost half adding four or more protections and some adding more than 20.
- The problem is growing across time. The number of drugs that had a patent added on to them almost doubled during the time period. The addition of certain other types of barrier increased even more, with additions of orphan drug exclusivities tripling.

5.3.2 Recycling and Repurposing Old Drugs

Our first metric examined the extent of recycling and repurposing of old drugs. We did this by looking at the number of drugs that were newly approved each year compared to the number of drugs that had patents and exclusivities added to them in the Orange Book that year. In other words, within all of the drugs on the market that had patents and exclusivities added to them each year, which ones were drugs that were newly approved that year, and which ones were drugs that had been approved in the past?

This metric is significant because it indicates how much patent and exclusivity activity is the result of innovation in the pharmaceutical industry and how much of it is attributable to the recycling or repurposing of old drugs. If the number of drugs with patents and exclusivities added to them in the Orange Book each year were to exceed the number of new drugs approved each year, this would suggest that many drugs are receiving patents and exclusivities – not for innovation represented by a newly approved drug, but rather for changes made to old drugs that were approved previously.[58]

We should note that our analysis is likely to significantly understate the amount of repurposing and recycling of old drugs. We examined drugs at the new drug application level. Anecdotal evidence suggests that, with some product-hopping and evergreening behavior, companies change the name and make insubstantial formulation changes to the drug, submitting the new product under a different "new drug application" than the original one.[59] For example, the maker of the colitis drug Asacol, which already had a protective coating, wrapped the drug in an extra ineffective cellulose capsule. This occurred as part of a product hop – a strategy in which a brand-name company tries to shift the market to a new version of a drug before the generic can gain a foothold. In this case, the company named the new drug Delzicol and listed it as a separate "new drug application." Our data set did not connect different new drug applications to each other, and we could not capture behavior of this sort. Thus the dramatic results below are still only part of the dismal picture.

As is evident from Table 5.1, the number of drugs with additions to the Orange Book dwarfs the number of newly approved drugs in every single year between 2005 and 2015. On average, 77.62 percent of

Table 5.1 *Comparison of newly and previously approved drugs with Orange Book additions by year*

Year	Total no. of drugs with Orange Book additions in given year	No. of drugs approved that year that had Orange Book additions	Percentage of previously approved drugs with Orange Book additions*
2005	263	63	76.05%
2006	281	71	74.73%
2007	267	53	80.15%
2008	335	61	81.79%
2009	273	70	74.36%
2010	264	65	75.38%
2011	258	50	80.62%
2012	309	71	77.02%
2013	326	70	78.53%
2014	348	75	78.45%
2015	355	85	76.06%
Total	3279	734	77.62%

* Annual percentages have been rounded to the nearest 0.01. Total percentage is calculated using the total values of Orange Book additions and is rounded to the nearest 0.01.

Table 5.2 *Number of drugs newly approved with an added patent compared to number of drugs with an added patent in a year*

Year	No. of drugs with an added patent	No. of drugs that were approved that year that added a patent	No. of drugs not newly approved that year that added a patent	Percentage of previously approved drugs with Orange Book additions*
2005	166	45	121	72.89%
2006	213	53	160	75.12%
2007	191	37	154	80.63%
2008	263	42	221	84.03%
2009	201	53	148	73.63%
2010	205	51	154	75.12%
2011	201	38	163	81.09%
2012	239	50	189	79.08%
2013	267	63	204	76.40%
2014	288	61	227	78.82%
2015	300	76	224	74.67%
Total	2534	569	1965	77.55%

* Annual percentages have been rounded to the nearest 0.01. Total percentage is calculated using the total values of Orange Book additions and is rounded to the nearest 0.01.

drugs with Orange Book additions in a particular year were not new approvals from that year. This suggests a large degree of repurposing and recycling of existing drugs in the pharmaceutical industry and, concomitantly, less innovation and invention than the patent process is intended to create.

When looking at only patent additions, the narrative is the same. Moving to Table 5.2, 77.55 percent of drugs with a patent added to them between 2005 and 2015 were existing drugs. Moreover, this problem grew over the time frame of our study, with the number of existing drugs with added patents almost doubling from 2005 to 2015.

The concern with repurposing and recycling of old drugs is that while many of the changes made to those old drugs may earn new patents and exclusivities, they may not be significant from a patient benefit or therapeutic point of view. As such, society may be lavishing expensive rewards on suboptimal behavior.[60] The concern is even greater if one considers that many of these secondary patents may be of questionable validity.

This is not to suggest that secondary changes would have *no* value, to any patient, under any circumstances; rather, minor changes to dosage or delivery systems, for example, may have *some* amount of value to *some* patients. Similarly, applying an old drug to a different disease delivers the advantage of years of experience in the field, which can provide important information on safety. These advantages may not, however, justify the magnitude of the patent reward that is conferred. From society's standpoint, one might be better off with incentives that drive scientists back to the bench to look for advances of greater significance or at least provide no more than a minimal benefit for secondary protections.[61]

These results fall along the same lines as a French study using a different methodology to consider whether new drugs in that country represented advancement over prior drugs. Examining roughly the same period (that is, 2005–14), the study concluded that less than 10 percent of new drugs and new uses for old drugs in France provided a significant advantage, and more than 50 percent provided nothing new at all.[62]

5.3.3 Extending the Protection of Blockbuster Drugs

We looked next at the percentage of the roughly 100 bestselling drugs between 2005 and 2014 that had the protection cliff extended. Blockbuster drugs, of course, are the ones in relation to which the drug companies have the most to lose if their exclusivity period ends and the most to gain by extending the lifetime of the drug, even by only a few months. Thus, if widespread competition blocking behavior were to be found anywhere, we would expect it to be found here. The results from this metric – broken down between drugs that had their protection cliff extended at least once and drugs that had their protection cliff extended more than once – are shown in Table 5.3.

Out of the roughly 100 bestselling drugs between 2005 and 2014, more than 70 percent had their protection cliff extended at least once, and more than 50 percent had their protection cliff extended more than once. The magnitude of the behavior highlights the extent to

Table 5.3 *Percentage of top 106 bestselling drugs that had their protection cliff extended*

Year	No. of new top 50 drugs by year[63]	No. of these drugs that had their protection cliff extended at least once*	No. of these drugs that had their protection cliff extended more than once*
2005	50	39 (78%)	33 (66%)
2006	5	2 (40%)	2 (40%)
2007	5	4 (80%)	1 (20%)
2008	6	5 (83%)	3 (50%)
2009	6	4 (67%)	3 (50%)
2010	5	3 (60%)	2 (40%)
2011	9	7 (78%)	3 (33%)
2012	5	4 (80%)	3 (60%)
2013	10	5 (50%)	3 (30%)
2014	5	3 (60%)	1 (20%)
Total	106	76 (72%)	54 (51%)

* Annual percentages have been rounded to the nearest whole number. Total percentages have been calculated using total values and are rounded to the nearest whole number.

which stifling competition has become the norm in the drug industry. When over 70 percent of bestselling drugs have had their protection extended, it is clearly the go-to approach for profitability.[64]

5.3.4 Number of All Drugs (Not Only Blockbusters) That Had Market Barriers Added

Looking at the group as a whole, we wanted to determine the extent to which companies are adding patents and exclusivities. Is this a limited activity, confined to well-worn anecdotes that everyone repeats, or does it occur throughout the industry, regardless of whether the drug is a blockbuster? Our results demonstrate that adding patents and exclusivities is a common behavior, one endemic to pharmaceuticals. In fact, between 2005 and 2015, almost 40 percent of all drugs available on the market had patents, exclusivities, or other changes added to them.

Table 5.4 shows the total number of FDA-approved drugs available on the market in each year of our study. Table 5.5 shows the number of drugs that had a patent or exclusivity added to them as a percentage of the total number of drugs. The figure is broken down in terms of the

Table 5.4 *Total number of unique, small-molecule drugs listed in the Orange Book, 2005–15*

Year	Total no. of drugs listed (at the new drug application level)
2005	2,402
2006	2,354
2007	2,354
2008	2,353
2009	2,362
2010	2,397
2011	2,425
2012	2,436
2013	2,470
2014	2,533
2015	2,547
2005–15 (No. of unique drugs throughout the period)	3,372

Table 5.5 *Number of drugs with added patents and/or exclusivities out of all drugs, 2005–15*

Category	No. of drugs	Percentage of all drugs*
Drugs with an added patent	1,059	31.4% (1,059/3,372)
Drugs with an added exclusivity	978	29.0% (978/3,372)
Drugs with any relevant change/addition	1,322	39.2% (1,322/3,372)
All drugs available	3,372	100% (3,372/3,372)

* Annual percentages have been rounded to nearest 0.1. Total percentage has been calculated using total values.

number of drugs with an added patent, the number of drugs with an added exclusivity, and the number of drugs that had any relevant change made to it (which includes not only adding a patent and/or exclusivity, but also other significant changes, such as adding a use code.)

5.3.5 Serial Offenders

Some drugs in our data set had patent or exclusivities added to them in to the Orange Book only once during our 11-year time frame. Other drugs, however, repeatedly returned to the well, having one set of patents and exclusivities added to them, then another set added a few months later, and another round a few years after that, and so on. To capture this behavior, we measured the number of months during which a drug had a patent or exclusivity added to it in the Orange Book. This means that, regardless of whether the drug had one patent or ten patents added to it within a month, we considered that month as one instance of patent activity. We did this to keep our calculations as conservative as possible.

Table 5.6 shows that a troublingly large percentage of drugs returned to the well repeatedly. Out of the drugs that had at least one Orange Book addition, 80 percent had additions on more than one occasion. Moreover, 49 percent received additions on four or more occasions, and 20 percent received additions on seven or more occasions. As these results demonstrate, drugs that repeatedly bolster their

Table 5.6 *Number of times each drug had an Orange Book addition*

No. of patents and/or exclusivities added	No. of drugs (Total = 1,349)	Cumulative no. and percentage (i.e. at least 18+, at least 17, at least 16, etc.)
18+	29	29/1,349 (2.15%)
17	3	32/1,349 (2.37%)
16	10	42/1,349 (3.11%)
15	10	52/1,349 (3.85%)
14	10	62/1,349 (4.60%)
13	12	74/1,349 (5.49%)
12	13	87/1,349 (6.45%)
11	23	110/1,349 (8.15%)
10	25	135/1,349 (10.01%)
9	33	168/1,349 (12.45%)
8	55	223/1,349 (16.53%)
7	60	283/1,349 (20.98%)
6	81	364/1,349 (26.98 %)
5	125	489/1,349 (36.25%)
4	173	662/1,349 (49.07%)
3	208	870/1,349 (64.49%)
2	212	1082/1,349 (80.21%)
1	267	1349/1,349 (100%)

* Annual percentages have been rounded to nearest 0.01. Total percentage has been calculated using total values.

patent and exclusivity protections are not the rarity they might once have been. In similar fashion, one study of the top 12 bestselling drugs in the United States found that, with more than half of those bestsellers, the companies attempted more than 100 patent filings per drug.[65]

5.3.6 The Problem Is Growing across Time

There was a clear increase in the number of drugs with three or more added patents in a single year between 2005 and 2015. The figure more than doubles from 37 drugs in 2005 to 76 drugs in 2015. When the definition of a "high quantity" of patents was changed from three to five, the results were similar. The number of drugs with five or more added patents in a single year also doubled between 2005 and 2015, from 14 drugs in 2005 to 34 drugs in 2015.

Unfortunately, it is likely that, as more patents are added to a drug, the quality of the patents declines. Typically, the subsequent patents are more likely to be "secondary patents," which, instead of covering the active ingredient or base compound, cover modified forms of the active ingredient, associated uses of existing chemical compounds, new combinations of old chemical compounds, dosage regimens, and specific formulations (for example tablet versus capsule).[66] For instance, while the first patent added to a drug might cover the core active ingredient of the drug, the fifth patent might be covering a therapeutically negligible change to the formulation or composition of the drug. As such, the increase in the number of drugs with a high quantity of added patents in a year might be an indication that the pharmaceutical game-playing strategy of evergreening is becoming increasingly common.[67]

Figure 5.1 shows the number of drugs with three or more patents added in a year. Figure 5.2 shows the number of drugs with five or more patents added in a year.

5.3.7 What's in Vogue? Particular Exclusivities That Are Increasing across Time

Certain exclusivities appear to have become particularly popular across the time period we studied: orphan drug exclusivity and new uses.[68]

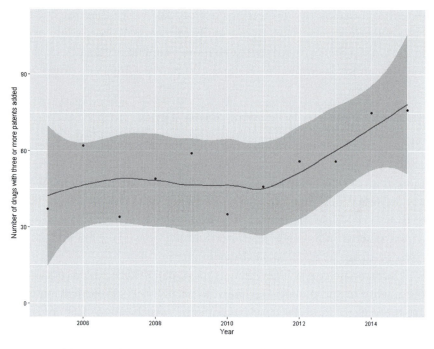

Figure 5.1 Number of drugs with three or more added patents in a year, 2005–15

5.3.7.1 Increase in Orphan Drug Exclusivity

Orphan drug exclusivity is a seven-year exclusivity granted to drugs that are approved and designated specifically to treat problems affecting populations of 200,000 individuals or fewer.[69] The exclusivity was established through the Orphan Drug Act, originally passed in 1983 and amended by the Hatch-Waxman Act in 1984.[70] The orphan drug program was intended to spur investment in neglected fields of medical research – that is, drugs to treat rare diseases that affect only a small number of people in the United States.[71] Policymakers feared that insufficient financial incentives exist to develop treatments for small patient populations and that, as a result, these populations would languish untreated.[72] Today, however, it seems that "everyone is an orphan," with orphan drugs accounting for more than 40 percent of drugs approved by the FDA.[73]

Part of the reason for the rapid expansion of the orphan drug program is the enormous value of the seven-year exclusivity. Most regulatory exclusivities awarded by the FDA extend a drug's

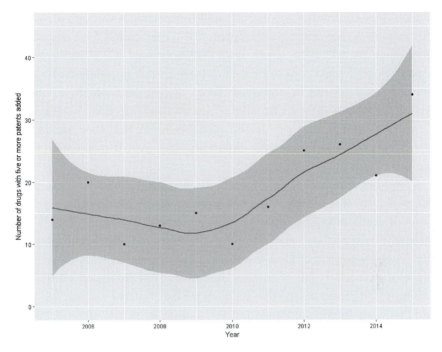

Figure 5.2 Number of drugs with five or more added patents in a year, 2005–15

protection by a few months, or perhaps a few years at most. For example, the pediatric exclusivity extends exclusive marketing and data rights for a drug by six months, and the exclusivity awarded for new clinical studies lasts for three years.[74]

At seven years, orphan drug exclusivity is by far the longest lasting of the forms of regulatory property granted by the FDA. With such strong exclusivity protection, manufacturers of orphan drugs are able to raise prices to shockingly high levels. The median cost for a patient to use an orphan drug for a single year is nearly $100,000, compared to roughly $5,000 for nonorphan drugs.[75] Given that just a few months of additional market protection can be worth hundreds of thousands of dollars for a drug company, winning an additional seven years is akin to winning the lottery.

More important, drug companies have figured out how to raise prices under orphan drug protections and then spread those high prices across patient populations much broader than the small groups envisioned when Congress passed the Orphan Drug Act. This technique is referred to as "spillover pricing."[76] The most common way in which drug companies accomplish spillover pricing is through off-label use, which occurs when doctors prescribe a medication for a use other than that for which the FDA originally approved it.[77] Consider the drug Epogen, which was approved to treat a small population afflicted with anemia related to end-stage renal disease and which, as such, received orphan drug designation.[78] After receiving this designation, however, Epogen was prescribed off-label to treat a wide variety of types of anemia, dramatically expanding the patient population that paid the high price of Epogen.[79]

Another approach for gaming the orphan drug exclusivity system is through "salami slicing."[80] This strategy involves dividing up the patient population into separate slices – perhaps separating those with an early stage of the disease from those with an end stage, or those who developed a genetic disease as a result of one mutation from those who developed it as a result of another mutation – and obtaining a different orphan drug exclusivity for each slice. By "salami slicing," if the original and intended population for a drug is greater than 200,000 and thus too large to qualify for orphan drug designation, the drug company can simply divide that original group up into subpopulations that are small enough to qualify.

A drug does not actually have to be newly developed to qualify for orphan drug exclusivity, and hence long-existing drugs can be revived and repurposed for an orphan drug indication. In fact, a troubling investigation by one media organization concluded that one-third of orphan drugs approved since the program began in 1983 were either repurposed mass-market drugs or drugs that received multiple orphan approvals.[81]

Consider the drug 3,4-diaminopyridine (3,4-DAP), which was used by patients with a rare neuromuscular disease, and which had been shown to be safe and effective as early as 1983.[82] Although the drug had never been officially approved, it had been provided to patients at no cost for many years thanks to a generous company and the FDA's "compassionate use" program.[83] In 2015, however, a different company submitted an application for a slightly modified version of the drug that does not require refrigeration, obtaining orphan drug designation in the process.[84] As a result, the company projected that it would be able to charge somewhere between $37,500 and $100,000 per patient per year – and it would be charging those same patients who had been receiving the drug for free.[85]

In our study, we found that the number of drugs for which orphan drug exclusivities were added to the Orange Book notably increased between 2005 and 2015, with a large jump between 2010 and 2011, and a steady climb upwards from 2011 through 2015. On the whole, between 2005 and 2015, the number of drugs with an added orphan drug exclusivity tripled from 9 drugs in 2005 to 27 drugs in 2015.[86] Figure 5.3 shows these results.

5.3.7.2 Increase in New Use Codes

There was a notable increase in the number of use codes added to the Orange Book within our time frame, rising from 115 use codes in 2005 to 364 in 2015. These results are corroborated by one study of use codes finding that the total number listed in the Orange Book nearly tripled between 2003 and 2013.[87]

The number of drugs with at least one added use code also exhibited an upwards trend between 2005 and 2015, more than

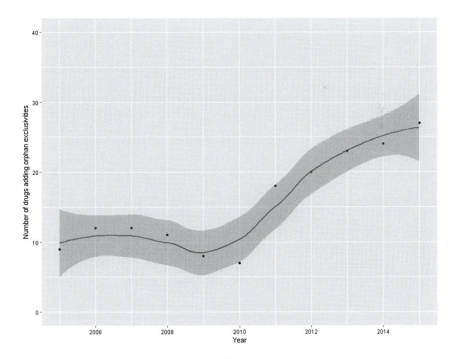

Figure 5.3 Number of drugs with an added orphan drug exclusivity, 2005–15

doubling from 63 drugs in 2005 to 173 drugs in 2015. One might attribute the rise in the number of drugs with at least one added use code to a general rise in the number of drugs with anything added to them in the Orange Book between 2005 and 2015. Even accounting for the rise in drugs with additions in the Orange Book, however, there is still a rise in the frequency of drugs with added use codes. In 2005, 63 of the 233 drugs with any relevant addition or change to the Orange Book (that is, 27 percent) had at least one added use code. In 2015, 173 of the 353 drugs that had any relevant addition or change made to them in the Orange Book (that is, 49 percent) had at least one added use code. Thus the fraction of drugs with added use codes in the Orange Book rose from less than a third to around half during the full period.

Our findings for the number of times a use code was added to a patent each year between 2005 and 2015 are shown below in Figure 5.4,[88] and the number of drugs that had at least one use code added to them in each of those years is shown in Figure 5.5.[89]

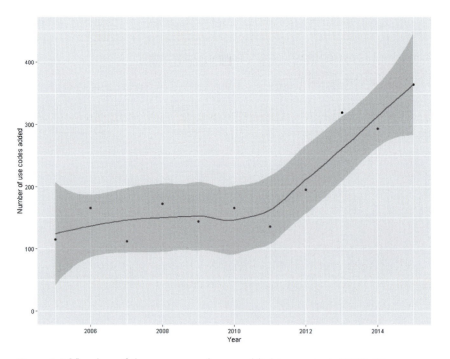

Figure 5.4 Number of times a use code was added to a patent, 2005–15

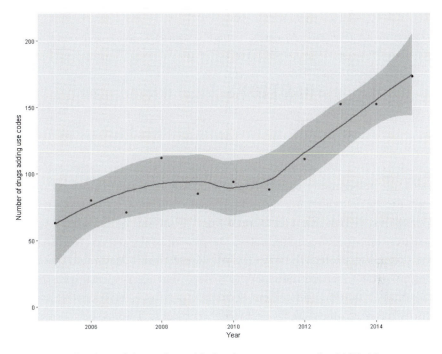

Figure 5.5 Number of drugs that added at least one use code, 2005–15

5.4 FINAL THOUGHTS ON EXTENDING THE PROTECTION CLIFF

In short, the vision presented in this study is not an image of innovation and competitive entry; rather, it is an image of repeatedly extending competition-free zones, which pushes a competitive market further and further out into the future. The problem is not only pervasive and persistent; it is also growing across time. It is this drive to extend protection that continues on in contracts with PBMs and other intermediaries, as drug companies use rebates and formulary strategies to prevent competitors from gaining traction in the market.

When the government itself bestows benefits that are stifling competition, society has both an obligation and an opportunity to act. One cannot enter into such action lightly, however, and any intervention must be designed with thought and care. Drug research is expensive, and companies must have sufficient incentive to travel down that risky road. Nevertheless, by incentivizing game-playing rather than innovation, society has clearly missed the mark.

6 SOLUTIONS

As John F. Kennedy explained, "the enemy of the truth is very often not the lie – deliberate, contrived, and dishonest – but the myth – persistent, persuasive and unrealistic."[1] Nowhere is the fog of myth greater than in the drug industry. Despite all of the parties who should be primed to protect the interests of patients and consumers – including pharmacy benefit managers (PBMs), pharmacists, health insurers, hospitals, doctors, and patient advocacy groups – the incentive structures align strongly in favor of higher prices. The system not only creates great pain for patients and taxpayers, but also provides convenient methods with which drug companies can carve out or reinforce competition-free zones.

As public fury mounts over high drug prices, policymakers have proposed – and will continue to propose – numerous small alterations. Many of these proposals could help in small ways. Moreover, such tinkering may be all that is politically feasible. Nevertheless, high drug prices and persistent pain for patients, governments, and taxpayers are unlikely to ease unless society can fundamentally alter the perverse incentive structures at work. And, at the end of the day, if we lack the political will to face the issues head on, we will have ourselves to blame as well. With these challenges in mind, this chapter turns to some possible solutions.

6.1 PROPOSALS WITH POTENTIAL (BUT PROBLEMS)

Many of the drug industry's pledges and fixes may be of limited value, and, in some cases, counterproductive. Consider the controversial pledge some drug companies have made to control prices by limiting list price increases to below 10 percent.[2] On the one hand, it is certainly better than an increase above 10 percent; on the other hand, it provides cover for increasing prices to that level and discourages anything below it. With a pledge like that, companies get little public relations benefit from increasing only 5 percent or 6 percent, as opposed to 9 percent, and they could get hammered by shareholders and capital markets for going much lower than 10 percent. Thus 10 percent helps to set a floor for price increases, rather than simply a ceiling.

Companies also can dodge the pledge by raising the price by 9 percent multiple times in a year.[3] And, of course, the pledge is nothing more than a promise, which the company could choose to abrogate, if it so wished.

Similarly, company pledges to roll back prices may not always be what they appear. When pharmaceutical company Merck announced that it would lower prices to help patients,[4] the announcement was greeted with less than the rousing applause the company might have hoped for. Journalists quickly pointed out that the reduction would not apply to the company's top-selling cancer and diabetes products, and would affect only minor products.[5]

Price pledges are not the only "good intentions" that may have less-than-good results. With the complex financial flows of the healthcare system, the best of intentions can have unintended consequences.[6] Several of the perverse incentives described in Chapters 3 and 4 stemmed from provisions in the Affordable Care Act of 2010 related to Medicare that were intended to help to control the costs of drugs to seniors, but which have had quite different results.

Consider also the curious case of requiring "equal access for all classes of trade." In the 1990s, a federal district court case under Judge Charles Kocoras, *In re Brand Name Drug Litigation*, considered the antitrust implications of the fact that drug companies might give better prices on drugs to large pharmacies, or "favored purchasers," than to small retailer pharmacies.[7] Such agreements were considered to disadvantage small players in the industry, helping to shore up the market positions of both large pharmacies and large drug companies.[8]

The settlement of the case served as a warning bell for those in the industry, suggesting the requirement of equal access to all classes of trade in the industry.[9] Drug companies and PBMs have responded, however, by developing an even more dangerous type of agreement. Rebates are now tilted toward market share of a drug. Such an agreement might offer both the small retail pharmacy and the PBM the same thing: a certain level of rebate if a certain percentage of the patients who use a particular drug (or any in that class of drugs) purchases the company's version.

This type of agreement exploits both market-share advantages and information asymmetries. The PBM knows everything a particular patient is buying at any location, while the retailer knows only what the patient buys at that retail outlet. Thus, even if the percentage is reached, the small retail pharmacy may have difficulty proving it and cannot claim the highest level of rebate.

The problem is not necessarily a particular order by a particular judge; the problem is a system that avoids open and vigorous competition. Secret deals and misaligned incentives are unlikely to be fixed by targeted judicial and regulatory orders. They are not necessarily bad orders and may be the best one can get politically, but, at the end of the day, they are doomed to remain one step behind.

6.1.1 Value-Based Pricing

Another proposal for taming drug prices is called "value-based pricing," or a version of that known as "outcomes-based pricing." The basic notion of value-based pricing is that drug companies should be compensated for the value that they provide with their drug treatments. A key problem, as the National Academies of Science (NAS) concluded, lies in the question of how to determine when and the extent to which an intervention with a particular drug has been of value.[10] This is particularly true given that the scientific field lacks a straightforward method of determining even what would count as *evidence* of value.[11]

A variant of value-based pricing would look at outcomes. In this particular approach, drug companies would provide a drug, and the payer would receive a rebate if the drug were to fail to save a patient's life, provide a cure, or work as expected.[12] For example, Novartis is testing this approach with an expensive drug for the treatment of pediatric patients with acute lymphoblasic leukemia.[13] The company will charge for the drug only if patients respond to treatment after one month of therapy. Thinking back to the notion of evidence of value, would improvement after one month of therapy justify a highly expensive drug? If the patient receives some benefit, but their life is extended by only a few months, would that be sufficient?

Pricing and patient care data would be key for monitoring these value-based contracts. Imagine a vertically integrated PBM–insurer–pharmacy, which already has an incentive to share data with its rebate-conferring drug company partners. These will be the only entities controlling this essential information, which is necessary for evaluating the drug company's value claims. Such information and data analysis asymmetries will only expand and grow more problematic, making it nearly impossible for payors and government entities to engage in independent auditing.

In addition, putting aside the sticky issue of determining the extent to which a drug "provided value," outcomes-based pricing could present serious moral hazards. In simplified form, drug companies essentially are saying, "I will give you my expensive drug. If the patient dies, you either get a rebate or don't pay in the first place." This could create an uncomfortable incentive structure, in which insurers, PBMs, hospitals, and doctors get paid more if the patient dies. Why would one want a system in which the provider does better financially if the patient dies? That is particularly of concern if the drug company's payments are arriving in the form of rebates, rather than in the form of free initial use. Society particularly might be concerned if rebates were to be given to a hospital at key times of the year that could be distributed to executives and staff or used to improve a hospital's books at the end of a reporting period. Moreover, some of the risks associated with the complex diseases, for which many of these outcomes-based models are proposed, are not solely attributable to the drug treatment. As a result, the structure could have an impact on incentives to provide complimentary care that may be costly or burdensome on a hospital.

I recognize that many readers may bristle at the moral concerns raised here. And I do want to articulate my deep conviction that our healthcare system is staffed with people who genuinely care about their patients and do their best to provide compassionate care. However, as this book demonstrates repeatedly and as behavioral economics counsels, human beings are – well, human beings. We behave according to the incentives presented to us; we value the short term over the long term; we overvalue our own position and what we might lose; and we have a remarkable ability to rationalize our own behavior. Anyone who doubts the last point should consider the foibles of politicians and public figures throughout the ages, let alone in the era of social media. Most importantly, we do not travel with an artificial intelligence brain whispering into our ear the long-range effects and complex calculations of various choices. At the end of the day, we are subject to the pettiness of our limited rationality, buffeted by incentives that drive us to enact behaviors that might seem a tad unappealing in the cold light of day.

Nevertheless, value-based pricing is gaining popularity among drug companies and many commentators.[14] Most tellingly, value-based programs are already moving into place. For example, Oklahoma approved a value-based purchasing approach for its Medicaid program in 2018.[15] This movement toward value-based pricing is occurring despite the fact that it might actually raise prices. For example, in discussing the industry's support for value-based pricing, the executive vice president of PhRMA, pharmaceutical industry's trade association, made the following comments in the context of new, breakthrough drugs coming to market:

> [W]ill it have a big price tag? It might. If we really are moving toward a value-based health care system, then medicines that truly represent value should merit a larger price, and we're comfortable with saying that should be the case.[16]

When the pharmaceutical industry tells us that prices are going to be high in a value-based system, perhaps we should listen.

Drug companies certainly would like to find some basis other than cost for measuring the price of their medicines. The marginal cost of producing a particular pill may be quite low – and certainly not high enough to justify the eye-popping prices tags on the shelves these days. Even if we throw in costs for research and development on that drug directly, the numbers may not add up. And they may still not add up even if we throw in costs for the company's failures.[17] Thus drug companies themselves have to look for other ways of justifying pricing.

One can certainly understand the appeal of value-based pricing given that pricing and intellectual property goodies, such as patents and exclusivities, seem devoid of any connection to patient value. As noted in Chapter 2, my own life and comfort may be of incalculable value to me, even when the likelihood of success is low or the additional lifespan provided is minimal. How does one value an extraordinarily expensive cancer drug that extends life by only two months? The United States has been particularly queasy about approaching the issue of value, and the U.S. Food and Drug Administration (FDA) is not permitted to consider value when approving a drug. In contrast, European approval authorities may choose not to approve a drug if the drug does not appreciatively improve life in proportion to its price.[18]

As we turn toward value-based measures, the notion of value must be cabined. As one commentator explained, the value of giving my child a polio vaccine may be US$1 million per dose, because it would be worth that to avoid my child succumbing to polio.[19] The US healthcare system would collapse, however, if each vaccine were to cost $1 million per dose. And, indeed, everything we do with pharmaceuticals may have value, but can we afford all of that, particularly when our ability to value life and comfort is subject to such irrationality?

In contemplating value, society should think in terms of what I would call "cumulative value." If the national budget for drug spending is a certain amount (or the average person's budget for drug spending is a certain amount), how much of that amount does it make sense to spend on this particular advance? Otherwise, if value is open-ended and has no sense of total upper boundaries, we could value ourselves into budget oblivion.

6.1.2 Direct Negotiations by Medicare

Another proposal that has received considerable attention relates to having Medicare negotiate for drug prices directly with pharmaceutical companies.[20] The issue plays out in the following manner: The Medicare prescription drug benefit is administered by states through private healthcare plans. Each private plan (generally through its PBM) negotiates drug prices. In debates more than a decade ago, Congress concluded that a marketplace of private plans competing with each other would be better than a direct government drug benefit.[21] Federal legislation goes to great lengths to forbid any participation by the federal government, specifying that the Secretary of Health and Human Services, who oversees Medicare, "(1) may not interfere with the negotiations between drug manufacturers and pharmacies and [health plans]; and (2) may not require a particular formulary or institute a price structure for reimbursement of [drugs covered by Medicare]."[22] In contrast, certain other federal programs, such as Veterans Administration (VA) drug benefits and Medicaid, have greater latitude for federal regulators and have enjoyed more success in holding down prices.[23] (Medicaid provides benefits to the poor, while Medicare provides benefits to those over the age of 65. Both are federal programs administered by the states.)

Giving federal regulators a greater role in the process might provide the leverage of greater buying power. The Medicare program accounts for 29 percent of the money spent on prescription drugs in the United States. That market presence provides purchasing muscle, along with the government's ability to coordinate without facing antitrust concerns. Nevertheless, allowing federal regulators to have negotiating power for Medicare drugs may not provide the silver bullet some may be hoping for – at least not on its own. Medicare is an enormously complex program, which breeds numerous opportunities for manipulation. For example, as explained in Chapter 3, even basic rebates do not fully pass through under Medicare – a circumstance that already creates incentives that push prices higher. Moreover, the pharmaceutical industry has proven quite adept at outflanking the federal government in the face of complex legislative and regulatory schemes. The process becomes a "Whac-a-mole" game, in which the federal government tries to find loopholes, and industry finds a new pathway.

Finally, in the past the Congressional Budget Office (CBO) has expressed some skepticism that giving federal regulators negotiating power for Medicare would bring about substantial cost savings unless the government were willing to exclude certain drugs and limit the utilization of others.[24] The CBO's analysis is almost 15 years old now, however, which may make its conclusions less salient. All of this is not to suggest that giving negotiating power to federal regulators within the

Medicare system would be unhelpful; only that much more would be needed in addition.

6.1.3 Slay the Dragon

With public outcry increasing, legislators and regulators at all levels are scrambling for solutions and, as always, for someone to blame. In that context, calls are emerging to radically reform, or even to eliminate, PBMs. To offer a truly loose analogy, if PBMs are like to bar owners, then Prohibition is on the horizon. But will it help?

To answer that question, one must understand that two related problems are occurring in the drug distribution system. One problem is the system of rebates and other persuasion payments that create upward pressure on prices. Eliminating or neutering PBMs could certainly help with this problem. It could defuse the odd system in which artificial price rises create mad money for PBMs. Thus, one would expect to see some stabilization and improvement in drug pricing, with concomitant benefits for patients and taxpayers.

The system of rebates and other payments, however, is only one of the two problems. The second is the pressure exerted by drug companies to keep lower-priced competitors from gaining traction in the market – and this second problem is unlikely to evaporate even if PBMs magically disappear.

Imagine a world without PBMs. Among other changes, drug companies would have to negotiate directly with health insurance plans over the prices of their drugs. However, just as drug companies have been sharing some of their monopoly rents with PBMs to block out lower-priced competitors, drug companies could shift to sharing some of their monopoly rents with health insurance companies in a similar manner. The same type of factors would still be in play. To reiterate only a few: A company with a drug coming off patent would still have the volume position that would allow it to offer attractive inducements to insurance plans – inducements that the new, lower-priced entrant could not beat. Companies with a stable of drugs – some with stronger protection, some with weaker protection – could bargain across all of those drugs, once again sharing some of the monopoly rents from one drug to strangle nascent competition. The benefits of ensuring competition among drug companies, if it is possible for one health insurer to pursue such a goal alone, would be enjoyed by all plans, so no single player would choose to take that path. The fact that health insurance executives need to meet financial expectations could enhance a drug company's ability to offer enticements. The short-term allure of persuasion payments could tempt insurers far more than the uncertain long-term benefits of competition.

The health insurance market is less concentrated than the PBM market – which boasts three powerful players holding, among them, 85 percent of the market. One would hope that some competitive pressures would push health insurers toward more rational behavior. Nevertheless, health insurance markets exhibit their own concentration problems – albeit not as dramatic as those of the PBM markets.[25] Moreover, the type of factors noted above will still favor the efforts of drug companies to strangle nascent competition. Competition, with its salutary effect on pricing, is unlikely to flourish.

Moving the activity from the PBM level to the health insurance level could have an unfortunate side effect. Many federal laws, includ-ing those related to antitrust, exempt insurance companies from federal regulation, leaving that domain to the states.[26] For example, the McCarran-Ferguson Act restricts the ability of the Federal Trade Commission (FTC) to regulate insurance markets, limiting the FTC to regulating the business of insurance only to the extent that it is *not* regulated by state law.[27] McCarran-Ferguson dates back to 1945, and repeated attempts to repeal it have been rebuffed.[28] Thus, if the primary locus of activity shifts to interactions involving health insurers, the federal government's role will be severely limited.

Federal and state actors each have critical roles to play in battling problems in the pharmaceutical market, and it is always better to enter a battle with allies at your side. Sidelining the powerful federal govern-ment would create a distinct disadvantage. Thus moving the PBMs aside could have the effect of seriously hampering reform efforts.

Perhaps the greatest risk of aiming all of the firepower at PBMs is the possibility of exhaustion. Passing legislation over the objection of the pharmaceutical industry is extremely challenging, particularly without handing over some other benefit to the industry.[29] Congress and other regulators could expend enormous effort to neutralize the

PBMs, then declare victory and bring the troops home. At the end of the day, while prices might stabilize or back off to some degree, the heart of the problem would remain, but the political will would be spent.

6.2 WHAT WILL WORK?

6.2.1 Market Information

Markets, like gardens, grow best in the sun. They wither without information. Thus, when an industry's pricing information and rebate relationships are secret, deeply hidden, or obscured even from payors, one should not be surprised to see significant competitive distortions and problematic outcomes. Quite simply, entrants and prospective entrants power the economic engines of competition, and information provides the fuel for those engines.

To begin restoring sanity to pharmaceutical markets, information must flow. That includes transparency about pricing information. All aspects of the deals, including rebates and financial benefits in any form, should be visible, at a minimum, to the payers and the government. Governments, however, have limited resources and face numerous demands. In light of these limitations, in the best of all circumstances, the full range of information would be visible to competitors and to the public. In particular, in an open and democratic society, we would be foolish to bypass the power of the press and individual citizens in their ability to ferret out objectionable behavior, especially in the modern age of crowdsourcing and social media. One can understand why industry would not wish to see this, but why would society put shackles around its great twin powers: the free market and an informed citizenry? These are among the core values upon which the United States rests, although certainly not the only ones.

6.2.1.1 Changes at the Federal Level

The best opportunities for shining light into the deep, dark crevices of pharmaceutical pricing lie at federal legislative and regulatory levels.

Any number of federal laws could be amended to mandate information transparency. This could be done through amendments to the Food and Drug Act of 1906, which regulates the manufacture and marketing of all prescription and nonprescription medication, the Employee Retirement Income Security Act of 1974 (ERISA), which sets standards for pensions and health plans in private industry,[30] or by an expansion of the Physician Payments Sunshine Act of 2010.[31] The agencies that administer these programs, along with the agencies that administer Medicare and Medicaid, could similarly mandate transparency.

More indirectly, transparency could be accomplished through regulation by the federal agencies that fund pharmaceutical research. Many of the drugs that end up in our medicine cabinets begin with the federal funding of academic research by agencies such as the National Institutes of Health (NIH). Regulations issued by such bodies could mandate that those who receive funding must include transparency stipulations for those who license or purchase the resulting inventions.[32]

6.2.1.2 Changes at the State Level

States also have the power to mandate transparency. This is certainly true when the state is an employer, administrator of a program, or other payor, and it is likely true for all health insurance activity within the state's borders.[33] States also may have the power to mandate particular aspects of information openness by means of state pharmacy substitution laws, related to substituting generic prescriptions for brands, and other state regulatory processes. In fact, states continue to be at the forefront of battling these difficult issues. States have passed or proposed 178 bills (enacting 44 of them) relating to price transparency, clawbacks, price gouging, gag rules (which keep pharmacists from pointing customers toward the cheapest alternatives), and PBM regulation.[34]

The proposals range from bold to timid, and the road ahead is not for the faint of heart. The pharmaceutical industry is expected to mount fierce opposition to these laws, including filing suits on grounds of trade secret laws, the First Amendment, and various other US constitutional provisions.[35] Such challenges already have been filed in California, Nevada, Maryland, and North Dakota.[36]

Some respected academics and government reports also have argued that drug-pricing information should be kept secret, based on the notion that if drug companies know the true prices that their competitors are offering for drugs, the companies will collude to keep prices high.[37] Although well-meaning, those analyses are misguided. To begin with, some of these perspectives are based on a study from the 1990s of bidding in the cement industry in Denmark.[38] It is a limited data point from an industry that has struggled with collusion.[39] One would need far more convincing evidence to support shrouding an entire industry in darkness, particularly when that darkness is hiding behavior so damaging to the nation's citizens.

In general, it is quite odd to suggest that keeping price information secret is good for competition. When things are secret, any collusion that exists will be extremely difficult to uncover. Moreover, the notion that price information is a recipe for collusion defies the experience of the nation's free market economy, in which pricing information normally is not hidden from consumers, government entities, and auditors.

If price information truly is such a dangerous catalyst for collusion, the current system is certainly no panacea. As described throughout this book, there are numerous ways in which the current secrecy helps entrenched players to insulate themselves from competition. Price secrecy may also help to maintain the position of dominant players. A subset of large players will be able to discover the prices, with the result that the collusive behavior will be impossible to detect, along with other improper behavior that is occurring. In the end, the players we worry most about may be able to obtain the information, while mid-sized competitors, which are best suited to inject true competition, are left in the cold. Finally, if we are truly convinced that drug companies will collude in their bidding with PBMs, we could always mandate that the information have a delayed release, as opposed to insisting that the information must never see the light of day.

6.2.1.3 The Al Capone Approach

With bar owners as our image, perhaps we should return to the era of Prohibition and borrow a strategy effective in relation to that era's famous gangster Al Capone. The Federal Bureau of Investigation (FBI) finally was able to jail Capone not for his many crimes related to bootlegging alcohol, murder, and mayhem, but for tax evasion.[40] In other words, sometimes the indirect approach can be effective when the direct approach may be difficult to accomplish.

For example, mandating transparency certainly is one approach, but other mechanisms might work as well. Consider a recent exchange between Express Scripts (one of the big three PBMs) and the Securities and Exchange Commission (SEC).[41] The series of letters involves the PBM's accounting treatment of various items and the disclosure involved in that treatment. In the exchange, the SEC objects to the fact that Express Scripts does not separately disclose the rebates and other payments it receives from pharmaceutical companies, as well as other detailed information.

Express Scripts may be making a good faith effort to comply with accounting standards, given the unusual timing and funding flows of the industry. Nevertheless, the exchange is a poignant reminder of the SEC's power. If accounting regulations designed and applied to the PBM industry were to require a different level of disclosure, the shadowy world of pricing might find itself in the sunlight.

In its comments to Express Scripts, the SEC conveys surprise that the PBM seems to be treating the money flow from drug companies as though the drug companies were the PBM's customers – when in fact, the health plans are the customers. Here is the SEC's language: "It is unclear why you believe accounts receivable from pharmaceutical manufacturers are a component of customer receivables considering that pharmaceutical manufacturers do not appear to be your customer."[42]

The choice to lump the revenue flow from pharmaceutical companies in with the revenue flow from health plans may simply be sloppy accounting, and Express Scripts readily agrees to separate out the two figures going forward.[43] Nevertheless, Dr. Freud might suggest that there are no accidents: It would be quite easy for a PBM to begin thinking of drug companies as its clients, rather than keeping the interests of health plans and patients in mind.[44]

In particular, financial disclosures such as these highlight the extent to which *nonrebate* revenue from drug companies may constitute a significant part of a PBM's business. In the case of Express Scripts, its 2017 annual report suggests that nonrebate revenue from drug companies could be up to $1.4 billion – a significant figure in comparison to Express Script's $5.4 billion in operating income.[45]

From society's perspective, one might hope that the law would channel a PBM into thinking of the good of the patients served by the formularies it is crafting. Attempts to claim that PBMs have a duty to patients have fallen flat, however, running up against issues related to ERISA, the mammoth federal law that governs most health plans and pensions.[46] A different understanding of the role of ERISA could shift the landscape considerably, opening the door to claims that the PBMs are breaching their fiduciary duty to patients.

As an additional alternative to mandating that PBMs and drug companies make their pricing information public, governments might be able to achieve similar results by acting in their capacity as buyers. In this case, the government entities would be borrowing a page from the federal procurement book. For example, companies selling to federal defense agencies must disclose a host of information on pricing in sole bidding circumstances. Until 2013, the statute was known by the memorable acronym TINA (the Truth in Negotiations Act), but it is now saddled with the far less memorable title, the Truthful Cost or Pricing Data Act.[47] Commercial items such as drugs, however, are exempt from this statute.[48]

A state or federal government agency could promulgate a regulation that, in its capacity as a buyer of health insurance products, the agency requires full pricing information to be provided. Although such an approach would mandate disclosure only when the government is a buyer, the government is a buyer in a wide swath of purchases. In this manner, governments would not have to mandate that drug company–PBM interactions must be revealed in all circumstances, yet a wealth of critical information would be revealed. Thus, rather than flatly mandating transparency, the government could accomplish much of the same result simply by virtue of its rights as "little old buyer, me."

In short, when the direct route is not feasible, there are times when an indirect route might get you there as well. In other words, governments might follow the Al Capone example.[49]

6.2.2 Reduce Concentration and Rethink Markets

6.2.2.1 The Shape of Markets

Rising prices and competition concerns raise questions about the level of concentration in various levels of the drug delivery chain. The PBM markets are dominated by three players, which among them hold up to 85 percent of the commercial insurers market; PBMs also have merged with large pharmacy chains, along with purchasing specialty pharmacies. Concentration also has increased in the generic drug industry, insurance markets, wholesale markets, and in local hospital markets – although perhaps not to the severe extent seen in the PBM market.[50] In light of these concerns, federal and state competition agencies should tread carefully when it comes to approving merger and purchase requests from major players, either at the same level of the distribution chain horizontally or between players at different levels of the distribution chain vertically.[51]

6.2.2.2 Market Power and Multiplicity Effects

In examining markets themselves, competition agencies would do well to focus on the potential anticompetitive effects possible as a result of the PBM contracting and incentive structures described throughout this book. One does not need market domination in a particular drug to create these effects, and federal market penetration measures may fail to capture properly the effects of those behaviors.[52] This is particularly true in the context of deals that exploit volume across multiple drugs. If competition measures focus only on the market power of each individual drug in a company's stable, the power of overall volumes and the multiplicity effects will be overlooked.

The varying ways of exerting power in pharmaceutical markets described in this book should be a wake-up call to state and federal regulatory agencies, whose definitions of market power should be updated to consider multiplicity effects. In particular, given that antitrust authorities evaluate actions by looking at a relevant market,[53] the definition of "relevant market" is key.

During the 1990s era of federal government action against Microsoft, the notion of relevant markets expanded to include the notion of nascent markets.[54] Antitrust authorities recognized that an existing company might exert power not only to threaten competitors in a current market, but also to prevent the creation of new markets that might threaten its dominance.[55] In other words, measuring only existing markets allows actions that can strangle the baby in its cradle, before a new technological or splinter market ever struggles to its feet. This is a tremendously important advance, but in light of modern multiplicity effects, more is needed.

This is not the first time that multiplicity effects in markets have stymied antitrust concerns. In the context of patent trolling, courts and antitrust authorities do not have the tools for combating the potential to affect prices in one market by targeting companies across that market with a large portfolio of patents that will be too expensive to fight off, even if most of the patents are unrelated to that market and many of them are weak.[56]

In a similar vein, one cannot fully measure the potential competitive impact of agreements related to a particular drug and its substitutes without looking at the full range of drugs and markets that might be leveraged through that activity. In short, modern markets require the development of a multiplicity of analyses that allow antitrust authorities to understand and measure ripple effects, along with the complex effects of volume and bundling.

6.2.2.3 Hub-and-Spokes Structures and Artificial Intelligence

Competition agencies also may need to be sensitive to the potential for hub-and-spokes structures. A hub-and-spokes arrangement can be understood in the following general terms: Market competitors may not get together on price or other specifications; such horizontal collusion is at the core of forbidden behavior under antitrust laws. In a hub-and-spokes arrangement, middle parties can create the mechanism for collusion among the competitors, enforcing agreements that have the effect of maintaining price controls or blocking lower-priced competitors from access that would harm the power of the group.[57] The middle player is the hub, which connects all of the competitors arrayed around it on spokes. Although that may not be the case with the drug industry, when prices are rising dramatically and middle players hold significant sway, one would want to monitor the situation carefully.

The relationship between the concentrated PBM industry and PBM consultants may also contribute to the potential for collusion – certainly among the PBMs and possibly through them – among the drug companies. Consultants to the PBM industry offer advice based on databases of prices and formulary costs. Particularly where there is a concentrated industry and a small number of consultants, competitors do not need to speak to each other, but can nevertheless converge on similar prices and terms.

A cutting-edge area of concern within the consultant sphere is the potential for collusion established through artificial intelligence (AI) programs.[58] Without AI, human analysts are likely to reach differing conclusions about the precise behavior that would lead to optimal results – at least if there is no collusion. Suppose, however, that AI programs have the ability to cycle through the behavioral options in a complex, layered manner that consistently reaches approximately the same results. Different entities could have perfectly coordinated efforts, while pointing to the AI to say, "The computer made me do it." How would one prove collusive intent in a circumstance like that? The challenges of AI for planning behavior will require creative rethinking of antitrust doctrines.

Finally, from a competition standpoint, the most interesting change on the horizon may be arising within the market itself. Amazon, Berkshire Hathaway (Warren Buffet's behemoth), and J.P. Morgan have formed a new venture to disrupt the PBM and pharmaceutical distribution system.[59] Using their own businesses as a lab, the trio hopes to develop ways of delivering health care to the more than one million employees of their companies in a way that reduces the high prices, administrative costs, and waste of the current system. When giants walk, the earth trembles. The Amazon/Berkshire Hathaway/J.P. Morgan venture is a market solution that has fascinating potential, assuming that the government regulations favoring entrenched players do not get in the way.

6.3 ONE AND DONE

As described in Chapter 5, a drug company's position in the market and ability to string that position out across time create the underlying power structures that feed into keeping competitors from gaining traction once they get to market. Drug companies with a dominant position and a stable of drugs that have many patents strung out among them are in the best position to bargain with PBMs so that their drugs emerge victorious in the formulary scramble.

As with other aspects of pharmaceutical pricing, numerous small changes to the patent and exclusivity system have been made, and are likely to be suggested. Tinkering approaches, however, are likely to result in continued cat-and-mouse games, in which government authorities attempt to close a strategic avenue, and drug companies develop another one. One approach for cutting through the complexity would be to implement a "one and done" principle for the protection of drug innovation.

Under a one-and-done system, a drug would receive *one* period of exclusivity, and only one. The choice of which "one" could be left entirely in the hands of the pharmaceutical company, with the election made at the moment of drug approval. Perhaps development and approval on the drug has gone swiftly and smoothly, so the remaining life of one of the drug's patents is of greatest value. Perhaps those processes languished through many setbacks, such that designation as an orphan drug or some other benefit would bring greater reward. The choice would be up to the company itself, based on its own calculation of the maximum benefit. The result, however, would be that a pharmaceutical company must choose whether its period of exclusivity should be a patent, or an orphan drug designation, or a period of data exclusivity for safety and efficacy data, or something else – but not all of the above and more.

Crafting one-and-done implementation at the FDA level underscores the fact that these problems and solutions are designed for pharmaceuticals, not other types of technology. Although there are similarities within the patent system for all inventions, given the drug approval processes (including the Hatch-Waxman system for the approval of generic drugs and the biosimilars pathway for approval of follow-on biologics), pharmaceuticals are different.

Much of "one and done" could be implemented through legislative changes to the FDA drug approval system, which would apply to patents granted going forward. Statutory amendments could specify

that, once a company elects a particular patent or exclusivity, competitors wishing to obtain approval of a generic version of the drug through
the Hatch-Waxman system need only certify to that one exclusivity.

The election could be crafted so that it mandates relinquishment of
any other patent or exclusivity claims relating to the generic drug being
approved. This approach would be somewhat analogous to an election,
which currently exists under the Hatch-Waxman Act. When a generic
applicant makes a "paragraph IV" certification claiming that the
brand-name company's patents are invalid or do not apply to the drug,
the brand-name company has a period of time in which to challenge
that certification in court. If the brand-name company fails to challenge
the assertion, it relinquishes various rights, particularly the right to an
automatic 30-month stay of the generic's approval. Without the 30-
month stay, the brand-name company would have to prove likelihood
of success on the merits and other preliminary injunction factors to
keep the generic off the market during the period of the litigation.[60]
Similarly, in the proposed system, the company's choice to designate a
particular form of exclusivity upon approval could serve to relinquish
its right to challenge the generic under any other exclusivity.

Although the concept of "one and done" would include both patents
and exclusivities – allowing inventors to choose one coverage period
among the entire group – one could craft an approach for patents only.
Although a limited approach, it would be easier to draft and possibly
more politically palatable. One pathway could be to expand the judi-
cially created doctrine that prevents patent holders from what is known
as "obviousness-type double patenting."[61] The doctrine is intended to
prevent the approval of claims from a second patent where the new
claims are not clearly distinct from those of the first.[62] In theory, one
could craft a sister doctrine to prevent secondary patents from the
perspective that the core of the invention is no more than the original
chemical formulation.[63] Anything else is merely an obvious adaptation
of what was the core of the invention, modified with existing technology.

In designing this approach, one could borrow a page from the
Supreme Court's approach in the doctrine of patentable subject
matter. That Court has cast doubt on numerous patents by taking an
expansive view of what falls within the category of an unpatentable law
of nature and then holding that:

[I]f a law of nature is not patentable, then neither is a process reciting the law of nature, unless that process has additional features that provide practical assurance that the process is more than a drafting effort designed to monopolize the law of nature itself.

In other words, the Supreme Court Justices took aim at patents in which they felt that, putting aside what already exists in nature or elsewhere, there is (as Gertrude Stein would say) "no more 'there' there."

The Justices established a two-part test in which one should first determine whether the patent is directed to one of the ineligible categories – abstract ideas, natural phenomena, etc. – and then should look to see if the patent has something more:

We have described step two of this analysis as a search for an "inventive concept" – i.e., an element or combination of elements that is "sufficient to ensure that the patent in practice amounts to significantly more than a patent upon the [ineligible concept] itself."[64]

The Supreme Court's "patentable subject matter" doctrine was greeted by howls of protest, and it has been the subject of repeated attacks by the patent bar and by the Federal Circuit, which has never been known for fealty to the Court.[65] The complaints have argued that the doctrine is confusing and unworkable because it is impossible to pin down how a patent holder can satisfy the Court's two-part test. That, indeed, may be the Court's point: Its quartet of cases may have been intended to eliminate much, if not all, of the types of patent considered in those cases. A similar type of doctrinal development could be applied to the doctrine of obviousness-type double patenting.

Of course, one could argue that many secondary patents are obvious adaptations of the original invention and existing technology, and that, as such, they should already fail on obviousness grounds anyway. Indeed, a more vigorous and robust application of the current obviousness doctrine could go a long way toward reducing behaviors such as a company piling on additional patents.

Either invigorating the doctrine of obviousness or expanding the doctrine of obviousness-type double patenting could be accomplished through judicial or legislative changes. Although adjusting obviousness doctrines is an easier approach, it does have the drawback of including only patents, while the broader one-and-done approach could address all patents and exclusivities.

If all of these suggestions are too politically unpalatable, one might at least consider pushing secondary patents into some form of short exclusivity, rather than a full patent term. One could argue that secondary formulations might have some value to some patients, even if the value does not justify 20 years. Although this solution has advantages over the current morass, it would not strike at the heart of the problem – at least not on its own.

If Congress adopted a more expansive one-and-done approach, one could argue that the length of a patent should be extended. After all, patent holders would be losing the ability to stretch their patents – an ability they have enjoyed for some time. Doing so would reflect the compromise struck with the Hatch-Waxman Act, which provided additional time for a patent in exchange for the expedited approval process for generic entrants. Of course, one could also argue that the various techniques employed to extend one's protection cliff either distort the intent of the system or constitute outright abuse. Nevertheless, Congress did indeed intend to allow delay of the protection cliff in at least some cases with the creation of certain exclusivities. Moreover, it may be politically expedient to follow the path blazed by Hatch-Waxman, although allowing extensions beyond a year or two could undermine the benefits gained by a comprehensive one-and-done system.

In a similar vein, Congress could choose to standardize the periods of protection offered by various exclusivities, which currently range from six months to seven years. As described in section 6.4 on simplification, the complexity of these various systems provides opportunities for game-playing. Standardization may reduce those opportunities.

Some commentators may be tempted to claim that any relinquishment of patent or exclusivity rights constitutes a taking of private property. In particular, one scholar has asserted that patent rights are constitutionally protected property and, as such, would be subject to the Fifth Amendment Takings Clause.[66] Even that author, however, acknowledges that "modern courts and scholars ... seem to agree in a rare case of unanimity that the historic record reflects no instance of a federal court holding that the Takings Clause applies to patents."[67]

In a 2018 case upholding the *inter partes* review system at the U.S. Patent and Trademark Office (USPTO), the Supreme Court specifically avoided ruling on the question of whether patents are property for the purpose of the Takings Clause.[68] In a paragraph that begins by noting, "[w]e emphasize the narrowness of our holding" and presents a litany of what the decision does not address, the Court cryptically concludes by noting that "our decision should not be misconstrued as suggesting that patents are not property for purposes of the Due Process Clause or the Takings Clause." The Justices then cite two cases related to sovereign immunity and whether the state can be sued for using a patented item without paying for it.[69] In contrast, the two dissenting Justices use language that would move the status of patents much closer into the realm of traditional property rights. This suggests that whether, and the extent to which, patents are treated as property for constitutional purposes is likely to arise in future Supreme Court cases.

The notion of patents as full property rights – akin to the type of core property rights protected by the Constitution – would require ignoring significant aspects of patent history and theory. Patent rights are theoretically, doctrinally, and practically distinct from real property, making the notion of an absolute right to exclude particularly inapplicable.[70] Even basic patent doctrines have, from time immemorial, provided for overlapping rights, such that more than one patent holder may have the right to exclude others from the exact same space.[71] More important, unlike real property such as land, patent rights are granted by the government for limited times and for limited purposes – namely, promoting the progress of the useful arts[72] for the benefit of society. With patents, the utilitarian roots of their theory and design bear little resemblance to natural rights theories of the types of property protected by the Constitution.

One particularly cogent modern description of the issue appears in a dissent to the 2015 Supreme Court decision in the *Teva* case, in which the dissenters reviewed the history of patent rights in contrast to core property rights:

> The Anglo-American legal tradition has long distinguished between "core" private rights – including the traditional property rights represented by deeds – and other types of rights. These other

rights [include] "privileges" or "franchises," which public authorities have created purely for reasons of public policy and which ha[ve] no counterpart in the Lockean state of nature. Notwithstanding a movement to recognize a core property right in inventions, the English common law placed patents squarely in the final category as franchises.[73]

As the text of the dissent also explained, the U.S. Constitution's "[f]ramers adopted a similar scheme."[74]

In short, patents are not core property rights and attempting to characterize them as such threatens the reverence that the nation has traditionally held for core property rights. Although concerns may play out in the context of due process, the notion that the Takings Clause would prevent Congress from shortening the length of time or the interaction among various patent rights[75] would be misguided, at best.

6.4 RUTHLESS SIMPLIFICATION

For those who like complexity, the system of intellectual property rights for pharmaceuticals is a garden of delights. From the Hatch-Waxman legislation through the Biologics Price Competition and Innovation Act of 2009 (the Biosimilars Act), to the maze of regulatory exclusivities and beyond, the judicial and regulatory processes surrounding intellectual property rights for drugs are among the most complex corners of our legal system.

Of course, some complexity in pharmaceuticals is inevitable. The intellectual property rights systems for drugs must, of necessity, interact with approval processes, and those approval processes must operate with exquisite awareness of public health and safety. These are heady responsibilities. Nevertheless, the system has become so complex and convoluted that it threatens to collapse in on itself.

And, of course, complexity breeds endless opportunities.[76] It ensures that the legislators and regulators will always be at least a step behind in an endless game of cat and mouse. Year after year, government actors must attempt to block strategic behaviors that have developed even as the industry develops new ones.[77] In such a process, it is clear that our incentives structure is badly misaligned with societal goals.

Putting the system back on track will require ruthless simplification. It means stripping away the intricate details that are so appealing to those who must forge compromises among interest groups, compromises that sow the seeds of current and future strategic behavior. In short, what has become business as usual for the pharmaceutical industry must become a thing of the past.

The 180-day period of exclusivity for first-filing generics is a classic example of a complexity that provides game-playing opportunities, one that is ripe for simplification. It is an extremely complicated and intricate piece of legislation. Unfortunately, as described in Chapter 5, the system has provided a method for generics and branded pharmaceutical companies to form anticompetitive agreements within which the generic agrees to stay off the market in exchange for some form of payment.[78]

A simplified approach, in which the six-month period of exclusivity attaches only if the patent is actually invalidated, could reduce the game playing. Along the same lines, one scholar has suggested that governments should reduce complexity by viewing any transfer of contemporaneous value conferral as a payment.[79] Frankly – and although it is akin to heresy to suggest this – one could argue that the entire first-filer exclusivity period should be eliminated. There may be sufficient market opportunities for generics without that incentive – particularly given the high price of branded pharmaceuticals – and the game playing it has spawned may outweigh the benefits of having such a system.

A broader tactic for simplification would involve taking a standards-based approach instead of, or in addition to, a rules-based approach. The goal with a standards-based approach would be look at the overall effect of a behavior in an effort to thwart those who follow the letter of the law, but manage to arrive at a destination that the law intends to forbid. Such an approach can be useful when those being governed may be able to find loopholes to defeat governmental intent. The tax code's "step transaction" doctrine provides a classic example of a standards approach, allowing tax authorities to collapse all steps of a transaction if the steps are part of an overall plan to avoid taxation.[80]

Of course, a legal restriction packs a powerful punch only if authorities are willing to wield that restriction. Consider citizen petitions filed at the FDA for the purpose of delaying competitive entry. In an effort to limit the impact of that type of behavior, Congress passed legislation providing that the FDA must rule on a citizen petition within 150 days.[81] This is an example of a rules-based solution to a problem.[82] In the same legislation, Congress granted the FDA the ability to summarily deny a citizen petition if the petition has "the primary purpose of delaying the approval of an application."[83] An example of a standards-based approach, the summary denial provision suffers from two problems.[84] First, the petition is toothless. At worst, the sham tactic fails more quickly, and the company trying the tactic moves onto another approach. Second, the FDA has yet to summarily deny a single petition – and this despite empirical evidence that the majority of petitions are filed as a last-ditch effort to hold off competition[85] and that almost all petitions are denied.[86] A standard is useless if no one is willing to apply it and if the results of its application are meaningless.

Although one tends to think of penalties in terms of dollars assessed to a company, that need not be the case. Pharmaceutical companies can pay hundreds of millions of dollars in fines and still find a tactic to have been worth the cost. In 2015, pharmaceutical company Teva paid $1.2 billion in FTC fines and class-action settlements regarding its pay-for-delay tactics to block generic competitors of its narcolepsy drug Provigil.[87] Despite this hefty bill, the company still profited from the delay to the tune of roughly $2 billion.[88]

In addition to, or in the place of, fines, Congress or a regulatory agency could provide that a misbehaving company will lose certain regulatory privileges. The government also could impose penalties on the lawyers involved in behaviors that violate the standards. For example, under the SEC's system to deter fraudulent filings, the Enforcement Division can impose punishment on the company making the filing, and the Litigation Division can suspend the attorney from practice before the Commission.[89] This could provide a model for responding to bad behavior in the drug industry and could be applied at either the state or federal level, depending on the level at which the bad behavior occurs.

In short, a standards-based approach could make it more difficult for companies to profit from sophisticated strategies designed to exploit complex systems. Standards are useless, however, unless someone has the power and the will to enforce them.

6.5 PAVING A BETTER ROAD

One-and-done and ruthless simplification, coupled with transparency measures, could go a long way toward returning the system of pharmaceutical innovation to its proper competitive pathway. There will, of course, be much wailing and gnashing of teeth. The drug industry has become comfortably accustomed to working with a system that provides space for creating noncompetitive environments. The industry will not relinquish this environment with ease and grace, and the nation is likely to hear impassioned pleading that pharmaceuticals cannot withstand any reform of the current system.[90] Foreshadowing such public relations battles, the chief executive officer of pharmaceutical company Allergan published a 2017 op-ed in the *Wall Street Journal* arguing that the 2011 patent reforms, which created a new post-grant review process for patents, left the company with no choice but to transfer its patents to Indian tribes to avoid having its patents reviewed.

When companies plead with the government for beneficial treatment by arguing that they cannot withstand competition, one should be deeply skeptical. Our challenge as a society is to restore the balance provided by the patent system itself, in which the inventor of a truly innovative product receives a limited period of time in which to attempt to garner a return, following which open competition reigns supreme. The system has strayed far from that ideal.

As a final thought, imagine the landscape a decade from now. Where will we be if drug prices have continued to soar, if basic medications cost tens of thousands of dollars a year and more complex medications cost millions, and if drug development continues to focus on churning and repurposing existing drugs, with little true innovation? Is that the future we wish to usher in? Perhaps, instead, we will have stepped back from the precipice – bringing some measure of sanity and rationality to an industry that has defied efforts to introduce competition. Or perhaps we should all reach for anti-anxiety medication. . .

At least today, it's a mere $1,285 for 30 tablets.[91]

NOTES

Chapter 1

1 Meg Tirrell, *First U.S. Drug Priced at More Than $1 Million May Be on the Horizon*, CNBC (May 7, 2018), www.cnbc.com/2018/05/07/uss-first-drug-priced-at-more-than-1-million-may-be-on-the-horizon.html.

2 *See id.*

3 Meg Tirrell, *A U.S. Drugmaker Offers to Cure Rare Blindness for $850,000*, CNBC (Jan. 3, 2018), www.cnbc.com/2018/01/03/spark-therapeutics-lux turna-gene-therapy-will-cost-about-850000.html.

4 *See* Paul Kleutghen et al., *Drugs Don't Work If People Can't Afford Them: The High Price of Tisagenlecleucel*, HEALTH AFF. (Feb. 8, 2018), www.healthaffairs.org/do/10.1377/hblog20180205.292531/full/.

5 Riardo Alonso-Zaldiviar, *Feds: Skimping Can't Save Seniors from Rising Med Cost*, AP NEWS (Jun. 4, 2018), www.apnews.com/2a4936fd7bc44 ba699662c21bd5869a2, citing U.S. DEP'T. OF HEALTH & HUM. SERV., OFFICE OF INSPECTOR GENERAL, OEI–03–15-0080, INCREASES IN REIM-BURSEMENT FOR BRAND-NAME DRUGS IN PART D (2018); *see also* Ned Pagliarulo, *To Shame Drugmakers, CMS Publicizes Price Hikes*, BIOPHARMA DIVE (May 16, 2018), www.biopharmadive.com/news/to-shame-drugmakers-cms-publicizes-price-hikes/523693/; CTR. FOR MEDICARE & MEDICAID SERV., Fact sheet, DRUG SPENDING INFORMATION PRODUCTS (2018).

6 *See id.*

7 *See* EVALUATEPHARMA, ORPHAN DRUG REPORT 2017 (2017), http://info .evaluategroup.com/rs/607-YGS-364/images/EPOD17.pdf. On the whole, prices for branded drugs rose 12.4 percent in 2015 and have increased 10 percent or more annually for each of the prior three years. *See* Neeraj Sood, Dana Goldman & Karen Van Nuys, *Follow the Money to Understand How Drug Profits Flow*, STAT (Dec. 15, 2017), www.statnews.com/2017/12/15/ prescription-drug-profits-pbm/, citing Murray Aitken, *Medicines Use and Spending in the U.S.: A Review of 2015 and Outlook to 2020*, IMS INST. FOR HEALTHCARE INFORMATICS 2, 8 (2016). *See also* Fiona Scott Morton & Lysle T. Boller, *Enabling Competition in the Pharmaceutical Markets*, Working Paper 30, HUTCHINS CTR. ON FISCAL & MONETARY POL'Y AT BROOKINGS

(May 2017), www.brookings.edu/wp-content/uploads/2017/05/wp30_scott morton_competitioninpharma1.pdf; Carly J. Goeman, *The Price Isn't Right: Shareholder Proposals as Opportunities for Institutional Investors to Restore Firm Value and Reduce Pharmaceutical Prices*, 2 COLUM. BUS. L. REV. 748, 755, n. 22 (2017) (stating that "Valeant's product Nitropress rose by 525% in price" and "Isuprel rose 212%"); Brendan Murphy, *Getting High on Profits: An Analysis of Current State and Federal Proposals to Rein in Soaring Drug Prices*, 12 J. HEALTH & BIOMED. L. 37, 37 (2016) (criticizing Martin Shkreli's decision to hike the price of Daraprim by 5,000 percent overnight); Jordan Paradise, *A Profile of Bio-Pharma Consolidation Activity*, 25 ANN. HEALTH L. 34, 41 (2016) (noting that the price for "the type 2 diabetes drug Glumetza ... rose 800 percent"); Hannah Brennan, Amy Kapczynski, Christine H. Monahan & Zain Rizvi, *A Prescription for Excessive Drug Pricing: Leveraging Government Patent Use for Health*, 18 YALE J.L. & TECH. 275, 284 (2016) (describing soaring drug prices caused by profit margins reaching an estimated 42 percent); U.S. GOV'T ACCOUNTABILITY OFFICE, BRAND-NAME PRESCRIPTION DRUG PRICING: LACK OF THERAPEUTICALLY EQUIVALENT DRUGS AND LIMITED COMPETITION MAY CONTRIBUTE TO EXTRAORDINARY PRICE INCREASES (Dec. 2009) [hereinafter 2009 GOV'T ACCOUNTABILITY OFFICE REPORT]; Michael G. Daniel et al., *The Orphan Drug Act: Restoring the Mission to Rare Diseases*, 39 AM. J. CLIN. ONCOL. 210 (2015) (citing the example of Imatinib, a treatment for chronic myelogenous leukemia, which cost $30,000 a year when it was introduced in 2001, but the price of which had more than tripled to $92,000 a year by 2012).

8 Dylan Scott, *Inside the Impossibly Byzantine World of Prescription Drug Prices*, STAT (Dec. 21, 2015), www.statnews.com/2015/12/21/prescription-drug-prices-confusion/ (describing secretive discount and rebate systems and explaining that the list price is the company's opening bid).

9 *See* U.S. Dep't. of Health & Hum. Serv., *supra* note 5 (documenting the rise in total spending despite the fact that rebates increased from $58 billion to $102 billion during the period).

10 Ed Silverman, *Spending Growth on Prescription Drugs Will Double This Year*, STAT (Feb. 14, 2018), www.statnews.com/pharmalot/2018/02/14/prescription-drugs-spending-cms/, citing Gigi A. Cuckler, *et al.*, *National Health Expenditure Projections, 2017–26: Despite Uncertainty, Fundamentals Primarily Drive Spending Growth*, 37 HEALTH AFF. 482, 486 (2018); *see also* Norman R. Augustine, Guru Madhavan & Sharyl J. Nass, *Making Medicines Affordable: A National Imperative*, NAT'L ACADEMIES OF SCI., ENG'G, AND MED. 76 (2017) [hereinafter NAS REPORT] (showing that, although the rate of increase in spending for prescription drugs in 2016 slowed from the year before to only 5.8 percent, that growth rate was still double the rate of increase in 2013; spending rates in 2014 and 2015 rose by 10.3 percent and 12.4 percent, respectively).

11 NAS Report, *supra* note 10, at 25, citing Office of the Assistant Sec'y for Planning & Evaluation, Observations on Trends in Prescription Drug Spending 1 (2016) (noting that spending on prescription drugs is increasing and is expected to grow more quickly than overall health spending). *See also* U.S. Dep't. of Labor, Bureau of Labor Statistics, Prescription Drugs in the U.S. City Average, All Urban Consumers, Seasonally Adjusted (2018) (showing a 2.4 percent increase in the CPI for prescription drugs from January 2017 to January 2018); Silverman, *supra* note 10 (noting a 2.9 percent increase in spending on prescription drugs in 2017).

12 *See How Critics Say Drug Companies Play "Games" to Stave off Generic Competitors*, CBS News (Feb. 2, 2018) (quoting industry spokesperson); *see also* Rachel Schmidt & Shinobu Suzuki, *The Medicare Prescription Drug Program (Part D): Status Report*, Medicare Payment Advisory Comm'n 11 (Jan. 11, 2018) (showing that growth in brand price more than offset effects of generic use in Medicare Part D).

13 *See* Robin Feldman & Evan Frondorf, Drug Wars: How Big Pharma Raises Prices and Keeps Generics off the Market 16, 86, 97 (2017).

14 *See* Patricia Kime, *VA, DoD Spend More than $450M on Costly Hepatitis Drug*, USA Today (Jan. 8, 2015), www.usatoday.com/story/news/politics/ 2015/01/08/government-hepatitis-drug-costs/21462363/; *cf.* Pauline Bartolone, *California Pays Insurers Millions More for Hepatitis C Drugs*, NPR (Jan. 28, 2016), www.npr.org/sections/health-shots/2016/01/28/464708911/ california-pays-insurers-millions-more-for-hepatitis-c-drugs (noting that the state of California spent $387 million to treat 3,624 patients with the new hepatitis C drugs).

15 NAS Report, *supra* note 10, at 110 (explaining that patient "sticker shock" at the pharmacy leads them to forgo filling the prescription or extend their medication by reducing dosages). *See also* Robyn Tamblyn, *The Incidence and Determinants of Primary Nonadherence with Prescribed Medication in Primary Care: A Cohort Study*, 160 Ann. Intern. Med. 441 (2014) (study showing that patients with higher co-pays, recent hospitalizations, other severe health problems, or combinations of these factors were less likely to fill their prescriptions); President's Cancer Panel, Promoting Value, Affordability, and Innovation in Cancer Drug Treatment A Report to the President of the United States from the President's Cancer Panel 17 (Mar. 2018), https://prescancerpanel.cancer.gov/report/drugvalue/pdf/Pre sCancerPanel_DrugValue_Mar2018.pdf(detailing that higher out-of-pocket costs make it less likely that patients will adhere to recommended treatment regimens and undergo financial hardship); Nat. Cancer Inst., Nat. Insts of Health, Financial Toxicity and Cancer Treatment (PDQ®) – Health Professional Version (2018), www.cancer .gov/about-cancer/managing-care/track-care-costs/financial-toxicity-hp-pdq

(a study on the financial burden of cancer treatments, noting how high costs have resulted in cancer patients selling property and other assets, incurring medical debt, reducing spending on necessities, changing housing, and declaring bankruptcy).

16 *See* Linda Cahn, *Don't Get Trapped By PBMs' Rebate Labeling Games*, MANAGED CARE (Jan. 1, 2009), www.managedcaremag.com/archives/2009/ 1/don-t-get-trapped-pbms-rebate-labeling-games (industry consultant explaining that audit materials are limited to client-specific materials and that, given that rebates are not client-specific, the PBM can refuse to provide information about them); Michael Hiltzik, *How 'Price-Cutting' Middlemen Are Making Crucial Drugs Vastly More Expensive*, LA TIMES (2017), www .latimes.com/business/hiltzik/la-fi-hiltzik-pbm-drugs-20170611-story.html (quoting another insurance industry consultant, who says that "insurers generally don't have the right to audit PBMs' collections and distributions . . . The PBMs will say the rebate contracts are between them and the pharmaceutical companies, and it is none of our business"); *see also* Neil Weinberg & Robert Langreth, *Inside the "Scorpion Room" Where Drug Price Secrets Are Guarded*, BLOOMBERG (May 4, 2017), www.bloomberg.com/ news/articles/2017-05-04/in-scorpion-room-auditor-gets-scant-look-at-drug-contracts ("PBMs still often put auditors in secure rooms, limit the number of contracts they can see and restrict and review note-taking, according to people in the industry and contracts reviewed by Bloomberg"); Stephen Barlas, *Employers and Drugstores Press for PBM Transparency*, 40 PHARMACY & THERAPEUTICS 206, 206 (2015) (quoting an accredited healthcare fraud investigator, who says that "PBMs make it near impossible to audit both their 'secret agreements' for rebates with pharmaceutical companies and retail network agreements with pharmacy chains").

Chapter 2

1 A 2014 study from the Tufts Center for the Study of Drug Development found that developing a new drug costs approximately US$2.5 billion, which includes the costs of compound failures. *See* TUFTS CTR. FOR THE STUDY OF DRUG DEV., COSTS OF DEVELOPING A NEW DRUG (2014), https://static1 .squarespace.com/static/5a9eb0c8e2ccd1158288d8dc/t/5ac66afc6d2a732e8 3aae6bf/1522952963800/Tufts_CSDD_briefing_on_RD_cost_study_-_Nov_ 18%2C_2014.pdf. This finding has been challenged on multiple fronts. *See* Steve Morgan et al., *The Cost of Drug Development: A Systematic Review*, 100 HEALTH POL. 4 (2011), www.ncbi.nlm.nih.gov/pubmed/21256615 (analyz-ing 13 different studies to estimate that drug development costs range from $161 million to $1.8 billion); Aaron E. Carroll, *$2.6 Billion to Develop a Drug? New Estimate Makes Questionable Assumptions*, NY TIMES (Nov. 18, 2014), www.nytimes.com/2014/11/19/upshot/calculating-the-real-costs-of-developing-

a-new-drug.html (suggesting that the disparity in the findings stems from methodological mistakes in the Tufts study and noting that the Tufts Center is funded by pharmaceutical companies); TUFTS CTR. FOR THE STUDY OF DRUG DEV., *Financial Disclosure*, https://csdd.tufts.edu/financial-disclosure/ (last visited Oct. 28, 2018). Additionally, a study analyzing the U.S. Securities and Exchange Commission (SEC) filings for ten cancer drugs found that the average cost of developing a single cancer drug was $648 million. *See* Vinay Prasad & Sham Mailankody, *Research and Development Spending to Bring a Single Cancer Drug to Market and Revenues after Approval*, 177 JAMA INTERN. MED. 1569 (2017). Moreover, the Tufts study focuses only on the development of new drugs, while many released drugs are merely repurposed old ones. *See* Chapter 5, *infra*.

Although high drug prices could, in theory, help successful companies to go on to develop more new products, studies suggest that very little of pharmaceutical company profits go back into research and development. *See* Donald W. Light & Joel Lexchin, *Foreign Free Riders and the High Price of U.S. Medicines*, 331 BMJ 958 (2005) (finding that only 1.3 percent of pharmaceutical industry spending is directed to basic research). In addition, one recent study concluded that Novartis' new Car-T drug Kymriah is overpriced, even including enough profit to underwrite both research and development successes and failures for the company. *See* Paul Kleutghen et al., *Drugs Don't Work If People Can't Afford Them: The High Price of Tisa-genlecleucel*, HEALTH AFF. (Feb. 8, 2018), www.healthaffairs.org/do/10.1377/hblog20180205.292531/full/. Including these assumptions, the study estimated that the cost of the drug should be $160,000 for the one-time infusion rather than the current $475,000 planned by Novartis. *See id.*

2 *U.S. Pharmaceutical Industry: Statistics and Facts*, STATISTA, www.statista.com/topics/1719/pharmaceutical-industry/ (last visited Oct. 28, 2018).

3 *See* Robin Feldman, *Regulatory Property: The New IP*, 40 COLUM. J.L. & ARTS 53, 67–68 (2016) (detailing the history of more than a dozen forms of nonpatent exclusivities).

4 For detailed descriptions of the system under the Hatch-Waxman Act (more formally known as the Drug Price Competition and Patent Term Restoration Act of 1984), *see generally* ROBIN FELDMAN & EVAN FRONDORF, DRUG WARS: HOW BIG PHARMA RAISES PRICES AND KEEPS GENERICS OFF THE MARKET 21–22, 26–33 (2017), citing Wendy H. Schacht & John R. Thomas, *The Hatch-Waxman Act: A Quarter Century Later*, CONGRESSIONAL RESEARCH SERVICE 1 (Mar. 13, 2011); Matthew Avery, *Continuing Abuse of the Hatch-Waxman Act by Pharmaceutical Patent Holders and the Failure of the 2003 Amendments*, 60 HASTINGS L.J. 171 178, nn. 55–56 (2008).

5 Treximet combines sumatriptan and naproxen in multilayered tablets. Janet Freilich, *Patent Infringement in the Context of Follow-on Biologics*, 16 STAN. TECH. L. REV. 9, 42, n. 186 (2012). Soon after Treximet was brought to market,

GlaxoSmithKline sold the branded drug for $18 per pill, even though the individual components sumatriptan and naproxen were available for a total of about $5. Tracy Staton, *Treximet: Cautionary Tale of Payer Price Revolt*, FIERCEPHARMA (2009). Pernix later acquired the drug. More recent sources indicate that the average cost for a Treximet prescription of nine tablets is $1,050.15, but this can vary depending on the pharmacy. PERNIX THERAPEUTICS, Press release, *Pernix Signs Agreement to Acquire Treximet Tablets for Migraine from GSK* (May 14, 2014), http://ir.pernixtx.com/phoenix.zhtml?c=84041&p= irol-newsArticle&ID=2123202; *Treximet: Sumatriptan and Naproxen*, GOODRX (2018), www.goodrx.com/treximet. There is currently no generic version of the drug available, and generic manufacturers have been blocked from entering the market by patent infringement claims. *See Treximet Prices, Coupons and Patient Assistance Programs*, DRUGS.COM (2018), www.drugs .com/price-guide/treximet; Christopher M. Holman, *In Defense of Secondary Pharmaceutical Patents: A Response to the UN'S Guidelines for Pharmaceutical Patent Examination*, 50 IND. L. REV. 759, 801 (2017) (noting that "[v]arious generic drug companies sought to bring a generic version of Treximet to the market, and were sued . . . for infringement"); *Pozen Inc. v. Par, Pharma., Inc.*, 800 F. Supp. 2d 789, 809 (E.D. Tex. 2011).

6 ROBIN C. FELDMAN, MAY YOUR DRUG PRICE BE EVER GREEN 2 (2018) (observing that, "rather than creating new medicines, pharmaceutical companies are recycling and repurposing old ones," and referring to empirical data that, "78% of the drugs associated with new patents were not new drugs coming on the market, but existing drugs").

7 U.S. GOV'T ACCOUNTABILITY OFFICE, GAO-16-706, GENERIC DRUGS UNDER MEDICARE: PART D GENERIC DRUG PRICES DECLINED OVERALL, BUT SOME HAD EXTRAORDINARY PRICE INCREASES 1 (Aug. 2016) [hereinafter 2016 GOV'T ACCOUNTABILITY OFFICE REPORT].

8 Under Hatch-Waxman, a first filing generic that submits an abbreviated new drug application with a complete Paragraph IV certification receives a six-month period in which no other generic company may receive approval to enter the market: 21 U.S.C. §355(j)(5)(B)(iv). Paragraph IV certification refers to an abbreviated new drug application (ANDA) applicant's certification that the original patent is either "invalid or will not be infringed by the manufacture, use, or sale of the new drug for which the application is submitted": 21 U.S.C. §355(j)(2)(A)(vii)(IV). During this period, the only versions on the market will be the original brand and the first-filing generic, along with any generic versions that the brand-name company might choose to introduce or authorize. *See* Feldman & Frondorf, *supra* note 4, at 59 (describing the concept of "authorized generics," i.e. generic, unbranded versions of a drug introduced by the brand-name company).

9 MEDICARE PAYMENT ADVISORY COMM'N, REPORT TO THE CONGRESS: MEDICARE PAYMENT POLICY 408–09 (2017) [hereinafter MEDPAC 2017

REPORT], citing Jonathan D. Alpern, William M. Stauffer & Aaron S. Kesselheim, *High-Cost Generic Drugs: Implications for Patients and Policymakers*, 13 NEW ENG. J. MED. 1859 (2014); Why Are Some Generic Drugs Skyrocketing in Price? Hearing Testimony before U.S. Senate Subcomm. on Primary Health and Aging, 2014 Leg., 113th Sess. S. Hrg 113–859 (statement of Aaron S. Kesselheim, Associate Professor, Medicine, Harvard Medical School); Adam Fein, *Retail Generic Drug Inflation Reaches New Heights*, DRUG CHANNELS (Aug. 12, 2014), www.drugchannels.net/2014/08/retail-generic-drug-inflation-reaches.html. *See also* 2016 GOV'T ACCOUNTABILITY OFFICE REPORT, *supra* note 7, at 13 (showing 351 cases of a history of extraordinary price increases for generic drugs within a single year); Chintan V. Dave et al., *High Generic Drug Prices and Market Competition: A Retrospective Cohort Study*, 167 ANN. INTERN. MED. 145 (2017).

10 Brian A. Hearn, Nicola Amendola & Giovanni Vecchi, *On Historical Household Budgets*, INST. FOR NEW ECON. THINKING 6 (2016), https://papers.ssrn.com/sol3/papers.cfm?abstract_id=2793438; Thomas J. Campbell, *Labor Law and Economics*, 38 STAN. L. REV. 991, 1005, n. 82 (1986), citing EDWIN MANSFIELD, MICROECONOMICS 251 (1982); Kenneth M. Casebeer, *Unemployment Insurance: American Social Wage, Labor Organization & Legal Ideology*, 35 B.C. L. REV. 259, 280, 298 (1994).

11 For a full description of buying distortions in the healthcare market, *see generally* Feldman & Frondorf, *supra* note 4, at 13 (noting that the "pharmaceutical market does not operate much like a standard market at all"); Clifford D. Stromberg, *Health Law Comes of Age: Economics and Ethics in a Changing Industry*, 92 YALE L.J. 203 (1982), reviewing WILLIAM J. CURRAN & E. DONALD SHAPIRO, LAW, MEDICINE AND FORENSIC SCIENCE (3rd ed.) (1982); Abigail Moncrieff, *Understanding the Failure of Health-Care Exceptionalism in the Supreme Court's Obamacare Decision*, 142 CHEST 559, 559 (2012) (arguing that the Supreme Court's failure to employ healthcare exceptionalism in a constitutional challenge to the Patient Protection and Affordable Care Act was an "odd" holding that disregards the uniqueness of the healthcare market).

12 Fiona Scott Morton & Lysle T. Boller, *Enabling Competition in the Pharmaceutical Markets*, Working Paper 30, HUTCHINS CTR. ON FISCAL & MONETARY POL'Y AT BROOKINGS 2 (May 2017), www.brookings.edu/wp-content/uploads/2017/05/wp30_scottmorton_competitioninpharma1.pdf   (2017) (explaining that externalities and information asymmetries prevent consumers from optimal substitution because they do not bear full costs and lack medical expertise or reliable information with which to identify therapeutic equivalents).

13 Nicholas Drew, *Two Federally Subsidized Health Insurance Programs Are One Too Many: Reconsidering the Federal Income Tax Inclusion for Employer-Provided Health Insurance in Light of the Patient Protection and Affordable Care Act*,

54 B.C. L. Rev. 2047, 2056 (2013) (describing the government subsidy for employer-provided health care created by section 106 of the Internal Revenue Code); Yair Listokin, *Equity, Efficiency, and Stability: The Importance of Macroeconomics for Evaluating Income Tax Policy*, 29 Yale J. on Reg. 45, 49 (2012) (noting a government subsidy excluding "employer-provided health insurance from income tax"); Max Huffman, *Competition Policy in Health Care in an Era of Reform*, 7 Ind. Health L. Rev. 225, 261 (2010) (observing that healthcare costs are paid with "before-tax dollars").

14 The United States and New Zealand are the only two industrialized nations that allow direct-to-consumer advertising (DTCA) for prescription medication. *See* Bruce Patsner, *Problems Associated with Direct-to-Consumer Advertising (DTC) of Restricted, Implantable Medical Devices: Should the Current Regulatory Approaches be Changed?*, 64 Food Drug L.J. 1, 3 (2009) ("... aside from New Zealand, DTCA is banned in every other Western industrialized nation except the United States"); *see also* Erin J. Asher, *Lesson Learned from New Zealand: Pro-Active Industry Shift toward Self-Regulation of Direct-to-Consumer Advertising Will Improve Compliance with the FDA*, 16 Alb. L.J. Sci. & Tech 599, 614 (2006) ("New Zealand is currently the only other industrialized country in the world besides than the United States to allow DTC advertising").

15 Ctr. for Medicare & Medicaid Serv., *Open Payments*, www.cms.gov/openpayments/ (last visited Oct. 28, 2018) (Open Payments is a government program under the Affordable Care Act that details the value and nature of payments made from companies to physicians).

16 *See* Letter from Marina Lao, Deborah L. Feinstein & Francine Lafontaine, Fed. Trade Comm'n Staff to Congressman Joe Hoppe & Congresswoman Melissa Hortman 4–5 (June 29, 2015), www.ftc.gov/system/files/documents/advocacy_documents/ftc-staff-comment-regarding-amendments-minnesota-government-data-practices-act-regarding-health-care/150702minnhealthcare.pdf. *See generally* Christopher Whaley et al., *Association between Availability of Health Service Prices and Payments for these Services*, 312 JAMA 1670, 1670–76 (2014); U.S. Gov't Accountability Office, GAO-11–791, Health Care Price Transparency: Meaningful Price Information Is Difficult for Consumers to Obtain Prior to Receiving Care 2 (2011), www.gao.gov/assets/590/585400.pdf [hereinafter GAO report]. *See generally* Fed. Trade Comm'n, Workshop, *Examining Health Care Competition*, www.ftc.gov/news-events/events-calendar/2015/02/examining-health-care-competition (last visited Oct. 28, 2018); High Prices, Low Transparency: The Bitter Pill of Health Care Costs: Hearing Before the S. Comm. on Finance, 113th Cong. 8 (2013) (statement of Paul B. Ginsburg, Ph.D., Ctr. for Studying Health System Change and National Institute for Health Care Reform), www.scribd.com/document/322903642/SENATE-HEARING-113TH-CONGRESS-HIGH-PRICES-LOW-TRANSPARENCY-THE-BITTER-PILL-OF-HEALTH-CARE-COSTS.

17 *See id.* One study concluded that the effects of cost-containment efforts are reduced when drug companies advertise to consumers. Richard Hansen et al., *The Association of Consumer Cost-Sharing and Direct-to-Consumer Advertising with Prescription Drug Use*, 1 Res. Soc. & Admin. Pharma. 139 (2005), www.ncbi.nlm.nih.gov/pubmed/17138472.

18 *See generally* Wendy Netter Epstein, *Revisiting Incentive-Based Contracts*, 17 Yale H. Health Pol´y L. & Ethics 1 (2017) (addressing skewed economic incentives in health care); William P. Kratzke, *Tax Subsidiaries, Third-Party-Payments, and Cross-Subsidization: America's Distorted Health Care Markets*, 40 U. Mem. L. Rev. 279 (2009), citing E. Haavi Morreim, *Diverse and Perverse Incentives of Managed Care: Bringing Patients into Alignment*, 1 Widener L. Symp. J. 89, 95, 139 (1996); Arnold S. Kling, Crisis of Abundance: Rethinking How We Pay for Health Care 53–54 (2006); Uwe E. Reinhardt, *Reorganizing the Financial Flows in American Health Care*, 12 Health Aff. 172, 176 (Supp. 1993); David Gratzer, The Cure: How Capitalism Can Save American Health Care 42 (2006); Clive Crook, *The Slippery Economics of Health Care*, The Atlantic (Oct. 2005), www.theatlantic.com/magazine/archive/2005/10/the-slippery-economics-of-health-care/304394/ (discussing the lack of consumer incentives in healthcare decision making); Jennifer Prah Ruger, *Health, Capability, and Justice: Toward a New Paradigm of Health Ethics, Policy and Law*, 15 Cornell J.L. & Pub. Pol´y 403, 476 (2006) (noting efforts to manufacture economic incentives through "inappropriate" and "deleterious" insurance deductibles and co-payment schemes to help healthcare purchases mimic typical economic rationales); *see also* Paige Kelton, *Some Pharmacists Barred from Helping Patients Save Money*, Action News Jax (Feb. 22, 2018), www.actionnews jax.com/news/local/some-pharmacists-barred-from-helping-patients-save-money/705277162 (quoting one commentator that the "key question is not: What's it worth to save a child's life… If that was the question, the polio (vaccine) they gave me when I was 6 years old would have cost a million dollars. The right question is: What is the price that will maximize accessibility and affordability, while maintaining a robust R&D pipeline").

19 In the United States, 8.5 percent of total healthcare spending is for individuals in the last year of life. *See* Alan R. Weil, *Advanced Illness and End-of-Life Care*, 36 Health Aff. 1167 (2017), www.healthaffairs.org/doi/pdf/% 2010.1377/hlthaff.2017.0741; Courtney Davis et al., *Availability of Evidence of Benefits on Overall Survival and Quality of Life of Cancer Drugs Approved by European Medicines Agency: Retrospective Cohort Study of Drug Approvals 2009–2013*, 359 BMJ j4530 (2017), www.ncbi.nlm.nih.gov/pmc/articles/ PMC5627352/ (finding that "[t]he magnitude of the benefit on overall survival ranged from 1.0 to 5.8 months (median 2.7 months)").

20 National Academies of Sciences, Engineering, and Medicine, Making Medicine Affordable: A National Imperative 24 (2018),

www.nap.edu/catalog/24946/making-medicines-affordable-a-national-impera
tive; *see also* Murray Aitken, *Understanding the Dynamics of Drug Expenditure
in the U.S.*, Quintiles IMS Institute 5 (2017), http://phrma-docs.phrma
.org/download.cfm?objectid=4FCE2890-A496-11E7-833F0050569A4B6C
(noting that retail prescription drug spending averaged 4.8 percent growth
between 2006 and 2015); Dana O. Sarnak, David Squires & Shawn Bishop,
Paying for Prescription Drugs around the World: Why Is the U.S. an Outlier?,
Commonwealth Fund Exhibit 1 (2017), www.commonwealthfund.org/
publications/issue-briefs/2017/oct/paying-prescription-drugs-around-world-
why-us-outlier; Aimee Picci, *Martin Shkreli-Style Drug Price Hikes are Every-
where*, Moneywatch (Feb. 2, 2016), www.cbsnews.com/news/martin-
shkreli-style-drug-price-hikes-are-everywhere/, citing Robert Langreth &
Rebecca Spalding, *Shkreli Was Right; Everyone's Hiking Drug Prices*, Bloomberg (Feb. 2, 2016), www.bloomberg.com/news/articles/2016-02-02/
shkreli-not-alone-in-drug-price-spikes-as-skin-gel-soars-1-860 (noting that
"[a]bout 20 of the top prescription drugs have at least quadrupled" their
prices from 2014 to 2016).

21 MedPAC 2017 Report, *supra* note 9, at 408.

22 Express Scripts, Value Beyond: Delivering More than Medicine –
Annual Report 4 (2016), https://expressscriptsholdingco.gcs-web.com/
static-files/777166b9–6d1a-4b3f-b979-f798b856955c [hereinafter Express
Scripts].

23 U.S. Gov't Accountability Office, Brand-Name Prescription Drug
Pricing: Lack of Therapeutically Equivalent Drugs and Limited
Competition May Contribute to Extraordinary Price Increases 11
(2009) [hereinafter 2009 Gov't Accountability Office Report].

24 *See id*; *see also* Brenda Goodman & Andy Miller, *The High Cost of Surviving
Rabies*, WebMD (Feb. 20, 2018), www.webmd.com/a-to-z-guides/news/
20180220/the-high-cost-of-surviving-rabies (noting that the cost of the
rabies shot regimen increased nearly 400 percent between 2008 and 2018).

25 Ass'n for Accessible Medicines, Generic Drug Access and Savings
in the U.S. 33 (2017), https://accessiblemeds.org/sites/default/files/2017-07/
2017-AAM-Access-Savings-Report-2017-web2.pdf (the Association for
Accessible Medicines was formerly the Generic Pharmaceutical Association,
and the information for the report was compiled by the Quintiles IMS
Institute).

26 *See How Critics Say Drug Companies Play "Games" to Stave Off Generic
Competitors*, CBS News (Feb. 2, 2018), www.cbsnews.com/news/drug-com
panies-alleged-tactics-delay-cheaper-generic-drugs/ (quoting a representative of the pharmaceutical industry group PhRMA, saying that 90 percent
of all medicines are generic and that over 1,000 new generics were approved
in 2017 – the highest of anywhere in the world); *cf.* Michael Mezher, *FDA on
Pace for Record Generic Approvals in 2018*, Reg. Aff. Prof. Soc. (Sept. 6,

2018),   www.raps.org/news-and-articles/news-articles/2018/9/fda-on-pace-for-record-generic-approvals-in-2018.

27 *See* MEDPAC 2017 REPORT, *supra* note 9, at 408 (concluding that price increases in the brands are overwhelming the effects of using lower-cost generic drugs, even as the use of generics continues to climb).

28 Neeraj Sood, Dana Goldman & Karen Van Nuys, *Follow the Money to Understand How Drug Profits Flow*, STAT (Dec. 15, 2017), www.statnews.com/2017/12/15/prescription-drug-profits-pbm/, citing Murray Aitken, *Medicines Use and Spending in the U.S.: A Review of 2015 and Outlook to 2020*, IMS INST. FOR HEALTHCARE INFORMATICS 2, 8 (2016).

29 *See* ELI LILLY AND CO., 2016 LILLY INTEGRATED SUMMARY REPORT 15 (2016).

30 Ed Silverman, *Several Drug Makers Just Raised Their Prices by Nearly 10 Percent, and Buyers Expect More Price Hikes*, STAT (2018), www.statnews.com/pharmalot/2018/01/02/price-hikes-inflation-survey/.

31 Joseph Walker, *For Prescription Drug Makers, Price Increases Drive Revenue*, WALL ST. J. (Oct. 5, 2015), www.wsj.com/articles/for-prescription-drug-makers-price-increases-drive-revenue-1444096750. The *Wall Street Journal*'s coverage of pharmaceutical price increases was later a finalist for a Pulitzer: THE PULITZER PRIZES, *2016 Pulitzer Prizes*, www.pulitzer.org/prize-winners-by-year/2016 (last visited Oct. 28, 18); *see also* Lydia Ramsay, *We Just Got a Better Idea of How Much Drug Companies Rely on Price Hikes, and It Doesn't Look Good*, BUS. INSIDER (Apr. 19, 2017), www.businessinsider.com/drug-price-increases-represented-pharma-earnings-growth-2017-4.

32 MEDPAC 2017 REPORT, *supra* note 9, at 427, n. 37. Most biologics fall within a subset of specialty medicines. *See id.*

33 PEW CHARITABLE TRUSTS, Fact sheet, SPECIALTY DRUGS & HEALTH CARE COSTS (2015), www.pewtrusts.org/en/research-and-analysis/fact-sheets/2015/11/specialty-drugs-and-health-care-costs.

34 *See* Norman R. Augustine, Guru Madhavan & Sharyl J. Nass, *Making Medicines Affordable: A National Imperative*, NAT′L ACADEMIES OF SCI., ENG′G, AND MED. 76 (2017) [hereinafter NAS REPORT], citing AMERICA′S HEALTH INS. PLANS, SPECIALTY DRUGS: ISSUES AND CHALLENGES: ADVANCING EFFECTIVE STRATEGIES TO ADDRESS SOARING COSTS WHILE ENSURING ACCESS TO EFFECTIVE TREATMENTS AND PROMOTING CONTINUED MEDICAL INNOVATION 6 (2015), www.ahip.org/wp-content/uploads/2015/07/Issue Brief_SpecialtyDrugs_7.9.15.pdf; Murray Aitken, *Medicines Use and Spending in the U.S.: A Review of 2015 and Outlook to 2020*, IMS INST. FOR HEALTHCARE INFORMATICS 13 (2016). Spending increases of specialty drugs are reported on an invoice price basis, referring to the amounts that pharmacies and hospitals pay to distributors for medicines. *See also* 2009 GOV′T ACCOUNTABILITY OFFICE REPORT, *supra* note 23, at 2, 11 (noting that, between 2000 and 2008, a few specialty drugs used to treat conditions such

as fungal or viral infections or heart disease experienced price increases of 1,000 percent or more).

35 EXPRESS SCRIPTS, *supra* note 22, at 4 (Express Scripts, the institutional author of this report, is a PBM).

36 Dylan Scott, *Inside the Impossibly Byzantine World of Prescription Drug Prices*, STAT (Dec. 21, 2015), www.statnews.com/2015/12/21/prescription-drug-prices-confusion/ (describing secretive discount and rebate systems and explaining that the list price is the company's opening bid; quoting the acting administrator of the federal Centers for Medicare and Medicaid Services as saying that "we have list prices, wholesale prices, average wholesale prices, rebates, supplemental rebates, mark-ups … Most of that information is not available or well understood by the public," and University of Pittsburgh Professor Walid Gellad as referring to pricing as a black hole and noting that "[i]t's impossible to understand what people are paying").

37 Industry reports indicate that the gap between prices and rebate prices has increased in recent years. *See* Adam J. Fein, *Payor Power: Why Eli Lilly, Janssen, and Merck Deeply Discount Their Drug Prices*, DRUG CHANNELS (Apr. 5, 2018), www.drugchannels.net/2018/04/payer-power-why-eli-lilly-janssen-and.html (noting from publicly reporting earnings that, comparing 2016 to 2017, Janssen's average discount rose from 32 percent off list to 42 percent off list, Merck's rose from 41 percent to 45 percent off list, and Lilly's grew only marginally, from 50 percent to 51 percent off list).

38 *See* Neeraj Sood, *Understanding Competition in Prescription Drug Markets: Entry and Supply Chain Dynamics*, FED. TRADE COMM'N WORKSHOP SLIDES 101 (2017), www.ftc.gov/news-events/events-calendar/2017/11/understand ing-competition-prescription-drug-markets-entry-supply [hereinafter FTC WORKSHOP SLIDES]; *see also* Murray Aitken, *Medicines Use and Spending in the U.S.: A Review of 2016 and Outlook to 2021*, QUINTILES IMS INST. 2 (2017), www.iqvia.com/institute/reports/medicines-use-and-spending-in-the-us-a-review-of-2016.

39 *See* Scott, *supra* note 36.

40 *See* COINNEWS MEDIA GROUP LLC, *Current U.S. Inflation Rates: 2008 to 2018* (2018), www.usinflationcalculator.com/inflation/current-inflation-rates/.

41 MEDPAC 2017 REPORT, *supra* note 9.

42 For an example of a plan requiring that the patient pay 100 percent of the costs of drugs up to a certain limit, see the Anthem insurance plan described at First Am. Consolidated Class Action Compl., at para. 13, *In re Express Scripts/Anthem ERISA Litigation*, 2018 U.S. Dist. LEXIS 3081 (S.D.N.Y. 2016) [hereinafter ANTHEM CLASS ACTION COMPLAINT] (No. 16–3399); *see also* CIGNA Insurance Plan Documents (2018) (on file with author) (showing patient pays for medication in full until $2,500 family threshold).

43 NAS REPORT, *supra* note 34, at 99–100.

44 *See id.* at 98; Jalpa Doshi et al., *Specialty Tier-Level Cost Sharing & Bio. Agent Use in the Medicare Part D Initial Coverage Period among Beneficiaries with*

Rheumatoid Arthritis, 68 ARTHRITIS CARE & RES. 1623 (2016); Jeah K. Jung et al., *Coverage for Hepatitis C Drugs in Medicare Part D*, 22 AM. J. OF MANAGED CARE 220 (2016); Jennifer M. Polinski, Penny E. Mohr & Lorraine Johnson, *Impact of Medicare Part D on Access to and Cost Sharing for Specialty Biologic Medications for Beneficiaries with Rheumatoid Arthritis*, 61 ARTHRITIS CARE & RES. 745 (2009); Jinoos Yazdany et al., *Coverage for High-Cost Specialty Drugs for Rheumatoid Arthritis in Medicare Part D*, 67 ARTHRITIS & RHEUMATOLOGY 1474 (2015).

45 MEDPAC 2017 REPORT, *supra* note 9, at 404.

46 Patient Protection and Affordable Care Act., Pub. L. No. 111–148, 124 Stat. 119 (2010).

47 NAS REPORT, *supra* note 34, at 98.

48 *See id.*

49 Ed Silverman, *Spending Growth on Prescription Drugs Will Double This Year*, STAT (Feb. 14, 2018), www.statnews.com/pharmalot/2018/02/14/prescrip tion-drugs-spending-cms/, citing Gigi A. Cuckler, *et al.*, *National Health Expenditure Projections, 2017–26: Despite Uncertainty, Fundamentals Primarily Drive Spending Growth*, 37 HEALTH AFF. 482, 486 (2018); *see also* Norman R. Augustine, Guru Madhavan & Sharyl J. Nass, *Making Medicines Affordable: A National Imperative*, NAT'L ACADEMIES OF SCI., ENG'G, AND MED. 76 (2017) [hereinafter NAS REPORT] (showing that although the rate of increase in spending for prescription drugs in 2016 slowed from the year before to an increase of only 5.8 percent, that growth rate was still double the rate of increase in 2013; spending rates in 2014 and 2015 rose 10.3 percent and 12.4 percent, respectively); NAS REPORT, *supra* note 34, at 25, citing OFFICE OF THE ASSISTANT SEC'Y FOR PLANNING AND EVALUATION, OBSERVATIONS ON TRENDS IN PRESCRIPTION DRUG SPENDING 1 (2016) (noting that spending on prescription drugs is increasing and is expected to grow more quickly than overall health spending); U.S. DEP'T. OF LABOR, BUREAU OF LABOR STATISTICS, PRESCRIPTION DRUGS IN THE U.S. CITY AVERAGE, ALL URBAN CONSUMERS, SEASONALLY ADJUSTED (2018) (showing a 2.4 percent increase in the CPI for prescription drugs from January 2017 to January 2018); Silverman, *supra* note 49 (noting a 2.9 percent increase in spending on prescription drugs in 2017); *cf.* Robert Langreth, Blacki Migliozzi & Ketaki Gokhale, *The U.S. Pays a Lot More for Top Drugs Than Other Countries*, BLOOMBERG (2015), www.bloomberg.com/graphics/2015-drug-prices/?plat form=hootsuite (Bloomberg study concluding that those in the United States pay more for top drugs, even after accounting for discounts).

50 FTC WORKSHOP SLIDES, *supra* note 38, at 83; Liyan Chen, *The Most Profitable Industries in 2016*, FORBES (Dec. 21, 2015), www.forbes.com/sites/ liyanchen/2015/12/21/the-most-profitable-industries-in-2016/ (showing brand drugs among the top ten most profitable industries).

51 *See* ELI LILLY AND CO., 2016 FINANCIAL REPORT F22 (2017), https:// investor.lilly.com/static-files/77e65332-ec0d-460e-b29b-2f740617a5b2.

52 EXPRESS SCRIPTS, *supra* note 22, at 4.

53 *See id.*; *see also* Michael Hiltzik, *How 'Price-Cutting' Middlemen Are Making Crucial Drugs Vastly More Expensive*, LA TIMES (2017), www.latimes.com/business/hiltzik/la-fi-hiltzik-pbm-drugs-20170611-story.html (noting that Express Scripts reported a 34 percent increase in profits for a total of $3.4 billion in 2016 on slightly less revenue – $100.2 billion versus $101.8 billion the prior year).

54 *See* UNITED HEALTH GROUP, Form 10-K, ANNUAL REPORT 37 (Dec. 31, 2016); Hiltzik, *supra* note 53.

55 *See* Jennifer Rae Fleming, *The Blurred Line between Nursing Homes & Assisted Living Facilities: How Limited Medicaid Funding of Assisted Living Facilities Can Save Tax Dollars While Improving the Quality of Life of the Elderly*, 15 U. MIAMI BUS. L. REV. 245, 261 (2007) ("Each state administers its own Medicaid program while the federal Centers for Medicare & Medicaid Services (CMS) (formerly the Health Care Financing Administration) in the United States Department of Health and Human Services monitors the state-run programs and establishes requirements for service delivery, quality, funding, and eligibility standards"); *see also* Barbara S. Klees, Christian J. Wolfe & Catherine A. Curtis, *Brief Summaries of Medicare & Medicaid: Title XVIII and Title XIX of The Social Security Act as of November 1, 2009*, CTR. FOR MEDICARE & MEDICAID SERV., DEP'T. OF HEALTH & HUMAN SERV. 17 (2009), www.cms.gov/Research-Statistics-Data-and-Systems/Statistics-Trends-and-Reports/MedicareProgramRatesStats/downloads/MedicareMedicaidSummaries2009.pdf("DHHS has the overall responsibility for administration of the Medicare program. Within DHHS, responsibility for administering Medicare rests with CMS"); *see id.*, at 18 ("each State establishes its own eligibility standards; determines the type, amount, duration, and scope of services; sets the rate of payment for services; and administers its own program").

56 Under self-insurance, an employer assumes all financial risk for all employee healthcare costs. Employee claims are paid directly from the company's financial assets and are tax-deductible by the employer. The employer is also responsible for any costs associated with administering the health plan. In one subset of self-insurance called "administration services only (ASO) arrangements," the employer buys only the claims administration function from a third-party company, often a PBM, as opposed to the insurance protection function itself. *See* JEFFREY D. MAMORSKY, HEALTH CARE BENEFITS LAW §3.04[3], 19–20 (2005).

57 The rise of the PBM industry was, in part, a response to the 2003 Congressional amendment to Medicare that, for the first time, provided senior citizens and other Medicare beneficiaries with voluntary prescription drug benefits beginning in 2006. The PBMs manage the drug benefit systems for their clients using services such as assembling retail pharmacy networks,

establishing drug formularies for the client, and using mail order pharmacy options. *See generally* FED. TRADE COMM´N, PHARMACY BENEFIT MAN-AGERS: OWNERSHIP OF MAIL-ORDER PHARMACIES (2005) [hereinafter FED. TRADE COMM´N 2005 REPORT].

58 The quote is a reference to a classic comedy routine by Abbott and Costello. *See* BASEBALL ALMANAC, *Who's on First? By Abbott and Costello,* www.baseball-almanac.com/humor4.shtml (last visited Oct. 28, 2018).

59 *See* Morton & Boller, *supra* note 12, at 21–22 (rebates are percentage discounts used by manufacturers to gain market share from PBM enrollees).

60 *See e.g.,* ANTHEM CLASS ACTION COMPLAINT, *supra* note 42, at 28; *See e.g.,* EXPRESS SCRIPTS, ANNUAL REPORT 2015 (2016), https:// expressscriptsholdingco.gcs-web.com/static-files/777166b9-6d1a-4b3f-b979-f798b856955c. Wholesale acquisition cost (WAC) is a similar benchmark used in these contracts and as a starting point in negotiations. *See id.* Wholesalers mark up the drug from the WAC by a certain percentage, which leads to the average wholesale price (AWP). For example, if a drug has a WAC of $250, its AWP across the nation might be $250 + 20% = $300. *See* Julie Appleby, *Tracking Who Makes Money on a Brand-Name Drug,* KAISER HEALTH NEWS (Oct. 6, 2016), https://khn.org/news/tracking-who-makes-money-on-a-brand-name-drug/; *see also* WellPoint, Inc. & Express Scripts, Inc., Pharmacy Benefit Mgmt. Services Agreement (EX-10.30) (Dec. 1, 2009) (specifying that the AWP refers to the average wholesale price of a prescription drug "as established and reported by the Pricing Source" and that a drug's applied AWP will be the AWP for the actual 11-digit National Drug Code).

61 Commercial publishers of AWP data include Truven Health Analytics, Red Book, Medi-Span, and First Data Ban National Drug Data File Plus. Drug companies report the average wholesale price to these third parties using indexes that include the National Drug Code (NDC), which is a universal drug product identifier for prescription and nonprescription drugs. U.S. FOOD & DRUG ADMIN., NATIONAL DRUG CODE DIRECTORY (2017).

62 *See e.g.,* U.S. HEALTH & HUM. SERV., OFFICE OF INSPECTOR GENERAL, HHS OIG OEI-05-05-00240, MEDICAID DRUG PRICE COMPARISON: AVERAGE MANUFACTURERS PRICE TO PUBLISHED PRICES (2005) (examining the difference between AWP, WAC, and AMP for all Medicaid reimbursed drug codes, i.e. 24,101 NDCs); U.S. HEALTH & HUM. SERV., OFFICE OF INSPECTOR GENERAL, OEI-03–05-00200, MEDICAID DRUG PRICE COMPARISON: AVERAGE SALES PRICE TO AVERAGE WHOLESALE PRICE (2005). (In these analyses, the HHS OIG found that differences between AMP and AWP for generic drugs is about 70 percent, and the difference between AMP and AWP for single-source and multisource branded drugs is about 25 percent. Additionally, the HHS OIG found that WAC is about 20 percent lower than AWP for Medicare and Medicaid-reimbursed drugs. Average

sales price (ASP) was found to be lower than AWP and WAC, and is now used under Part B to reimburse for drugs used in hospital and clinic settings. It is the lowest indexed price because it includes reductions for rebates and discounts.)

63 *See supra* note 60 (describing the relationships between AWP and the markup fees that wholesalers receive). Concerns also have been raised about a practice known as "repackaging," i.e. where PBMs or their mail-order pharmacies repackage a drug to obtain a new NDC code at a new and usually higher AWP. In the FTC's 2005 report, PBMs reported that repackaging rarely occurred. For example, one study participant reported repackaging in only 1 out of roughly every 1 million prescriptions filled. FED. TRADE COMM´N 2005 REPORT, *supra* note 57, at xiii. Recent anecdotal reports by community pharmacists and others suggest that this practice may be increasing. *See* FTC WORKSHOP SLIDES, *supra* note 38, at 117.

64 *U.S. ex rel. Behnke v. CVS Caremark Corp.*, No. 14-cv-00824 MSG (E.D. Pa. 2014); *see also* Lucas Sullivan, *Aetna Whistleblower, Who Says CVS Gouged Medicare and Medicaid Customers, is Put on Leave*, COLUMBUS DIS-PATCH (June 5, 2018), www.dispatch.com/news/20180517/aetna-whistle blower-who-says-cvs-gouged-medicare-and-medicaid-customers-is-put-on-leave (describing the 2016 complaint that was unsealed in April 2018).

65 *U.S. v. CVS Caremark Corp.*, *supra* note 64, at 24 ("the Caremark defend-ants carefully managed the MAC prices so as to hit the minimum aggregate discount it had guaranteed Aetna, but not to allow Aetna to get the benefit of any lower prices").

66 *See id.*, at 24, 36–38.

67 Provisions between drug companies and PBMs that condition rebates on maintaining or exceeding the prior year's percentage of an insurer's patients who filled their prescriptions in that drug class with that drug may operate as a method of helping larger pharmacies (and larger PBMs that own large pharma-cies) to avoid competition from smaller players. For details of this technique, and the manner in which it maintains the market position for both large drug companies and large pharmacies, *see infra* section 3.1 (on why PBMs may prefer higher prices) and section 4.1.2 (on the financial incentives for pharmacies).

68 *See* Morton & Boller, *supra* note 12, at 19. A health plan "does not provide essential health benefits unless it" covers at least either "one drug in every... category and class" or "the same number of prescription drugs in each category and class as the EHB-benchmark plan." 45 CFR § 156.122(a)(1) (2017).

69 42 U.S.C. § 1395w-104(b)(3)(G)(iv); *see also* Morton & Boller, *supra* note 12, citing Mark Duggan & Fiona Scott Morton, *The Effect of Medicare Part D on Pharmaceutical Prices and Utilization*, 100 AM. ECON. REV. 594, 603, n. 14 (2010).

70 *See* EXPRESS SCRIPTS, *supra* note 22, at 11 ("Most clients choose formular-ies designed to be used with financial incentives, such as three-tier

co-payments, which drive preferential selection of plan-preferred generics and branded drugs over their non-formulary alternatives"); *see also* Allison Dabbs Garrett & Robert Garis, *Leveling the Playing Field in the Pharmacy Benefit Management Industry*, 42 VAL. U.L. REV. 33, 34 (2007) ("A common structure is the three-tier plan. The first tier... typically provides for a co-pay of around $10 for generic drugs. The middle tier, with a slightly higher co-pay, allows for the purchase of brand-name drugs that have been determined by the PBM to be the preferred brand drugs in the formulary for treating a particular disease or condition. The third tier, allows plan participants to purchase non-preferred brand drugs with the payment of the highest copay"). In addition to requiring the highest co-pay, the third tier may include a lower percentage coverage. Modern formularies may have up to six tiers, including two levels of cost-sharing each for generic, brands, and specialty drugs. The most restrictive specialty tier relies entirely on co-insurance (under which the patient pays a percentage of the cost or the full cost up to a specified amount), rather than a co-pay (under which the patient pays a fixed amount). Given the high price of specialty drugs, paying co-insurance is a particularly heavy burden for a patient to bear.

Tiering can have a significant effect on a patient. A 2017 survey of patients on private plans found that co-pays increased from $11 for first-tier drugs to $110 for fourth-tier drugs, that average co-insurance rates rose from 17 percent per drug in the first tier to 38 percent in the third tier, and that, in addition to co-pays and co-insurance, some health plans required additional deductibles for drugs, separate from the general annual deductible. GARY CLAXTON et al., EMPLOYER HEALTH BENEFITS 2017 ANNUAL SURVEY 150, 154, 159 (2017), http://files.kff.org/attachment/Report-Employer-Health-Benefits-Annual-Survey-2017.

71 *See e.g., id.* (listing the PBM's services provided); *see also* NAS REPORT, *supra* note 34, at 52 (explaining that higher-tiered drugs require greater co-pays from patients, thereby discouraging use of the drug; narrowing indications for which a drug may be used also constrains volume; excluding the drug entirely from coverage is the most powerful leverage).

72 Mark Meador, *Squeezing the Middleman: Ending Underhanded Dealing in the Pharmaceutical Benefit Management Industry through Regulation*, 20 ANNALS OF HEALTH L. 77, 82 (2011) (explaining that PBMs are not required to share information about rebates with plan sponsors, and so often remain silent and pocket some or all of the money saved through rebates).

73 *See* Hiltzik, *supra* note 53. One bright spot on the horizon is a recent decision from a California court rejecting an attempt by pharmacists to claim First Amendment protection against efforts to force the revelation of certain pharmacy fees and pricing. *See Beeman v. Anthem Prescription Mgmt. Inc.*, 2007 U.S. Dist. LEXIS 103220 (C.D. Cal. 2007). To the extent that drug companies challenge legislative attempts to mandate disclosure of this

information on First Amendment grounds, the California decision may provide a useful analogy for the governmental position.

74 Hiltzik, *supra* note 53 (noting that insurers "generally don't have the right to audit PBMs rebate collections and distribution"); CHANGE TO WIN, CVS CAREMARK: AN ALARMING MERGER, TWO YEARS LATER 9 (2009), http:// prescriptiondrugdiscounts.net/files/cvs%20an-alarming-merger.pdf.

75 Hiltzik, *supra* note 53. Scott Gottlieb, Comm'r of the FDA, recently referred to this system as "Kabuki drug-pricing constructs – constructs that obscure profit taking across the supply chain that drives up costs; that expose consumers to high out of pocket spending; and that actively discourage competition." Scott Gottlieb, Comm'r of Food & Drugs, *Remarks at America's Health Insurance Plans' National Health Policy Conference: Capturing the Benefits of Competition for Patients* (Mar. 7, 2018). The voluminous number of claims combined with constantly fluctuating prices creates enormous data analysis challenges for those who might want to audit closely. The volume of data is one reason why insurance companies hired PBMs in the first place, leaving one to wonder whether the PBMs have simply become too big to audit.

76 *See* FED. TRADE COMM'N 2005 REPORT, *supra* note 57, at 24, n. 6 (asserting that some PBM contracts with plan sponsors state that the PBM has several MAC lists for generic pricing and allow the PBM to select which list it will use with a particular plan sponsor).

77 In health system lingo, this is referred to as the "point of sale."

78 *See* Sood *et al.*, *supra* note 28; *see also* FTC WORKSHOP SLIDES, *supra* note 38, at 100. One can see the power of these three players, in particular, from the fact that, in 2016, the California Public Employee Benefits System (CalPERS) had only three finalists in the bidding for contract to manage prescriptions for the nearly 500,000 members and their families enrolled in non-HMO health plans. Hiltzik, *supra* note 53. Only the big three can compete for the major prizes.

79 Jon Roberts, CVS/Caremark Executive Vice President & President, *Gaining Lives with Our Unique PBM Capabilities* 27 (2014), http://investors .cvscaremark.com/~/media/Files/C/CVS-IR-v3/documents/16-12-2014/jon-roberts-presentation.pdf.

80 US GENERAL ACCOUNTING OFFICE, PHARMACY BENEFIT MANAGERS: EARLY RESULTS ON VENTURES WITH DRUG MANUFACTURERS 4–5 (1995), www.gao.gov/assets/230/221921.pdf (noting that, following a slew of drug companies purchasing PBMs, the FTC finally intervened when Eli Lilly purchased PCS and established safeguards against potentially anticompetitive consequences); *In the Matter of Merck & Co, Inc. & Merk-Medco Managed Care, LLC*, Administrative – Before the Fed. Trade Comm. (1999) (No. C-3853) (requiring an "open formulary" along with other conditions in response to a complaint that Merck was receiving favorable

treatment on Medco's formulary); MERCK & CO., INC., *Letter to Shareholders: Important U.S. Federal Income Tax Information Concerning the Medco Health Solutions, Inc. Stock Distribution* (2003), https://s21.q4cdn
.com/488056881/files/doc_downloads/spinoff/MRK_Medco_shareholders_
letter.pdf (noting that shareholders "received 1206 shares of Medco Health common stock for each share of Merck common stock" owned); Milt Freudenheim, *With Ties Lingering, Medco Leaves Merck,* NY TIMES (2003), www
.nytimes.com/2003/08/20/business/with-ties-lingering-medco-leaves-merck
.html (describing Medco's spin-off from Merck); FED. TRADE COMM'N, Press release, *FTC Gives Final Approval to Lilly Order; Pledges Continued Monitoring for Anticompetitive Practices* (July 31, 1995), www.ftc.gov/news-events/press-releases/1995/07/eli-lilly-and-company (noting SmithKline's acquisition of Diversified Pharmaceutical Services in a press release also touching on concerns regarding the anticompetitive potential of similar acquisitions); Elizabeth L. Mitchell, *The Potential for Self-Interested Behavior by Pharmaceutical Manufacturers through Vertical Integration with Pharmacy Benefit Managers: The Need for a New Regulatory Approach,* 54 FOOD DRUG L. J. 151, 152–53, nn. 16–17 (noting that SmithKline ultimately sold Diversified Pharmaceutical Services for $700 million, having originally paid $2.3 billion for the PBM); *In the Matter of Eli Lilly and Company, a Corporation,* Administrative – Before the Fed. Trade Comm. (1999) (No. C-3594) (setting aside an order placing restrictions and obligations on Lilly's use of its PBM after Lilly sold it to Rite Aid).

81 Brian Feldman, *Big Pharmacies Are Dismantling the Industry that Keeps U.S. Drug Costs Even Sort-of under Control,* QUARTZ (Mar. 17, 2016); *see also* Milt Freudenheim, *Company News: Merck Completes $6 Billion Deal for Medco,* NY TIMES 3 (Nov. 19, 1993); Milt Freudenheim, *A Shift in the Power of Pharmaceuticals,* NY TIMES 1 (May 9, 1994); Milt Freudenheim, *Pharmaceutical Giant is Buying Operator of Drug-Benefit Plans,* NY TIMES A1 (Jul. 12, 1994). A new consolidation variant has arisen recently as insurance companies look to purchase PBMs, raising a different set of issues for competition authorities to contemplate. *See* Alex Kacik & Shelly Livingston, *Cigna-Express Scripts Deal Unlikely to Benefit Consumers,* MODERN HEALTHCARE (Mar. 12, 2018), www.modernhealthcare.com/article/20180312/
NEWS/180319984.

82 See *supra* note 80 and accompanying text.

83 Amy L. Cralam, The Serpent in the Garden of Eden: A Look at the Impact of Physician Financial Incentive Programs and Reconsideration of *Herdrich v. Pegram,* 16 J.L. & HEALTH 289, 308, 311 (2002).

84 *See* EXPRESS SCRIPTS, *Response to SEC Comment* (Jun. 26, 2017) (in which the PBM responds to an SEC request for more information on its rebate program and notes that "[w]e administer a rebate program through which we receive rebates and administrative fees from pharmaceutical

manufacturers"); Linda Cahn, *Don't Get Trapped By PBMs' Rebate Labeling Games*, MANAGED CARE (Jan. 1, 2009), www.managedcaremag.com/arch ives/2009/1/don-t-get-trapped-pbms-rebate-labeling-games; *see also* FTC WORKSHOP SLIDES, *supra* note 38, at 119 (Pharmacists' Association slide suggesting that information about prescriptions filled by plan members are often sold to manufacturers/data repositories and that the PBM may receive up to $1 per prescription.

85 The term "co-insurance" refers to payments that patients make within plans that require patients to pay a percentage share of costs – either a partial share or a full share up to a specified ceiling. The term "co-pay" refers to a portion of healthcare costs that a patient pays as a flat fee, irrespective of the cost of the medication. *See* ANTHEM CLASS ACTION COMPLAINT, *supra* note 42, at 2, n. 2.

86 Murray Aitken et al., *The Regulation of Prescription Drug Competition and Market Responses: Patterns in Prices and Sales Following Loss of Exclusivity*, Working Paper No. 19487, NAT´L BUREAU OF ECON. RES. (2013), www.nber.org/papers/w19487.

87 Joanna Shepherd, *Deterring Innovation: New York v. Actavis and the Duty to Subsidize Competitors' Market Entry*, 17 MINN. J.L. SCI. & TECH. 663, 706–07 (2016); *see also New York v. Actavis PLC*, 787 F.3D 638, 646 (2015) (noting that "[s]tate substitution laws are designed to" shift "drug selection . . . to pharmacists and patients, who have greater financial incentives to make price comparisons").

88 For a description of the tactics brand-name companies use to switch to new versions of a drug just before the generic competitor receives approval, to prevent substitution, *see* Feldman & Frondorf, *supra* note 4, at 66, 69–78.

89 Adam J. Fein, *2018 Economic Report on U.S. Pharmacies and Pharmacy Benefit Managers*, DRUG CHANNELS (2018), https://drugchannelsinstitute.com/files/ 2018-PharmacyPBM-DCI-Overview.pdf. For a detailed, but more complex, graphic that includes the flow of funds and pharmaceutical products through pharmacies and wholesalers, *see* Linette Lopez, *The Feds Just Asked a Huge Healthcare Company Who Their Real Clients are and the Answer is Totally Unsatisfying*, BUS. INSIDER (Dec. 7, 2017), https://nordic.businessinsider .com/robinhood-cofounder-baiju-bhatt-interview-2017-8/, citing HENRY C. EICKELBERG, THE PRESCRIPTION DRUG SUPPLY "BLACK BOX": HOW IT WORKS AND WHY YOU SHOULD CARE 9 (2015), www.americanhealthpo licy.org/Content/documents/resources/December%202015_AHPI%20Study_ Understanding_the_Pharma_Black_Box.pdf.

90 NAS REPORT, *supra* note 34, at 111–12.

91 *See* Feldman & Frondorf, *supra* note 4, at 1 (describing the Hatch-Waxman system for rapid entry of generic drugs); *cf.* Jennifer L. Graber, *Excessive Pricing of off-Patent Pharmaceuticals: Hatch it or Ratcher?*, 92 N.Y.U.L. REV. 1146, 1161 (2017), citing Anna Edney & Justin Sink, *Trump Calls Drug*

Pricing "Astronomical" and Promises Changes, BLOOMBERG POLITICS (Jan. 31, 2017), www.bloomberg.com/news/articles/2017-01-31/trump-meets-with-drugmakers-as-industry-fears-price-controls (noting President Trump's promise to find ways "to get new medicines to market faster").

Chapter 3

1 *See* EXPRESS SCRIPTS HOLDING CO., Form 10-K, ANNUAL REPORT 13, 18, 62 (Dec. 31, 2017); *see also* Joana Shepherd, *The Fox Guarding the Henhouse: The Regulation of Pharmacy Benefit Managers by a Market Adversary*, 9 NW. J.L. & SOC. POL´Y 1, 2 (2013) (noting that PBMs administer prescription drug benefits for health plan sponsors and also negotiate discounts from drug manufacturers in exchange for putting the manufacturers' drugs on pre-ferred medication lists).

2 *See* EXPRESS SCRIPTS HOLDING CO., *supra* note 1, at 4–5, 18–19.

3 Some forms are modeled as price protections; others, as anticipated rebate amounts.

4 *See* Mark Meador, *Squeezing the Middleman: Ending Underhanded Dealing in the Pharmaceutical Benefit Management Industry through Regulation*, 20 ANNALS OF HEALTH LAW 77, 82 (2011) (noting that PBMs take advantage of the price range in various price lists for generic drugs, negotiating with manufacturers for a lower price and setting reimbursement rates with plan sponsors using a higher list price, to maximize the spread); *cf.* Fiona Scott Morton & Lysle T. Boller, *Enabling Competition in the Pharmaceutical Markets*, Working Paper 30, HUTCHINS CTR. ON FISCAL & MONETARY POL´Y AT BROOKINGS 3 (May 2017), www.brookings.edu/wp-content/uploads/2017/05/wp30_scottmorton_competitioninpharma1.pdf (noting that PBMs may use rebates to grow profits by keeping a share of the high prices paid by insurers for costly medication).

5 *See* Morton & Boller, *supra* note 4, at 21–22(noting that contracts between plan sponsors and the PBM are often based on list price without rebates, in part because this incentivizes the PBM to bargain for larger rebates). Accounting methods for PBMs are also problematic: PBMs report their revenue based on the total value of drugs flowing through their contracts and their income as a percentage of that total revenue. Thus, their earnings-per-share (EPS) stock valuations increase as the total revenue increases – a figure that is, in part, a function of prices.

6 For an example of a particularly powerful PBM–insurer contract, *see* Michael Hiltzik, *How 'Price-Cutting' Middlemen Are Making Crucial Drugs Vastly More Expensive*, LA TIMES (June 9, 2017), www.latimes.com/business/hilt zik/la-fi-hiltzik-pbm-drugs-20170611-story.html (reporting that, in 2016, the California Public Employee Benefits System (CalPERS) awarded a five-year contract to OptumRx, one of the three major PBMs, to manage

prescriptions for the nearly 500,000 CalPERS members and their families enrolled in non-HMO plans).

7 Compl., at 6, *Boss et al. v. CVS Corp. et al.*, No. 17–01823 (D.N.J, Mar. 17, 2017) (arguing that payments other than rebates are provided under a variety of labels, including discounts, credits, concession fees, etc.); *see also* Linda Cahn, *Don't Get Trapped by PBMs' Rebate Labeling Games*, MANAGED CARE (Jan. 1, 2009), www.managedcaremag.com/archives/2009/1/don-t-get-trapped-pbms-rebate-labeling-games.

8 *See e.g.*, EXPRESS SCRIPTS HOLDING CO., *supra* note 1, at 12 (describing its pharmaceutical services as including aligning its expertise and industry insight with UBC, a consulting company that, among other services, partners with drug companies to help prescribers to navigate prescription drug coverage and pharmacy options through patient access programs, including patient assistance programs, reimbursement, alternate funding, and compliance services). Express Scripts acquired UBC in its purchase of another PBM (Medco) in 2012 and sold the subsidiary in 2017. Samantha Liss, *Express Scripts to Sell Subsidiary to Private-Equity Firm*, ST. LOUIS POST-DISPATCH (Nov. 27, 2017), www.stltoday.com/business/local/express-scripts-to-sell-subsidiary-to-private-equity-firm/article_26514461-225a-5e81-8abb-09efe0ab005b.html.

Administrative fees also do not get included in a manufacturer's calculation of the best price for Medicaid. *See* 42 C.F.R. § 447.505(c)(17) and (d)(1) (noting, respectively, that PBM rebates are excluded from manufacturer calculation of Medicaid best price and that best price is also net of administrative fees).

9 *See Follow the Dollar: Understanding the Pharmaceutical Distribution and Payment System Shapes the Prices of Brand Medicines*, PHRMA 8 (2017), www.ftc.gov/system/files/documents/public_comments/2017/12/00503-1426 14.pdf (pharmaceutical industry report claiming that administrative fees have increased rapidly in recent years).

10 Rebate agreements may also ensure a form of most-favored nation (MFN) status, ensuring that competitors do not have better access in any way, presumably even if the competitor offers a lower price. *See e.g.*, *Eisai, Inc. v. Sanofi Aventis U.S., LLC*, 821 F.3d 394, 400 (3d Cir. 2016) (with a contract clause preventing hospitals from giving competing drugs priority status).

11 *See* Compl., at 26, *Sanofi-Aventis U.S. LLC v. Mylan N.V.*, 2017 U.S. Dist. LEXIS 204886 (D.N.J. 2017) (No. 17–02763) (drug company Sanofi acknowledged that drug maker rebates in exchange for exclusive coverage "are not unheard of," but said that drug makers with monopolies "do not – and under US antitrust law cannot – condition large rebates to block new rival drugs from key access to the market"). As described in this chapter, a drug company does not need to have full monopoly power in any particular

drug to create blocking behavior nor are the drugs that suffer necessarily new drugs. *See infra* section 3.1.1 on the power of volume; *see also* Boss Compl., *supra* note 7, at 6 (arguing that however the rebates are named or described, they are a *quid pro quo* for formulary inclusion or placement).

12 *See* Andrew Pollack, *AbbVie Deal Heralds Changed Landscape for Hepatitis Drugs*, NY TIMES (Dec. 22, 2014), www.nytimes.com/2014/12/22/business/ pharmacy-deal-heralds-changed-landscape-for-hepatitis-drugs.html; Gail R. Wilensky, *"Negotiating" Drug Prices for Medicare*, HEALTHCARE FIN. MGMT. MAG. (Mar. 1, 2016), www.gailwilensky.com/includes/pdf/Negotiating_ Drug_Prices_for_Medicare_HFMA_March_2016.pdf. Subsequently, CVS Health Corp. struck a deal to make Gilead's hepatitis C medicines the exclusive treatments for its customers following rebate negotiations. *See* Robert Langreth & Caroline Chen, *Gilead Makes Exclusive Deal With CVS for Hepatitis C Drugs*, BLOOMBERG (Jan. 5, 2015), www.bloomberg.com/ news/articles/2015-01-05/gilead-makes-exclusive-deal-with-cvs-for-hepatitis-c-medicine; STAFF OF S. COMM. ON FINANCE, THE PRICE OF SOVALDI AND ITS IMPACT ON THE U.S. HEALTH CARE SYSTEM, S. Prt. 114–20, 114 (Dec. 2015) (citing an email from the director, Federal Government Affairs, at CVS Health Corp., stating that, "as new drugs came on to the market like Viekira Pak, we were able to negotiate discounts [with Gilead]"). In theory, when equally situated players compete to lower prices, the customer benefits. As noted later in the chapter, however, problems may arise when the players are not equally situated, such as when one player has a large stable of drugs with which to bargain and the other does not. And, as noted earlier, the entire rebate system pushes prices higher – prices that patients will frequently pay without the rebate, and which create other burdens and economic distortions.

13 STAFF OF S. COMM. ON FINANCE, *supra* note 12, at 88.

14 Secondary patents cover various adjustments to a drug's timing, dosage, or delivery mechanism, rather than cover the main chemical formula or innovation. Secondary patents, sometimes called "evergreen patents," may be added in an effort to extend the life of the drug's protection, and such patents can be more difficult to defend in court. For an explanation and empirical analysis of evergreening, *see* Robin Feldman, *May Your Drug Price Be Ever Green*, J. L. & BIOSCI. 1 (2018); *see also* Michael A. Carrier, Nicole L. Levidow & Aaron S. Kesselheim, *Using Antitrust Law to Challenge Turing's Daraprim Price Increase*, 31 BERKELEY TECH. L.J. 1379 (2017); Stacy L. Dogan & Mark A. Lemley, *Antitrust Law and Regulatory Gaming*, 87 TEX. L. REV. 685 (2009).

15 FED. TRADE COMM´N, Press release, *AstraZeneca to Pay $7.9 Million to Resolve Kickback Allegations* (Feb. 11, 2015).

16 Compl. for Damages and Other Relief under the *Qui Tam* Provisions of the Federal False Claims Act and Similar State Provisions, at 2, *United States of America et al. v. AstraZeneca LP et al.*, No. 10–00910 (D. Del. 2010).

17 *See id.*, at 17.

18 *See* ROBIN FELDMAN & EVAN FRONDORF, DRUG WARS: HOW BIG PHARMA
    RAISES PRICES AND KEEPS GENERICS OFF THE MARKET 71 (2017).

19 Of course, on the flip side, selling in volume is always better for a seller, and
    buyers who can offer to purchase greater volume have an advantage negoti-
    ating a better price. Thus, one might argue that the larger discount for
    volume is perfectly rational and a normal function of the market. The
    transaction raises a number of red flags signaling that this is not a normal
    market function. One can see such red flags in: (a) the inducement to exclude
    competitors, particularly lower-priced competitors; (b) the siphoning off of
    value to middle players; and (c) the fact that, in the end, the consumer is
    driven toward higher-priced purchases. For a discussion of greater buying
    power for a larger-volume purchaser, see Michael E. Porter, *How Competitive
    Forces Shape Strategy*, 59 HARV. BUS. REV. 2, 137–45, 140–41 (1979).

20 With drugs for which the molecule is really the same, for example, insulin, a
    drug company might try to push its market share up far more aggressively.
    See Norman R. Augustine, Guru Madhavan & Sharyl J. Nass, *Making
    Medicines Affordable: A National Imperative*, NAT'L ACADEMIES OF SCI.,
    ENG'G, AND MED. 99–100 (2017) (all health insurance drug plans, whether
    Medicare or private, have an exception process that permits coverage of a
    drug not on formulary, or can reduce out-of-pocket cost if a physician
    provides information about side effects that the patient experienced from a
    lower-tiered drug or offers another medical reason). One should note that
    this is generally difficult, time-consuming, and can take a long time for
    patients to do successfully, which discourages its usage except in extreme
    circumstances. It can require a specialized level of knowledge in many cases
    to argue successfully.

21 *See Suburban Mobile Homes v. AMFAC Communities*, 101 Cal. App. 3d 532,
    544 (1980) ("we emphasize that the power over the tying product [here, home
    sites] can be sufficient even though the power falls short of dominance and
    even though the power exists only with respect to some buyers in the market");
    cf. Jefferson Parish Hospital District No. 2 v. Hyde, 466 U.S. 2, 27 (1984) (the
    court holding that an entity controlling 30 percent of a market does "not
    generate the kind of market power that justifies condemnation of tying").

22 Robin Feldman, *Regulatory Property: The New IP*, 40 COLUM. J.L. & ARTS
    54, 64 (2016) (describing the various bargaining chips utilized in negoti-
    ations between PBMs and manufacturers); Robin Feldman et al., *Empirical
    Evidence of Drug Pricing Games: A Citizen's Pathway Gone Astray*, 20 STAN.
    TECH. L. REV. 39, 45 (2017); Feldman & Frondorf, *supra* note 18, at 49,
    86, 136.

23 *See* Feldman & Frondorf, *supra* note 18, at 33.

24 It is important to note that a patent is not a guarantee of a monopoly; it brings
    with it the right to exclude and the opportunity thereby to obtain a monopoly

position. There may be substitutes in the market, however, such as ibuprofen and acetaminophen, or the market may have no interest in the drug. For a deeper discussion of these issues, *see* ROBIN FELDMAN, RETHINKING PATENT LAW 23, n. 53 (2012), citing *Ill. Tool Works Inc. v. Indep. Ink Inc.*, 547 U.S. 28 (2006).

25 *See e.g.*, Compl., *U.S. v. Blue Cross Blue Shield of Mich.*, 809 F. Supp. 2d 665 (E.D. Mich. 2011) (challenging Blue Cross Blue Shield of Michigan's use of MFN clauses); *see also* Roy Levy, *The Pharmaceutical Industry: A Discussion of Competitive and Antitrust Issues in an Environment of Change*, FED. TRADE COMM'N 54 (1999).

26 Jonathan D. Rockoff, *Johnson & Johnson Says Discounts Cut the Prices for Its Drugs, Though Revenue Rose*, WALL ST. J. (Mar. 8, 2018), www.wsj.com/articles/johnson-johnson-says-discounts-cut-the-prices-for-its-drugs-though-revenue-rose-1520551413.

27 *See id.* The *Wall Street Journal* article also noted that another drug company, Merck, reported in February 2018 that aggregate prices of its drugs and vaccines, after discounts and rebates, fell 1.9 percent the prior year.

28 *See id.*

29 *See* Robin Cooper Feldman, *Defensive Leveraging in Antitrust*, 87 GEO. L.J. 2079, 2103–05 (1999); PHILLIP E. AREEDA & HERBERT HOVENKAMP, ANTITRUST LAW ¶1758 (3d ed., 2011) (a section on "package or bundled discounts").

30 *See* Morton & Boller, *supra* note 4, at 19.

31 One can see a faint hint that volume discounts might be providing a key element of PBM profitability. Looking at public disclosures from PBM Express Scripts, gross margin and operating profit seem to consistently start lower in the first quarter, improve each quarter thereafter, and then drop down again in the first quarter of the following year. It is possible that this trend signals the impact of volume discounts coming into play across time, but there is no way of confirming this hypothesis without more information related to rebates and deals with drug companies.

32 Compl., at 6, 21–23, *Shire U.S. Inc. v. Allergan, Inc.*, No. 17–7716 (D.N.J. 2017) (specifically, the complaint implies that Allergan's product portfolio, which includes many popular glaucoma drugs, provides the company with "the financial wherewithal to give … rebates that far exceed anything that Shire could offer on Xiidra").

33 *See id.*, at 4–5.

34 *See id.*, at 6–7.

35 Compl., at 1, *Pfizer Inc. v. Johnson & Johnson and Janssen Biotech, Inc.*, U.S. Dist. LEXIS 31690, No. 17–4180 (E.D. Pa. 2018).

36 *See id.*

37 *See id.*, at 2.

38 *See id.*, at 3. If insurers are allowed to reimburse for the biosimilar when Remicade has failed, the complaint alleges that the effects of the contract are

still exclusionary, because physicians are unlikely to turn to the biosimilar if the original drug failed. *See id.*, at 3–4.

39 *See id.*, at 5.

40 *See id.*

41 *See id.*

42 *See generally* Order Granting Final Approval of Class Action Settlement, Approving Plan of Distribution and Final J. and Order of Dismissal, *Castro, M.D., P.A. v. Sanofi Pasteur Inc.*, No. 11–7178, LEXIS 96001 (D.N.J. 2012) [hereinafter Sanofi Settlement Final Approval]; Order Granting Preliminary Approval of the Proposed Settlement, Approval of the Proposed Manner and Form of Notice, and Appointment of Escrow Agent and Settlement Administrator at 2, *Castro, M.D., P.A. v. Sanofi Pasteur Inc.*, No. 11–7178, LEXIS 96001 (D.N.J. 2012) [hereinafter Sanofi Settlement Preliminary Approval].

43 Class Action Compl., at 3, *Castro, M.D., P.A. v. Sanofi Pasteur Inc.*, No. 11–7178, LEXIS 96001 (D.N.J. 2012).

44 *See generally* Sanofi Settlement Final Approval, *supra* note 42; Sanofi Settlement Preliminary Approval, *supra* note 42, at 2.

45 *See* Feldman, *supra* note 29, at 2091, 2104, citing *SmithKline Corp. v. Eli Lilly Co.*, 575 F.2d 1056 (3d Cir. 1978).

46 *See generally SmithKline Corp. v. Eli Lilly & Co.*, 427 F. Supp. 1089 (E.D. Pa. 1976); *see also* Feldman, *supra* note 29, at 2104–05.

47 *See* Feldman, *supra* note 29, at 2105.

48 *See id.*; *SmithKline*, *supra* note 46, at 1091–92.

49 *See id.*

50 *SmithKline*, *supra* note 46, at 1091.

51 *See id.*, at 1112–14.

52 *See id.*, at 109, 1115–17.

53 *See id.*, at 1128.

54 *SmithKline*, *supra* note 45, at 1065; *cf. Masimo Corp. v. Tyco Health Care Group, LP.*, LEXIS 29977 34–37 (C.D. Cal. 2006) (unpublished case criticizing the reasoning in *SmithKline*).

55 *See* Feldman, *supra* note 29, at 2105.

56 *See* David A. Crane, *Bargaining over Loyalty*, Pub. Law Research Paper No. 313, U. Mich. (2013); *see also* Rafi Mohammed, *When It's Wise to Offer Volume Discounts*, Harv. Bus. Rev. (Oct. 25, 2013), https://hbr.org/2013/10/when-it-is-wise-to-offer-volume-discounts (describing how volume discounts may be offered to move customers away from rivals).

57 For a description of list prices, which can be based on average wholesale price (AWP) and are cynically also known as "Ain't What's Paid," *see supra* Chapter 2, notes 60–63 and accompanying text.

58 I am indebted to Jeff Mosenkis, who used this imagery in a podcast interview discussing my earlier work regarding the pharmaceutical industry. *See* Jeff

Mosenkis, *IPA's Weekly Links*, Chris Blattman Blog (Sept. 14, 2017), https://chrisblattman.com/2017/07/14/ipas-weekly-links-121/ (noting that if you listen to Feldman's interview, "You might need blood pressure medication").

59 Charles Ornstein & Katie Thomas, *Take the Generic, Patients Are Told. Until They Are Not*, NY Times (Aug. 6, 2017), www.nytimes.com/2017/08/06/health/prescription-drugs-brand-name-generic.html?mtrref=undefined.

60 *See id. See also* Henry Grabowski, Genia Long & Richard Mortimer, *Recent Trends in Brand-Name and Generic Drug Competition*, 17 J. of Med. Econ. 1, 6, 7 (2013); Andreas J. Dirnagl & Myrvet A. Cocoli, *Global Generic Pharmaceutical Industry Review: Corporate Research*, Bank of Tokyo-Mitsubishi 11 (Feb. 2016), www.krungsri.com/bank/getmedia/a5599675-701b-49d8-a857-33d247c773a0/BTMU-Research-201602-29.aspx; Ass´n for Accessible Med., Generic Drug Access & Savings in the U.S. 16 (2017), https://accessiblemeds.org/sites/default/files/2017-07/2017-AAM-Access-Savings-Report-2017-web2.pdf.

61 *See id.*

62 *See id.* In an example from medical care, rather than medicines, the FTC entered into a consent agreement in 2017 with a group of ophthalmologists in Puerto Rico. The complaint alleged that collusion by the physician group had forced a health plan and network administrator to abandon plans for a new lower-cost network. *See generally In the Matter of Cooperative de Medicos Oftalmologos de Puerto Rico*, Administrative – Before the Fed. Trade Comm. (No. C-4603) (2017), www.ftc.gov/system/files/documents/cases/170303c4603_cooperativa_order.pdf; Fed. Trade Comm´n, Press release, *Puerto Rico Opthamologist Group Settles FTC Charges that Members Agreed to an Illegal Boycott of Health Plan* (Jan. 19, 2017), www.ftc.gov/news-events/press-releases/2017/01/puerto-rico-ophthalmologist-group-settles-ftc-charges-members.

63 *See* Compl., at 2, *Schultz v. CVS Health*, No. 17–00359 (D.R.I. Aug. 7, 2017); Compl., at 2, *Grabstald v. Walgreens Boots Alliance, Inc.*, No. 17–05789 (N.D.Ill. Aug. 9, 2017) (alleging that plaintiffs would have paid less for generic drugs had they paid with cash instead of insurance); *see also* Notice of Voluntary Dismissal, *Schultz v. CVS Health*, No. 17–00359 (D.R.I. Aug. 7, 2017); Notice of Voluntary Dismissal, *Grabstald v. Walgreens Boots Alliance, Inc.*, No. 17–05789 (N.D.Ill. 2017) (providing notice of plaintiffs' voluntary dismissals of their cases).

64 *See also* Dep´t. of Justice, Press release, *CVS Caremark Corp. to Pay $36.7 Million to U.S., 23 States, and D.C. to Settle Medicaid Prescription Drug Fraud Allegations* (Mar. 18, 2008) (announcing that CVS Caremark agreed to pay $36.7 million to the U.S. government, 23 states, and the District of Columbia to settle claims that the company improperly switched patients from the tablet version of the ulcer and stomach-acid prescription drug Ranitadine to a more expensive capsule version, in order to increase Medicare reimbursements).

65 *See* Bob Herman, *The Drug Rebate Curtain*, Axios (Apr. 2, 2018),
    www.axios.com/drug-rebate-curtain-express-scripts-d3c93f14-e699-4a60-
    ac1d-9f81e5a658c0.html.

66 *See id.*

67 *See id; Duexis Prices, Coupons, and Patient Assistance Programs*, Drugs.com
    (Sept. 4, 2018), www.drugs.com/price-guide/duexis (indicating that the unit
    price of Duexis is $28.88 – much higher than the below-$1-unit costs of both
    Advil and Pepcid).

68 Katie Thomas, *Patients Eagerly Awaited a Generic Drug – Then They Saw the
    Price*, NY Times (Feb. 23, 2018), www.nytimes.com/2018/02/23/health/
    valeant-drug-price-syprine.html?emc=edit_th_180224&nl=todaysheadlines&
    nlid=497896550224.

69 *Teva Announces Launch of Generic Version of Syprine in the United States*, Bus.
    Wire (Feb. 9, 2018), www.businesswire.com/news/home/20180209005252/en/.

70 Thomas, *supra* note 68.

71 Response Letter from Eric R. Slusser, Exec. Vice President and Chief Fin.
    Officer, to Sec. & Exch. Comm'n (June 26, 2017) (on file with author) (in
    which PBM Express Scripts notes that some clients prefer to keep a greater
    percentage of rebates).

72 *See infra* note 90 and accompanying text; *see also* discussion of pass-through
    rebates found in section 3.1.3 (noting that when PBM contracts agree to pass
    through all or most of the rebates to their clients, the contracts may define
    rebates to exclude rebates paid with respect to utilization of specialty drugs).

73 *See id.*

74 *See* Herman, *supra* note 65.

75 *See id.*

76 Concerned about the role that PBMs may be playing in rising drug spending,
    a few states recently have tried to absorb the PBM functions themselves. For
    example, in July 2017, West Virginia's Medicaid agency took over for the
    PBMs, and the state's Department of Health and Human Resources reports
    that it saved roughly $30 million in the first six months. *See Health Care
    Policy: PBMs' Medicaid Role under Attack in Some States*, 6 Capitol Forum
    1, 2 (2018), www.ohiopharmacists.org/aws/OPA/pt/sd/news_article/152158/
    _PARENT/layout_interior_details/false. It would be difficult for states to
    remove PBMs from their Medicare and Medicaid services entirely, given
    the myriad services that PBMs provide at so many levels. Most importantly,
    history casts doubt on the notion that U.S. government programs are likely to
    run more smoothly and efficiently than free-market programs. The challenge
    involves fixing the perverse incentives and competitive barriers that are
    distorting the current market system.

77 Removal of Safe Harbor Protection for Rebates to Plans or PBMs Involving
    Prescription Pharmaceuticals and Creation of New Safe Harbor Protection,
    RIN No. 0936-AA08 (prop. July 18, 2018).

78 Charley Grant, *Risks Just Rose for Drug Middlemen*, WALL ST. J. (July 19, 2018), www.wsj.com/articles/risks-just-rose-for-drug-middlemen-1532016180.

79 Although there are a limited number of major players in the health insurance market, the market is less concentrated than the PBM market, with the top ten companies controlling just under half of the market. Neeraj Sood, *Understanding Competition in Prescription Drug Markets: Entry and Supply Chain Dynamics*, FED. TRADE COMM'N WORKSHOP SLIDES 101 (2017), www.ftc.gov/news-events/events-calendar/2017/11/understanding-competition-prescription-drug-markets-entry-supply [hereinafter FTC WORKSHOP SLIDES].

80 Response Letter from Eric R. Slusser, *supra* note 71, at 4.

81 *See* WILLIAM POUNDSTONE, PRISONER'S DILEMMA: JOHN VON NEUMANN, GAME THEORY, AND THE PUZZLE OF THE BOMB 201–03 (1993) (discussing the volunteer's dilemma).

82 *See infra* Chapter 6 (discussing proposals to allow the federal government to play a role in negotiations over drugs for Medicare).

83 As an example of the types of government action that can eliminate competition, *see* Feldman, *supra* note 22 (describing the history of more than a dozen regulatory exclusivities passed by Congress, generally approved in the same Congress in which the pharmaceutical industry had to swallow changes that the industry opposed).

84 Daniel Kahneman, Jack L. Knetsch & Richard H. Thaler, *Anomalies: The Endowment Effect, Loss Aversion, and Status Quo Bias*, 5 J. ECON. PERSPECTIVES 193, 194–97 (1991); Richard H. Thaler, *Integrating Economics with Psychology*, KUNGL. VETENSKAPS-AKADEMIAN 3 (2017), www.nobelprize.org/uploads/2018/06/advanced-economicsciences2017.pdf (stating that economist Herbert Simon "argued that, rather than finding optimal solutions that maximize lifetime expected utility, decision-makers typically try to find acceptable solutions to acute problems").

85 Martin D. Mobley, *Compensation Committee Reports Post-Sarbanes-Oxley: Unimproved Disclosure of Executive Compensation Policies and Practices*, 2 COLUM. BUS. L. REV. 111, 150, 171–74 (2005); *cf.* Julie Wokaty, *Investors Say Executive Pay Packages at Pharma May Incentivize Drug Pricing Risks*, INTERFAITH CTR. ON CORP. RESP. (Dec. 13, 2017), www.iccr.org/investors-say-executive-pay-packages-pharma-may-incentivize-drug-pricing-risks-0 (post from the Interfaith Center on Corporate Responsibility regarding shareholder resolution on drug pricing and access, with quote from a representative of the United Auto Workers Retiree Medical Benefits Trust that "misaligned incentive pay may encourage executives to sacrifice long-term, organic growth from drug discovery for short-term, 'quick fix' strategies that may pose business risks").

86 More specifically, the rule requires that 80 cents out of every premium dollar must go to pay medical claims and activities that improve quality of care.

Rate Review and the 80/20 Rule, HEALTHCARE.GOV, www.healthcare.gov/
health-care-law-protections/rate-review/ (last visited Oct. 29, 2018). If the
insurance company sells to large groups, which is generally defined as more
than 50 employees, the mandated percentage rises to 85 percent. *See id.*

87 *See id* (explaining the term "80/20 rule" and explaining that, along with rate
review, the rule helps to keep patient costs down). Some use the term
"medical loss ratio" to refer to the rule – as in, your medical loss ratio must
be at least 80 percent. *See id.*

88 Marshall Allen, *Why Your Health Insurer Doesn't Care about Your Big Bills*,
PROPUBLICA (May 25, 2018), www.propublica.org/article/why-your-health-
insurer-does-not-care-about-your-big-bills.

89 *See supra* Chapter 2, esp. notes 11–20, for more on the unique nature of the
healthcare market with respect to budgetary pressures.

90 Similarly, one health insurance consultant published language from a PBM
contract promising "100% pass through," followed by language that,
although appearing to guarantee a minimum amount of such payments per
prescription, would actually have the effect of undoing the prior language
and making the PBM responsible for only the minimum amount, regardless
of how much of a rebate the PBM collects from the drug company. *See* Cahn,
supra note 7 (quoting the following language, purportedly from a PBM
contract: "PBM will provide client with 100 percent of the rebates PBM
receives. PBM will make payments to client on a per-net-paid-claim basis,
regardless of the amount of rebates received by PBM. PBM will make such
payments in accordance with the amounts set forth in the table below (for
retail, 90-day retail, and mail order).").

91 *See e.g.*, EXPRESS SCRIPTS, VALUE BEYOND: DELIVERING MORE THAN MEDI-
CINE – ANNUAL REPORT 10 (2016), https://expressscriptsholdingco.gcs-web
.com/static-files/777166b9–6d1a-4b3f-b979-f798b856955c (touting its
information flow and explaining that "our claims processing system also
generates a database of drug utilization information that can be accessed . . .
to analyze utilization trends and prescribing patterns for more intensive management of the drug benefit, and on a prospective basis to help support
pharmacists in drug therapy management decisions"); *see also* Farasat A.S.
Bokhari & Gary M. Fournier, *Entry in the ADHD Drugs Market: Welfare
Impact of Generics and Me-Too's*, 61 J. OF INDUST. ECON. 339 (2013), www
.ncbi.nlm.nih.gov/pmc/articles/PMC4373170/; *see* FTC WORKSHOP
SLIDES, *supra* note 79, at 115 (noting that PBMs contract with virtually every
other entity in the drug supply chain, with the result that their data knowledge
and sheer size provide a huge advantage).

92 *See e.g.*, FEHBP's Pharmacy Benefits: Deal or no Deal? Before the Subcomm.
On Fed. Workforce, Postal Service, and DC, 11th Cong. (2009) (Testimony
of Patrick E. McFarland, Inspector General, U.S. Office of Personnel Management) (congressional testimony from the federal agency that administers

the Federal Employees Health Benefits Program, or FEHBP, explaining that drug cost structures are utterly nontransparent in a manner that invites bad pricing and contracting practices). Some insurers have begun to push back on the system, forming their own PBMs. *See* Bruce Jaspen, *Anthem Partners with CVS Health to Launch New PBM*, FORBES (Oct. 18, 2017), www.forbes.com/sites/brucejapsen/2017/10/18/anthem-partners-with-cvs-health-to-launch-new-pbm/#5ac8d7775740; *see also* CIGNA, Press release, *Cigna to Acquire Express Scripts for $67 Billion* (Mar. 8, 2018), www.cigna.com/newsroom/news-releases/2018/cigna-to-acquire-express-scripts-for-67-billion.

93 *See* section 3.1.1 on the power of volume.

94 Feldman, *supra* note 29, at 2081, 2099, n. 91, citing Joseph Farrell & Garth Saloner, *Installed Base and Compatibility: Innovation, Product Preannouncements, and Predation*, 76 AM. ECON. REV. 940, 943 (1986).

95 Feldman & Frondorf, *supra* note 18, at 34–41.

96 Thomas G. Krattenmaker & Steven C. Salop, *Anticompetitive Exclusion: Raising Rivals' Costs to Achieve Power over Price*, 96 YALE L.J. 209, 214 (1986); *see also* Robin Cooper Feldman, *Defensive Leveraging in Antitrust*, 87 GEO. L.J. 2079, 2086–87 (1999) (for an explanation of raising rivals' costs in the pharmaceutical context).

97 *See supra* notes 4–6 and accompanying text; *see also* Morton & Boller, *supra* note 4, at 22–23 (noting that if manufacturers set higher drug prices and rebates are measured in percentage terms, higher list prices mean that the profits earned by the PBM will rise when nothing else about the situation has changed).

98 Adam J. Barnhart & Jason Gomberg, *The AIDS Institute: Financial Incentives in Medicare Part D*, MILLIMAN 1, 6 (2016), http://theaidsinstitute.org/sites/default/files/attachments/Milliman%20Report%20-%20Final.pdf.

99 MEDICARE PAYMENT ADVISORY COMM'N, REPORT TO THE CONGRESS: MEDICARE PAYMENT POLICY 404 (2017), http://medpac.gov/docs/default-source/reports/mar17_entirereport.pdf.

100 *See id.*

101 *See id.*

102 CTR. FOR MEDICAID & MEDICARE SERV., Fact sheet, MEDICARE PART D: DIRECT AND INDIRECT REMUNERATION (Jan. 19, 2017), www.cms.gov/newsroom/fact-sheets/medicare-part-d-direct-and-indirect-remuneration-dir.

103 *See id.* (explaining the relationship between lower plan liability and higher government costs, and noting in particular that the substantial rise experienced in the government's costs results in part because "gross drug cost growth is concentrated in the catastrophic phase ... where Medicare covers 80% of drug costs").

104 Compl., at 32, *U.S. ex rel Sarah Benke v. CVS Caremark Corp.* (E. D. Pa. 2014) (No. 14–0824).

105 *See id.*, at 27 (presenting evidence that increasing the discounts to the health plan would hurt the PBM's earnings).

106 *See id.*, at 38.

107 *See id.*, at 39.

108 *See supra* Chapter 2, notes 42–45 and accompanying text; Augustine *et al.*, *supra* note 20, at 99.

109 *Cf.* Allen, *supra* note 88 (discussing the lack of incentive to control costs with self-funded plans in the context of hospital bills).

110 *See supra* notes 84–85 and accompanying text.

111 *See* Eric Sagonowsky, *Bring it on, Pharma: Finger-Pointing at Insurers Provokes AHIP Tweetstorm*, FIERCEPHARMA (Sept. 28, 2017), www.fiercepharma.com/pharma/insurance-lobby-phrma-duke-it-out-over-healthcare-costs.

112 Price rises may impose costs on the drug company in terms of reputation, and drug companies are certainly taking a beating in the press for high prices. In addition, a health insurance plan does have to pay the reimbursement at the time of the sale before any rebate might be gained. In reaction, the plan could push its PBM to put the drug on a less desirable tier, thereby affecting utilization.

113 If the drug company were simply to raise prices and fully return that higher level in rebates to the PBM, revenues would stay the same. The drug company's overall revenue might increase, however, by pulling in higher prices from those who were paying the full list price. This would include patients who have not reached their deductibles, could not obtain insurance coverage for the medication, or had no drug coverage at all. *See supra* Chapter 2, notes 41–49 and accompanying text (discussing those who pay the list price).

114 *See supra* Chapter 2, notes 40–45 and accompanying text.

115 *Cf.* Feldman & Frondorf, *supra* note 18, at 35–36 (using the term "competition-free zones" in describing how pay-for-delay deals between brand-name companies and generic hopefuls allow drug companies to use regulatory incentives for first-filing generic companies, with consumers paying the price).

Chapter 4

1 As described below in the text, the patient's contribution may be reduced by coupons or cards supplied by the drug company to the patient. *See* section 4.3.1 (on the problem with patient coupons).

2 *See* Rich Cauchi, *Prohibiting PBM "Gag Clauses" that Restrict Pharmacists from Disclosing Price Options: Recent State Legislation 2017–2018*, NAT'L CONF. OF STATE LEGISLATURES (2018), www.ncsl.org/Portals/1/Documents/Health/Pharmacist_Gag_clauses-2018-14523.pdf (describing these rules as "restrictions that mean a pharmacist is prohibited by a contract with a PBM from *informing consumers* that the drug they want to buy ... could be purchased at a lower cost if the consumers paid out of pocket rather than purchasing through their insurance plan" (emphasis added)); Robert Pear, *Why Your*

Pharmacist Can't Tell You That $20 Prescription Could Only Cost $8, NY TIMES (Feb. 24, 2018), www.nytimes.com/2018/02/24/us/politics/pharmacy-benefit-managers-gag-clauses.html, citing Thomas E. Menighan, chief executive the American Pharmacist Association, as saying that "the pharmacist cannot volunteer the fact that a medicine is less expensive if you pay the cash price and we don't run it through your health plan"). *See also id.* (describing how multiple states enacted laws to "make sure pharmacists can inform patients about less costly ways to obtain their medicines"); Paige Pelton, *Some Pharmacists Barred from Helping Patients Save Money,* ACTION NEWS JAX (Feb. 22, 2018), www.actionnewsjax.com/news/local/some-pharmacists-barred-from-helping-patients-save-money/705277162 (explaining that contracts may prohibit pharmacies from telling patients about savings when paying in cash).

3 Taking advantage of this circumstance, some drug companies have engaged in a behavior known as product hopping, i.e. where a drug company files for patents on minor modifications in dosage or delivery system of a drug and encourages doctors to prescribe the new formula, so that pharmacists cannot substitute the generic, which will have been approved only for the prior dosage or delivery system. *See* ROBIN FELDMAN & EVAN FRONDORF, DRUG WARS: HOW BIG PHARMA RAISES PRICES AND KEEPS GENERICS OFF THE MARKET 66–79 (2017); Stacey L. Dogan & Mark A. Lemley, *Antitrust Law and Regulatory Gaming,* 87 TEX. L. REV. 685 (2009).

4 US FOOD & DRUG ADMIN., DEVELOPMENT & APPROVAL PROCESS (DRUGS) ORANGE BOOK Preface (Feb. 5, 2018), www.fda.gov/Drugs/DevelopmentAp provalProcess/ucm079068.htm ("Drugs coded as AB under a heading are considered therapeutically equivalent only to other drugs coded as AB under that heading. Drugs coded with a three-character code under a heading are considered therapeutically equivalent only to other drugs coded with the same three-character code under that heading").

5 *See* Feldman & Frondorf, *supra* note 3, at 69–71 (describing product hopping); *see also* ROBIN C. FELDMAN & CONNIE WANG, MAY YOUR DRUG PRICE BE EVER GREEN, J. L. & BIOSCI. 1, 1, 8, 28, 49 (2018) (empirical study concluding that, on average, 78 percent of drugs associated with new patents in the FDA's records were for existing drugs as opposed to new ones).

6 In theory, a patient's ability to buy other items in the household budget basket will be constrained when costs increase for medicine. Although that concept is not entirely irrelevant in health care, healthcare markets do not behave in a manner analogous to ordinary markets. *See generally* Feldman & Frondorf, *supra* note 3, at 13 (noting that the "pharmaceutical market does not operate much like a standard market at all"); Clifford D. Stromberg, *Health Law Comes of Age: Economics and Ethics in a Changing Industry,* 92 YALE L.J. 203 (1982), reviewing WILLIAM J. CURRAN & E. DONALD SHAPIRO, LAW, MEDICINE AND FORENSIC SCIENCE (3rd ed.) (1982); Abigail Moncrieff, *Understanding the Failure of Health-Care Exceptionalism in the Supreme Court's*

Obamacare Decision, 142 CHEST 559, 559 (2012) (arguing that the Supreme Court's failure to employ healthcare exceptionalism in a constitutional challenge to the Patient Protection and Affordable Care Act was an "odd" holding that disregards the uniqueness of the healthcare market).

7 Feldman & Frondorf, *supra* note 3, at 86; *see also* Jennifer Hagerman, *Specialty Pharmacy: A Unique and Growing Industry*, APHA (2013), www.pharmacist.com/specialty-pharmacy-unique-and-growing-industry.

8 Michael A. Carrier, Nicole L. Levidow & Aaron S. Kesselheim, *Using Antitrust Law to Challenge Turing's Daraprim Price Increase*, 31 BERKELEY TECH. L.J. 1379, 1381 (2017) (noting that Daraprim was sold to a network of specialty pharmacies through an exclusive deal with Walgreens); Andrew Pollack, *Drug Makers Sidestep Barriers on Pricing*, NY TIMES (Oct. 19, 2015), www.nytimes.com/2015/10/20/business/drug-makers-sidestep-barriers-on-pricing.html (reporting that some patients were directed by doctors to specialty pharmacies carrying Horizon-manufactured Duexis, a combination of Motrin and Pepcid costing about $1,500 a month).

9 Feldman & Frondorf, *supra* note 3, at 85–86.

10 DEP'T. OF JUSTICE, U.S. ATTORNEY'S OFFICE, Press release, *Manhattan U.S. Attorney Announces $370 Million Civil Fraud Settlement against Novartis Pharmaceuticals for Kickback Scheme Involving High-Priced Prescription Drugs, along with $20 Million Forfeiture of Proceeds from the Scheme* (Nov. 20, 2015), www.justice.gov/usao-sdny/pr/manhattan-us-attorney-announces-370-million-civil-fraud-settlement-against-novartis.

11 The case alleged violation of antikickback statutes and the False Claims Act. *See id.*; *see also* John George, *AmerisourceBergen-owned Specialty Pharmacy to Pay $13.4M to Settle Kickback Allegations*, PHIL. BUS. J. (Aug. 24, 2017), www.bizjournals.com/philadelphia/news/2017/08/24/amerisourcebergen-pharmacy-bioservices-exjade.html (noting that the specialty pharmacy involved paid $13.4 million in the settlement as well).

12 John Carroll, *FDA Floats New Rules for Testing Alzheimer's Drugs*, SCIENCE (Feb. 16, 2018), www.sciencemag.org/news/2018/02/fda-floats-new-rules-testing-alzheimers-drugs (remarking that the FDA's draft guidance effectively increases the number of approvals for Alzheimer's drugs by opening an approval pathway for drugs targeting earlier stages of the disease and not only later stages); *see also* Caroline Chen & James Paton, *The FDA is Approving Drugs at a Staggering Pace*, BLOOMBERG (Oct. 6, 2017), www.bloomberg.com/news/articles/2017-10-06/flurry-of-drug-approvals-has-wall-street-eyeing-pharma-profits (noting how the FDA's recent high rates of drug approvals are tied to 2012 legislation widening the use of accelerated approvals); Food and Drug Association Safety and Innovation Act of 2012, Pub.L. 112–44, 126 Stat. 1084 (allowing the FDA to base accelerated approvals for certain drugs on markers that indicate the drug is "reasonably likely to predict clinical benefit").

13 *See* Chapter 3, sections 3.1.1 (on the power of volume) and 3.1.2 (on bundling drugs) (describing incentives for PBMs to favor a company's drug, particularly with market leaders and large volume drug companies); *see also* EXPRESS SCRIPTS, VALUE BEYOND: DELIVERING MORE THAN MEDICINE – ANNUAL REPORT 4, 13 (2016), https://expressscriptsholdingco.gcs-web.com/static-files/777166b9–6d1a-4b3f-b979-f798b856955c [hereinafter EXPRESS SCRIPTS] (PBM annual report explaining that, with its specialty pharmacies, Express Scripts purchases directly from the pharmaceutical companies and wholesalers).

14 CHANGE TO WIN, CVS CAREMARK: AN ALARMING MERGER, TWO YEARS LATER 9, 2 (2009), http://prescriptiondrugdiscounts.net/files/cvs%20an-alarming-merger.pdf [hereinafter UNIONS REPORT]. The report also cites a pharmacists' advocate explaining that pharmacists observed the PBM Care-mark referring to refrigerated injectable medications as "specialty drugs," so that they would have to be filled exclusively by the PBM's pharmacy despite the fact that all state pharmacies are required to have refrigeration, and classified high-cost oral oncology drugs as "specialty medication," although they do not require special care of administration. In contrast, the PBM does not classify inexpensive drugs, such as the Coumadin blood thinner, as spe-cialty, although the drug requires monitoring. *See id.*, at 7.

15 *Anthem, Inc. v. Express Scripts, Inc.*, No. 16–02048 (S.D.N.Y. filed Mar. 21, 2016).

16 *See* Second Amended Compl. at ¶ 26, *In re Express Scripts/Anthem ERISA Litigation*, 2018 U.S. Dist. LEXIS 3081 (S.D.N.Y. 2016) (No. 16–3399).

17 *See* CVS CAREMARK CORPORATION, *Prescription Benefits FAQ*, www.nhsd.org/cms/lib/PA01001961/Centricity/Domain/65/Prescription%20FAQs%204.1.2016.pdf (last visited Oct. 30, 2018) ("CVS Pharmacy is the only retail pharmacy that can provide ... a 90-day supply" of a prescription for Care-mark plan members in the Maintenance Choice program).

18 UNIONS REPORT, *supra* note 14, at 2–3; CVS CAREMARK CORP'N, 2008 ANALYST/INVESTOR MEETING TRANSCRIPT, STATEMENT OF HELENA FOULKES 55 (2008), http://library.corporate-ir.net/library/99/995/99533/items/294969/2008CVSCaremarkInvestorRelationsALL.pdf (a CVS Caremark executive discusses how CVS Caremark planned to issue10 million ExtraCare promotional benefits cards to patients enrolled in prescription benefits plans); CVS CARE-MARK CORP'N, *The CVS Caremark ExtraCare Health Card*, www.caremark.com/portal/asset/fsa_thp.pdf (last visited Oct. 30, 2018) (CVS Caremark provides discounts on certain CVS-brand items such as allergy and cold rem-edies, first aid materials, and oral hygiene products for holders of its ExtraCare Health card); *see also* CVS/PHARMACY, Press release, *CVS/Pharmacy Expands ExtraCare Program with New Pharmacy and Health Rewards* (Feb. 4, 2013), https://cvshealth.com/newsroom/press-releases/cvspharmacy-expands-extracare-program-new-pharmacy-health-rewards (announcing a

program within which customers can earn "free CVS money" for in-store items as a reward for filling a certain number of prescriptions at CVS/Pharmacy).

19 *See also* AKIN GUMP, Newsletter, *FTC Closes Antitrust and Unfair Competition Investigation of CVS Caremark Post-merger Marketing Practices* (Jan. 19, 2012), www.akingump.com/en/news-insights/ftc-closes-antitrust-and-unfair-competition-investigation-of-cvs-caremark-post-merger.html#_ftn3 (noting that under some PBM contracts, members are automatically enrolled in CVS Caremark's ExtraCare loyalty program, which may serve the purpose of driving consumers to CVS pharmacies instead of others).

20 *See e.g.*, Patricia M. Danzon, *Pharmacy Benefit Management: Are Reporting Requirements Pro- or Anticompetitive?*, 22 INT'L J. ECON. BUS. 245 (2015); EXPRESS SCRIPTS, *supra* note 13, at 10 (touting its information flow and explaining that its "claims processing system also generates a database of drug utilization information that can be accessed at the time a prescription is dispensed, on a retrospective basis to analyze utilization trends and prescribing patterns for more intensive management of the drug benefit, and on a prospective basis to help support pharmacists in drug therapy management decisions").

21 *See* Class Action Comp., *Sergeant Benevolent Assoc. Health & Welfare Fund v. Eli Lilly Co.* 06-CV-06322 (E.D.N.Y. 2006) (No. 06–6322). One press report, using quotations that could not be confirmed with the nonredacted court material, contained alleged quotes from internal documents that the letter would target doctors based on "the most recent . . . claims data," and that the campaign was "designed to influence key prescribers" to assist in a "tactical plan for Zyprexa." BLOOMBERG, *CVS Unit Played Both Sides, $6.8 Billion Lilly Lawsuit Reveals*, FIRSTWORD PHARMA (2009), www.firstwordpharma.com/node/367134?tsid=17#axzz59SxEvJjt; UNIONS REPORT, *supra* note 14, at 4; *cf.* EXPRESS SCRIPTS, *supra* note 13, at 11 (noting that "[o]ur physician connectivity program facilitates well-informed prescribing by delivering benefit and formulary evaluations and medication history, both electronically and in real-time, as physicians write prescriptions").

22 *See* UNIONS REPORT, *supra* note 14, at 5.

23 *See* BLOOMBERG, *supra* note 21 (describing internal communication about the physician letters).

24 *See* UNIONS REPORT, *supra* note 14, at 5 (displaying an image of the letter).

25 *See id.*, at 4–5; BLOOMBERG, *supra* note 21.

26 *See also* John Russell, *Lilly Pays CVS Caremark to Try to Get Doctors to Prescribe Cymbalta*, INDIANAPOLIS STAR (Oct. 18, 2009), http://indystar.newspapers.com/image/126786606/?terms=22lilly%2Bpays%2Bcvs%22 (describing letters mailed by CVS to physicians promoting Eli Lilly's antidepressant Cymbalta and designed to look like international mailings).

27 The case also alleged that the maker of Zyprexa pushed the drug for off-label uses for the treatment of dementia, when the company's internal research

showed that the drug did not counteract dementia. *See* Second Amended Compl., at ¶ 54–57, *In re Zyprexa Products Liability Litigation*, 424 F.Supp.2d 488 (E.D.N.Y. 2006) (No. 04–01596); *Eli Lilly Pushed Useless Drug for Dementia*, ALLGOV (June 15, 2009), www.allgov.com/news/controversies/eli-lilly-pushed-useless-drug-for-dementia?news=839025. Doctors are permitted to prescribe off-label uses for drugs, and recent court cases have affirmed that drug companies have the right to advertise those uses. *See* ROBIN C. FELDMAN, MAY YOUR DRUG PRICE BE EVER GREEN, J. L. & BIOSCI. 1, 35–36 (2018); *United States v. Caronia*, 703 F.3d 149 (2d Cir. 2012).

28 *See e.g.*, Class Action Compl., at 48–50, *Boss v. CVS Health Corporation et al.*, BL 328545 (D.N.J. 2017) (No. 17–1823) (alleging that Sanofi, Norvo Nordisk, and Eli Lilly engaged in an insulin price-fixing scheme); *see also* Jacklyn Wille, *Sanofi, CVS, Others Accused of Insulin Price Fixing*, BLOOMBERG LAW (2017), www.bna.com/sanofi-cvs-others-n57982085476/ (describing the collusion between drug manufacturers and PBMs that led to the *Boss v. CVS* case). *See also* Chapter 6, section 6.1.3 (describing other dangers of combined PBM–insurers).

29 *See* David Dayen, *The Hidden Monopolies that Raise Drug Prices*, THE AMERICAN PROSPECT (Mar. 28, 2017).

30 *See id.*; Bob Herman, *The Algorithm Black Box*, AXIOS (Apr. 2, 2018), www.axios.com/algorithm-black-box-express-scripts-18f3d873-77ce-40eb-9a0c-578b608d1b6e.html.

31 Dayen, *supra* note 29 ("pharmacists have no idea how much money they'll make on a sale until the moment they sell it").

32 Erika Fernando, *Pharmacists: Pharmacy Benefits Managers are Losing Us Money*, THV11 (Jan. 31, 2018), www.thv11.com/article/news/health/pharma cists-pharmacy-benefits-managers-are-losing-us-money/91-513375933.

33 *See id.*

34 *See* FED. TRADE COMM'N, PHARMACY BENEFIT MANAGERS: OWNERSHIP OF MAIL-ORDER PHARMACIES vi (2005).

35 *See id.*

36 *See e.g.*, Evan Hughes, *The Opioid that Made a Fortune for Its Maker – and for Its Prescribers*, NYT MAGAZINE (May 2, 2018), www.nytimes.com/interactive/2018/05/02/magazine/money-issue-insys-opioids-kickbacks.html (describing payments to doctors who prescribed opioids); *see also United States ex rel. Bilotta v. Novartis Pharm. Corp.*, 50 F. Supp. 3d 497 (S.D.N.Y. 2014).

37 *See* Ed Silverman, *Abbvie is Accused of Paying Kickbacks, Using a Stealthy Network of Nurses to Promote Humira*, STAT (Sept. 18, 2018), www.statnews.com/pharmalot/2018/09/18/abbvie-kickbacks-nurses-humira/?utm_source=STAT+Newsletters&utm_campaign=53506cf1bf-Daily_Recap &utm_medium=email&utm_term=0_8cab1d7961-53506cf1bf-149549257.

38 *See id.*; *United States ex rel. Bilotta v. Novartis Pharm. Corp.*, 50 F. Supp. 3d 497 (S.D.N.Y. 2014).

39 *See id.*

40 *See id.*; *see also* Ed Silverman, *Three More Drug Makers Allegedly Used Nurses to Promote Medicines*, STAT+ (Dec. 11, 2017), www.statnews.com/pharmalot/2017/12/11/nurses-kickbacks-amgen-bayer-gilead/ (discussing Gilead, Amgen, and Bayer); Ed Silverman, *Are Nurses the New Sales Reps? Why Pharma Should Be Worried*, STAT+ (Nov. 28, 2017), www.statnews.com/pharmalot/2017/11/28/nurses-kickbacks-sales-reps/ (discussing Eli Lilly).

41 See the description in section 4.1.2 of how Novartis created incentives and pressures for doctors to prescribe Exjade. *See supra* note 11 and accompanying text.

42 *See supra* Chapter 2, section 2.2.2 (on deals hidden from insurers) and Chapter 3, notes 106–10, and accompanying text. *See also* Chapter 3, section 3.2.1 (on general incentives for insurers not to push back on the system).

43 *See* Chapter 2, section 2.1 (on branded prescription drugs) and Chapter 3.

44 *Eisai, Inc. v. Sanofi Aventis U.S., LLC*, 821 F.3d 396, 400 (2016).

45 *See id.*, at 407.

46 *See id.*, at 399.

47 Norman R. Augustine, Guru Madhavan & Sharyl J. Nass, *Making Medicines Affordable: A National Imperative*, NAT'L ACADEMIES OF SCI., ENG'G, AND MED. 105–06 (2018) [hereinafter NAS REPORT].

48 Drug companies are not required by the Act to provide these price concessions up front, but it has become the practice to do so. *See also* 42 U.S.C. § 256b (1992); 340B HEALTH, *Overview of the 340B Drug Pricing Program*, www.340bhealth.org/members/340b-program/overview/ (last visited Oct. 30, 2018). *See* ENERGY & COMMERCE COMMITTEE, REVIEW OF THE 340B DRUG PRICING PROGRAM 10 (2018) (noting that the 340B program will save between 25 and 50 percent of AWP); Mike McCaughan, *The 340B Drug Discount Program*, HEALTH AFF. (Sept. 14, 2017), www.healthaffairs.org/do/10.1377/hpb20171024.663441/full/ (340B discounts average 34 percent and are often much higher).

49 *See* Casey Ross, *Trump Takes on Hospitals: The Facts behind Fight over 340B Drug Discounts*, STAT (Nov. 6, 2017), www.statnews.com/2017/11/06/340b-drug-discounts-fight/.

50 *See* ENERGY & COMMERCE COMMITTEE, *supra* note 48, at 13.

51 In general, drugs administered by a doctor are covered under Medicare Part B, and drugs that a patient purchases at a pharmacy are covered under Medicare Part D. CTR. FOR MEDICARE & MEDICAID SERV., MEDICARE DRUG COVERAGE UNDER MEDICARE PART A, PART B, PART C & PART D, CMS PRODUCT NO. 11315-P (2017).

52 *See* Cole Werble, *Health Policy Brief: Medicare Part B*, HEALTH AFF. (Aug. 10, 2017), www.healthaffairs.org/do/10.1377/hpb20171008.000171/full/ (describing the way in which the sequestration provisions of the Budget

Control Act of 2011 affect the statutory average sales price (ASP) *plus* 6 percent reimbursement amount mandated by the 2003 Medicare Modernization Act, such that the effective current rate is ASP *plus* 4.3 percent); *see also id.*, at exhibit 1.

53 *See supra* Chapter 3, note 88, and accompanying text.

54 Kelvin Chan, *How Do Medicaid and Medicare Set Drug Prices?*, Medium (Feb. 23, 2016), https://medium.com/unraveling-healthcare/how-do-medic aid-and-medicare-set-drug-prices-83411811d632.

55 Kathy Svitil, *Wine Study Shows Price Influences Perception*, Caltech (Jan. 14, 2008), www.caltech.edu/news/wine-study-shows-price-influences-percep tion-1374 (finding that "changes in the stated price of a sampled wine influenced not only how good volunteers thought it tasted, but the activity of a brain region that is involved in our experience of pleasure"); Dan Ariely, *Commercial Features of Placebo and Therapeutic Efficacy*, 299 JAMA 1016 (2008), https://jamanetwork.com/journals/jama/article-abstract/181562 (showing that consumers assume higher-priced items to be of higher value and may even perceive higher-priced drugs to work better).

56 NAS Report, *supra* note 47, at 93–94. One should note that coupons are not available for government insurance, because they would be considered a form of kickback. Michelle Andrews, *Why Can't Medicare Patients Use Drugmakers' Discount Coupons?*, Shots (May 9, 2018), www.npr.org/sections/ health-shots/2018/05/09/609150868/why-cant-medicare-patients-use-drug makers-discount-coupons ("Under the federal anti-kickback law, it's illegal for drug manufacturers to offer any type of payment that might persuade a patient to purchase something that federal health care programs like Medicare and Medicaid might pay for").

57 *See* Fiona Scott Morton & Lysle T. Boller, *Enabling Competition in Pharmaceutical Markets*, Working Paper 30, Hutchins Ctr. on Fiscal & Monetary Pol´y at Brookings 27 (May 2017), www.brookings.edu/wp-content/ uploads/2017/05/wp30_scottmorton_competitioninpharma1.pdf.

58 *See id.*, at 26.

59 Leemore Dafny, Christopher Ody & Matthew Schmitt, *When Discounts Raise Costs: The Effect of Copay Coupons on Generic Utilization*, 9 Am. Econ. J. Econ. Policy 2, 94 (fig. 1) (2017) (this measure does not capture actual coupon use, given that not all buyers use or are eligible to use coupons).

60 *See id. See also* Joseph S. Ross & Aaron S. Kesselheim, *Prescription Drug-Coupons: No Such Thing as a Free Lunch*, 26 N. Eng. J. Med. 1188, 1188–89 (2013); Michael Erman, *Insurance Tactic Drags down U.S. Drug Prices in Second Quarter: Analyst*, Reuters (Sept. 4, 2018), www.reuters.com/article/ us-usa-healthcare-drugpricing/insurance-tactic-drags-down-u-s-drug-prices-in-second-quarter-analyst-idUSKCN1LK2FX (citing Sector and Sovereign Research for the conclusion that U.S. drug prices fell in the second quarter of

2018 likely as a result of insurers using co-pay accumulators, which limit the financial assistance that drug companies provide to consumers).

61 David Grand, *The Cost of Drug Coupons*, 307 JAMA 2375 (2012), https:// jamanetwork.com/journals/jama/fullarticle/1182868; *see also* Leemore et al. *supra* note 59, at 27, n. 41 (noting that "a copay coupon ... for Lipitor ... may have resulted in loss of share for generic statins").

62 *Cf.* Feldman & Frondorf, *supra* note 3, at 22 (describing Hatch-Waxman's so-called Paragraph IV provision in which the first generic, in some circumstances, receives a six-month period in which no other generics may enter the market, as an incentive to do battle with the branded drug); *see also* Feldman & Frondorf, *supra* note 3, at 53–56.

63 *See* William G. Schiffbauer, *Let's Talk About Prescription Drug Copay Coupons: Do They Operate as Unregulated Secondary Insurance?*, BLOOMBERG LAW (Apr. 18, 2018).

64 Andrew Pollack, *Hemophilia Patient or Drug Seller? Dual Role Creates Ethical Quandry*, NY TIMES (Jan. 13, 2016), www.nytimes.com/2016/01/14/business/ hemophilia-patient-or-drug-seller-dual-role-creates-ethical-quandary.html; *see also* Philip Kucab, Katelyn Dow Stepanyan & Adriane Fugh-Berman, *Direct-to-Consumer Marketing to People with Hemophilia* 13 PUB. LIBRARY OF SCI. MED. 1 (2016); Morton & Boller, *supra* note 57, at 3 (noting that brands may offer kickbacks in the form of coupons, financial assistance, free meals, patient care, and other benefits to avoid moving demand to lower-priced alternatives).

65 Katie Thomas, *Patients Eagerly Awaited a Generic Drug. Then They Saw the Price*, NY TIMES (Feb. 23, 2018), www.nytimes.com/2018/02/23/health/ valeant-drug-price-syprine.html?emc=edit_th_180224&nl=todaysheadlines &nlid=497896550224.

66 NAS REPORT, *supra* note 47, at 94, citing Matthew S. McCoy et al., *Conflicts of Interest for Patient-Advocacy Organizations*, 376 NEW ENG. J. MED. 880 (2017).

67 Emily Kopp, Sydney Lupkin & Elizabeth Lucas, *Patient Advocacy Groups Take in Millions From Drugmakers. Is There a Payback?*, KAISER HEALTH NEWS (Apr. 6, 2018), https://khn.org/news/patient-advocacy-groups-take-in-millions-from-drugmakers-is-there-a-payback/.

68 Paul Thacker, *Big Pharma is Quietly Using Nonprofits to Push Opioids*, LA TIMES (Jul. 19, 2018), www.latimes.com/opinion/op-ed/la-oe-thacker-fun ders-opioid-misinformation-20180719-story.html#.

69 Austin Frerick, *The Cloak of Social Responsibility: Pharmaceutical Corporate Charity*, 153 TAX NOTES 1151 (2016); *see also* Morton & Boller, *supra* note 57 (discussing the implications of the Frerick paper). The Internal Revenue Service (IRS) may be starting to look askance at some of this activity. In 2017, the IRS opened an investigation into one such group to examine whether the charity gave impermissible benefits to the corporate donors who provided the money to purchase their own drugs for patients. *See* Robert

Langrath, *Charity Funded by Drugmakers Draws IRS Probe on Tax Exemption*, BLOOMBERG (June 29, 2017), www.bloomberg.com/news/articles/2017-06-29/charity-funded-by-drugmakers-draws-irs-probe-on-tax-exemption; Compl., at ¶ 7–8, *Chronic Disease Fund, Inc. v. United States of America*, 2:17-CV-00304 (W.D. Pa. 2017).

70 *See* Morton & Boller, *supra* note 57, at 29, citing Frerick, *supra* note 69.

71 *See* Morton & Boller, *supra* note 57, at 29 (noting that pharmaceuticals have a low marginal cost).

72 *See* Morton & Boller, *supra* note 57, at 29; *see also* Roger Colinvaux, *Enforcing the Enhanced Charitable Deduction*, URBAN INST. CTR ON NONPROFITS AND PHILANTHROPY AT URBAN-BROOKINGS TAX POL. CTR 1 (2012) (describing the history of the enhanced deduction, including that Congress first restricted corporate deductions of "income property" to the donor's cost and then eased that restriction as a means of incentivizing the donation of medical supplies rather than disposing of them).

73 Ariely, *supra* note 55.

74 These groups are not necessarily monolithic nor do they all benefit. For example, smaller and rural pharmacies may not benefit, and the same may be true of employers who self-insure.

75 *See e.g.*, Caroline Chen & Robert Langreth, *Gilead Executive Says Pharmacy Benefit Managers Keep Prices High*, BLOOMBERG (Mar. 3, 2017), www.bloomberg.com/news/articles/2017-03-03/gilead-executive-says-pharmacy-benefit-managers-keep-prices-high (Gilead executive pointing to PBMs and saying, "[i]f we just lowered the cost of Sovaldi from $85,000 to $50,000, every payer would rip up our contract"). *See* Eric Sagonowsky, *Bring it on, Pharma: Finger-Pointing at Insurers Provokes AHIP Tweetstorm*, FIERCEPHARMA (Sept. 28, 2017), www.fiercepharma.com/pharma/insurance-lobby-phrma-duke-it-out-over-healthcare-costs.

76 Charley Grant, *The Blame Game on Drug Prices is Getting Dangerous*, WALL ST. J. (Apr. 9, 2017), www.wsj.com/articles/the-blame-game-on-drug-prices-is-getting-dangerous-1491758834.

77 *See* Chapter 2, section 2.1 (on branded prescription drugs).

78 Feldman & Frondorf, *supra* note 3, at 8 (2017); *see also* US Const., art. I, § 8, cl. 8 (the Intellectual Property Clause of the Constitution, which states that, "The Congress shall have Power . . . [t]o promote the Progress of Science and useful Arts, by securing for *limited times* to Authors and Inventors the exclusive Right to their respective Writings and Discoveries. . ." (emphasis added)); *Pennock v. Dialogue*, 27 U.S. 1, 16–17 (1829) ("[The Constitution] contemplates . . . that this exclusive right shall exist but for a limited period . . ."); *Bonito Boatsm Inc. v. Thunder Craft Boats, Inc.*, 489 U.S. 141, 975 (1989) ("Congress may not create patent monopolies of unlimited duration . . ."); Letter from Thomas Jefferson to Oliver Vans (May 2, 1807), in THE WRITINGS OF THOMAS JEFFERSON 200–02 (Andrew A. Lipscomb, ed. 1903) ("Certainly an inventor

ought to be allowed a right to the benefit of his invention for some certain time. It is equally certain it ought not be perpetual; for to embarrass society with monopolies for every utensil existing, & in all the details of life, would be more injurious to them than had the supposed inventors never existed"); WILLIAM C. ROBINSON, THE LAW OF PATENTS FOR USEFUL INVENTIONS 42–43 (1890) (arguing that "[t]he duty which the state owes to the people to obtain for them, at the earliest moment, the practical use of every valuable invention in the industrial arts is . . . a higher and more imperative duty than which it owes to the inventor"); *see generally* Edward C. Walterscheid, *Defining the Patent and Copyright Term: Term Limits and the Intellectual Property Clause*, 7 J. INTELL. PROP. L. 315 (2000) (exploring term limits on rights granted in the Intellectual Property Clause).

79 *See* PETER LASLETT, JOHN LOCKE: TWO TREATISES OF GOVERNMENT –A CRITICAL EDITION 336–37, 341, 343, 351 (1967) (including a reprinting of the 1698 version of Locke's Two Treatises); *see also* Paul Brest, State Action and Liberal Theory: A Casenote on *Flagg Brothers v. Brooks*, 130 U. PA. L. REV. 1296, 1300 (1982) (noting that, in the Lockean modality, courts embrace the natural rights view of a sphere of autonomous private conduct immune from state regulation); Robin Feldman, Coming to the Community in IMAGINING NEW LEGALITIES: PRIVACY AND ITS POSSIBILITIES IN THE 21ST CENTURY 88 (Austin Sarat ed., 2012).

80 Intellectual property in the international arena at times rests on the notion of a creator's moral rights, but the intellectual property rights system in the United States has been decidedly utilitarian since the Founding Fathers inked the patent and copyright clause into the Constitution. *See* ROBIN FELDMAN, RETHINKING PATENT LAW 78 (2012).

81 For sources discussing the contrast between antitrust and patent law, *see e.g.,* Robin C. Feldman, *The Insufficiency of Antitrust Analysis for Patent Misuse*, 55 HASTINGS L.J. 399, 400–01 (2003) (discussing the inadequacy of antitrust law to address potential economic harms that may flow from granting a patent, since antitrust law doesn't recognize harms unless a patented drug gets a large enough market share to constitute a monopoly); *see generally* Robin Feldman, *Patent and Antitrust Differing Shades of Meaning*, 13 VA. J.L. & TECH 1 (2008) ("In reductionist form, the two concepts pose a natural contradiction: One encourages monopoly, while the other restricts it").

82 *See* Robin Feldman, *Regulatory Property: The New IP*, 40 COLUM. J.L. & ARTS 53, 67–68 (2016).

83 *See* Chapter 2, section 2.1 (on branded prescription drugs).

84 A 2014 study from the Tufts Center for the Study of Drug Development found that developing a new drug costs approximately $2.5 billion, which includes the costs of compound failures. *See* TUFTS CTR. FOR THE STUDY OF DRUG DEV., COSTS OF DEVELOPING A NEW DRUG (2014),

www.academia.edu/34807407/Cost_of_Developing_a_New_Drug_Tufts_
Center_for_the_Study_of_Drug_Development. This finding has been chal-
lenged on multiple fronts. *See* Steve Morgan et al., *The Cost of Drug Develop-*
ment: A Systematic Review, 100 Health Policy 4 (2011), www.ncbi.nlm
.nih.gov/pubmed/21256615 (analyzing 13 different studies to estimate that
drug development costs range from $161 million to $1.8 billion); Aaron E.
Carroll, *$2.6 Billion to Develop a Drug? New Estimate Makes Questionable*
Assumptions, NY Times (Nov. 18, 2014), www.nytimes.com/2014/11/19/
upshot/calculating-the-real-costs-of-developing-a-new-drug.html (suggesting
that the disparity in the findings stem from methodological mistakes in the Tuft
study, and noting that the Tufts Center is funded by pharmaceutical companies); Tufts Ctr. for the Study of Drug Dev., *Financial Disclosure*,
http://csdd.tufts.edu/about/financial_disclosure (last visited Oct. 30, 2018).

85 *See* 35 U.S.C. § 112 (Patent Act section mandating disclosure sufficient that
a person skilled in the art can make and use the invention).

86 *See* Feldman, *supra* note 82, at 68 (describing how the Hatch-Waxman Act
created a pathway for generics to use existing clinical trials data when they
enter the market); *see also* 21 U.S.C. § 355(j) (2012).

Chapter 5

1 *See e.g.,* Robin Feldman, Rethinking Patent Law 170–78 (2012)
(describing evergreening and providing case history examples); *see also infra*
notes 28–34, 58–64 and accompanying text (explaining evergreening and
identifying the quantity within our data set of those who apply repeatedly for
patent and exclusivity extensions).

2 *See generally* Robin Feldman & Evan Frondorf, Drug Wars: How Big
Pharma Raises Prices and Keeps Generics off the Market (2017);
Robin Feldman et al., *Empirical Evidence of Drug Pricing Games: A Citi-*
zen's Pathway Gone Astray, 20 Stan. Tech. L. Rev. 39 (2017); Michael
A. Carrier, Nicole L. Levidow & Aaron S. Kesselheim, *Using Antitrust*
Law to Challenge Turing's Daraprim Price Increase, 31 Berkeley Tech.
L.J. 1379 (2017), https://scholarship.law.berkeley.edu/btlj/vol31/iss3/5/;
C. Scott Hemphill, *An Aggregate Approach to Antitrust: Using New Data*
and Rulemaking to Preserve Drug Competition, 109 Colum. L. Rev. 629
(2009), https://ssrn.com/abstract=1356530; Michael A. Carrier, *Eight*
Reasons "No-Authorized-Generic" Promises Constitute Reverse Payment, 67
Rutgers U. L. Rev. 697, 716 (2016); Stacey L. Dogan & Mark A.
Lemley, *Antitrust Law and Regulatory Gaming*, 87 Tex. L. Rev. 685
(2009). One admirable empirical analysis exists, of the period 1988–
2005, which looks at secondary patents, rather than all forms of exclusivities. *See* Amy Kapczynski, Chan Park & Bhaven Sampat, *Polymorphs and*

Prodrugs and Salts (Oh My!): An Empirical Analysis of "Secondary" Pharmaceutical Patents, 7 PLoS ONE 1, 1 (2012).

3 *See* Feldman & Frondorf, *supra* note 2, at 49–65 (describing elaborate deals and combinations of deals undertaken to cloak agreements in which brand-name companies pay generics to delay market entrance).

4 Feldman et al., *supra* note 2, at 71–85 (empirical work establishing the extent to which citizen petitions filed at the FDA are last-ditch efforts by competitors to hold off generic entry); HERBERT HOVENKAMP et al., IP AND ANTITRUST: AN ANALYSIS OF ANTITRUST PRINCIPLES APPLIED TO INTELLECTUAL PROPERTY LAW § 12.5 (2002) (describing mechanisms "whereby the brand-name drug company takes advantage of its market power to shift pharmacists, doctors, and consumers to 'new' versions of drugs before a generic for the 'old' version is able to reach the market"); Mark S. Levy, *Big Pharma Monopoly: Why Consumers Keep Landing on "Park Place" and How the Game is Rigged*, 66 AM. U. L. REV. 247, 276–79, 291–93 (2017) (describing product-hopping techniques to thwart generic substitution).

5 *See e.g.,* 21 C.F.R. 314.53 (b) (stating, "Process patents, patents claiming packaging, patents claiming metabolites, and patents claiming intermediates are not covered by this section, and information on these patents must not be submitted to the FDA").

6 The sentence is a reference to a work by Welsh poet Dylan Thomas, which concludes with the line, "Do not go gentle into that good night. Rage, rage, against the dying of the light!" *See* DYLAN THOMAS, THE COLLECTED POEMS OF DYLAN THOMAS: THE ORIGINAL EDITION 122 (Paul Muldoon ed., 2010).

7 For more in-depth descriptions of the drug approval process, *see* U.S. FOOD AND DRUG ADMIN., DEVELOPMENT & APPROVAL PROCESS (DRUGS) (Oct. 5, 2017), www.fda.gov/Drugs/DevelopmentApprovalProcess/default.htm; *see also* U.S. FOOD AND DRUG ADMIN., HOW DRUGS ARE DEVELOPED AND APPROVED (Aug. 18, 2015), www.fda.gov/Drugs/DevelopmentApprovalPro cess/HowDrugsareDevelopedandApproved/default.htm; *see generally* BERNICE SCHACTER, THE NEW MEDICINES: HOW DRUGS ARE CREATED, APPROVED, MARKETED, AND SOLD (2005); *see generally* Kimiya Sarayloo, *A Poor Man's Tale of Patented Medicine: The 1962 Amendments, Hatch-Waxman, and the Lost Admonition to Promote Progress*, 18 QUINNIPIAC HEALTH L.J. 1 (2015); *see generally* Martin S. Lipsky & Lisa K. Sharp, *From Idea to Market: The Drug Approval Process*, 14 J. AM. BOARD FAM. PRACTIC. 362 (2001).

8 35 U.S.C. § 154(a)(2) (providing for 20 years of protection from the date of the patent application).

9 Aylin Sertkaya et al., *Key Cost Drivers of Pharmaceutical Clinical Trials in the United States*, 13 CLIN. TRIALS 117 (2016), www.ncbi.nlm.nih.gov/pubmed/ 26908540 (noting that costs for clinical trials can range from $1.4 million to $52.9 million, depending on the therapeutic area of the drug and the phase of the trial); *see* Rebecca S. Eisenberg & W. Nicholson Price,

Promoting Healthcare Innovation on the Demand Side, 4 J.L. & BIOSCI. 3, 8–9 (2017) (outlining the various incentives surrounding the high cost of clinical trials).

10 Feldman, *supra* note 1, at 54. The one exception to this rule is patents procured by nonpracticing entities, colloquially called "patent trolls." Given that these entities do not make any products, but simply assert patents against companies that make products, patent trolls are able to put their newly minted patents into use the minute they are granted. *See e.g.*, Joe Mullin, *Famous Patent "Troll's" Lawsuit against Google Booted out of East Texas*, ARS TECHNICA (Feb. 2017), https://arstechnica.com/tech-policy/2017/02/famous-patent-trolls-lawsuit-against-google-booted-out-of-east-texas/ (describing various patent infringement lawsuits by an ambitious nonpracticing entity, Eolas Technologies, against Microsoft, Google, Amazon, JC Penney, and Walmart).

11 Feldman & Frondorf, *supra* note 2, at 9.

12 Feldman & Frondorf, *supra* note 2, at 21–33 (describing in detail the history, design, and implementation of the complex Hatch-Waxman system).

13 The Hatch-Waxman system covers small-molecule drugs, not biologics. Biologics are large, complex cell-derived drugs, and replicating a biologic is much more challenging. The generic equivalent of a biologic drug is known as a "biosimilar," or an "interchangeable." Such drugs are governed by the Biologics Price Competition and Innovation Act of 2009 (the Biosimilars Act), rather than the Hatch-Waxman Act. Greater safety and efficacy testing is required for biosimilars than for generics. Biologics Price Competition and Innovation Act of 2009, Pub. L. No. 111–48, Title VII, Subtitle A, 124 Stat. 119 (2010).

14 Feldman & Frondorf, *supra* note 2, at 22 (citing 21 U.S.C. § 355(j)(2)(A)(i)–(v) (2012)).

15 *See id.*

16 Robin Feldman, *Intellectual Property Wrongs*, 18 STAN. J. OF L., BUS. & FIN. 250, 264 (2013), citing Mark A. Lemley, *Rational Ignorance at the Patent Office*, 95 NW. U. L. REV. 1495, 1500 (2001). Other scholars cite a slightly higher figure of 30 hours. *See* Lauren Cohen et al., *"Troll Check? A Proposal for Administrative Review of Patent Litigation*, 97 B. U. L. REV. 1775, 1786–87 (2017) (concluding that the average time for an individual examiner to review each of some 600,000 new applications filed per year is roughly 20 hours per application). *See id.* at n. 75 (mentioning that "More realistic estimates of examiner time per application put the average time available for these activities at about twenty hours per application, rather than thirty").

17 There were 8,195 patent examiners in FY 2016, compared to 4,177 in FY 2005. *Compare* U.S. PATENT & TRADE OFFICE, 2016 ANNUAL REPORT (2016), www.uspto.gov/sites/default/files/documents/PPAC_2016_Annual_Report .pdf *with* U.S. PATENT & TRADE OFFICE, PERFORMANCE & ACCOUNTABILITY

REPORT FOR FISCAL YEAR 2005 (2005), www.uspto.gov/sites/default/files/about/stratplan/ar/USPTOFY2005PAR.pdf. During the same period, the number of issued patents rose from roughly 150,000 to over 300,000. *See* Dennis Crouch, *FY2017: PTO on Course for Record Number of Issued Patents*, PATENTLY-O (Aug. 12, 2017), https://patentlyo.com/patent/2017/08/fy2017-course-patents.html.

18 Drug makers are required to list patents related to their medication within 30 days of issuance or within 30 days of a relevant approval making the previously issued patent listable, for example, with a new use. *See* 21 U.S.C. § 355 (c)(2). Generic drug makers are not required to certify to patents that are not "timely filed" if the generic application is submitted before the patent. If the patent is "timely listed" while a generic application is pending, the generic drug maker must certify to those patents, but no 30-month stay of litigation would result related to the lawsuit. *See* U.S. FOOD & DRUG ADMIN., PATENTS AND EXCLUSIVITY 1 (2015), www.fda.gov/downloads/drugs/developmentapprovalprocess/small businessassistance/ucm447307.pdf; 21 CFR § 314.53; *see also* Kurt Karst, *One Sponsor's Failure is Another Sponsor's Fortune: The Importance of Timely Listing (and Challenging) Orange Book Patents*, FDA LAW BLOG (Nov. 25, 2013), www.fdalawblog.net/fda_law_blog_hyman_phelps/2013/11/one-spon sors-failure-is-another-sponsors-fortune-the-importance-of-timely-listing-and-challenging-or.html.

19 Specifically, a company seeking approval of a generic version of the drug must provide a certification, regarding every patent listed in the Orange Book in relation to the drug, that the patent either has expired or will expire before the generic brings the drug to market, or stating that patent information has not been filed. Alternatively, the generic can challenge the validity of the patent or its application to a particular drug through the Paragraph IV process, which triggers litigation between the parties to resolve the matter. Paragraph IV litigation is a lengthy and expensive process. 21 U.S.C. § 355(j)(2)(A)(vii) (detailing the requirements for certification when filing an ANDA); Annie Gowen, Comment: Saving Federal Settlement Privilege after *Actavis*, 83 U. CHI. L. REV. 1505, 1510 (2016) (noting that "Paragraph IV litigation can be extremely expensive"). Thus brand-name companies have an incentive to liberally list patents in the Orange Book, placing the burden on generics to engage in litigation for the purpose of knocking the patents out.

20 The brand-name company, which already has approval to market, can continue the brand product or sell a lower-priced version to compete with the new generic. The brand's version is known as an "authorized generic." Feldman et al., *supra* note 2, at 50, n. 35.

21 This process continues to be the subject of extensive manipulation and anticompetitive behaviors. Feldman & Frondorf, *supra* note 2, at 34–65 (describing pay-for-delay deals in which the generic company settles its Hatch-Waxman suit by agreeing to stay off the market for a period of time in exchange for cash payments of other complex side deals).

22 Feldman & Frondorf, *supra* note 2, at 20 (citing Ernst R. Berndt & Murray Aitken, *Brand Loyalty, Generic Entry and Price Competition in Pharmaceuticals in the Quarter Century after the 1984 Waxman-Hatch Legislation*, Working Paper No. 16431, NAT'L BUREAU OF ECON. RES. 10 (2010), www.nber.org/papers/w16431.pdf); U.S. FOOD & DRUG ADMIN., *Generic Drugs Facts*, www.fda.gov/Drugs/ResourcesForYou/Consumers/BuyingUsingMedicine Safely/UnderstandingGenericDrugs/ucm167991.htm (last visited Oct. 30, 2018).

23 *See id.*, at 67–69 (noting that branded drugs making large yearly sales, such as the $1.3 billion annual sales of the drug Flonase, have the potential to gain hundreds of millions of dollars in only months of delay).

24 *See* FED. TRADE COMM'N, GENERIC DRUG ENTRY PRIOR TO PATENT EXPIRATION 16–17 (2002), https://perma.cc/MF3N-MDMZ.

25 For an extensive examination of pay-for-delay settlements, *see* Feldman & Frondorf, *supra* note 2, at 34–65.

26 *See* Nate Raymond, *AbbVie, AndroGel Partner Owe $448 Million in Antitrust Case: U.S. Judge*, REUTERS (June 29, 2018), www.reuters.com/article/us-abbvie-lawsuit/abbvie-androgel-partner-owe-448-million-in-antitrust-case-u-s-judge-idUSKBN1JP3A8; *Fed. Trade Comm'n v. AbbVie Inc., et al.* No. 14–5151 (E.D. Pa. 2018).

27 *See generally* Robin C. Feldman & Prianka Misra, *The Fatal Attraction of Pay for Delay*, CHI-KENT J. OF I.P. (forthcoming) (arguing that pay-for-delay agreements continue to flourish).

28 *See supra* note 1 and accompanying text.

29 *Cf.* Dorothy Du, *Novartis AG v. Union of India*: "Evergreening," Trips, and "Enhanced Efficacy" under Section 3(d), 21 J. INTELL. PROP. L. 223, 228 (2014) (describing evergreening as "the acquisition of secondary patents on reformulations or minor modifications of pharmaceutical products in order to unfairly extend the monopoly over the drug beyond the life of the initial patent"); Janice M. Mueller & Donald S. Chisum, *Enabling Patent Law's Inherent Anticipation Doctrine*, 45 HOUS. L. REV. 1101, 1106 (2008) (describing evergreening as "obtaining related patents on modified forms of the same drug, new delivery systems for the drug, new uses of the drug, and the like").

30 For a detailed description of these and other evergreening techniques, see Feldman & Frondorf, *supra* note 2, at 69–79.

31 *See* Kapczynski et al., *supra* note 2, at tab. 1 (showing that 64 percent of patents for a given number of drugs were for chemical compound, whereas 81 percent and 83 percent were for formulation and method of use, respectively).

32 *See id.*, at 1, 5.

33 *See* C. Scott Hemphill & Bhaven Sampat, *Drug Patents at the Supreme Court*, 339 SCIENCE 1386, 1387 (2013). For a general explanation of pay-for-delay, *see supra* notes 21–27 and accompanying text.

34 *See id.*

35 *See* Robin Feldman & Evan Frondorf, *Drug Wars: A New Generation of Generic Pharmaceutical Delay*, 53 HARV. J. ON LEGIS. 499, 529–30 (2016), citing *U.S. Pharmaceutical Sales-2013*, DRUGS.COM, www.drugs.com/stats/top100/2013/sales (last visited Oct. 30, 2018) (describing this technique in detail and explaining how AstraZeneca effectively shifted the market from Prilosec to Nexium by switching the former to an over-the-counter prescription drug – a move that helped to establish Nexium as the second-bestselling drug, with almost $6 billion in sales).

36 *See* Ashish Kumar Kakkar, *Patent Cliff Mitigation Strategies: Giving New Life to Blockbusters*, 25 EXPERT OPINION ON THERAPEUTIC PATENTS 1353, 1357 (2015).

37 *See id.*

38 *See* Chana A. Sacks et al., *Medicare Spending on Brand-Name Combination Medications vs Their Generic Constituents*, 320 J. AM. MED. ASS´N 650 (2018).

39 *See id.*

40 *See* Terry G. Mahn, *The Patent Use Code Conundrum – or Why FDA Can't Read (Patents)*, PHARMACEUTICAL COMPLIANCE MONITOR (Oct. 17, 2014), www.pharmacompliancemonitor.com/patent-use-code-conundrum-fda-cant-read-patents/7715/.

41 *See* Arti Rai, *Use Patents, Carve-outs and Incentives in the Drug-Patent Wars*, 367 N. ENGL. J. MED. 491, 491 (2012) (noting that brand-name drug manufacturers have attempted to defeat certain generic company strategies by listing use codes that substantially exceed the scope of the use patent).

42 *See* Mahn, *supra* note 40.

43 *See Caraco v. Novo Nordisk*, 132 S. Ct. 1670 (2012).

44 *See* Rai, *supra* note 41.

45 *See* Kurt Karst, *Adieu, "Orange Book FR Safety or Effectiveness Determinations List"; Hello, "Orange Book Patent Listing Dispute List,"* FDA LAW BLOG (June 6, 2017), www.fdalawblog.net/2017/06/adieu-orange-book-fr-safety-or-effectiveness-determinations-list-hello-orange-book-patent-listing-di/.

46 *Caraco*, 132 S. Ct., at 1675 (noting that, although the FDA requires brand manufacturers to submit descriptions of the scope of their patents, known as use codes, it does not attempt to determine whether that information is accurate, but simply assumes that the information is an accurate description of the breadth of their patent scope). For an unusual counterexample, consider the case of Johnson & Johnson's drug Depomed. The company filed with the FDA that it "became aware" that the patent claim was broader than that which was reflected in the use code on file. *Cf.* Kurt Karst, *A New Orange Book First: FDA Unilaterally Changes a Patent Use Code*, FDA LAW BLOG (Nov. 20, 2016), www.fdalawblog.net/fda_law_blog_hyman_phelps/2016/11/a-new-orange-book-first-fda-unilaterally-changes-a-patent-use-code.html.

Consistent with its ministerial role, the Agency acquiesced and added a use code. *See id.* In this case, however, the FDA pushed back against the company and withdrew the use code as uninterpretable – an action that one source described as extremely unusual. *See id.*

47 *See supra* note 18 (describing requirements for a listing to be considered "timely filed" and penalties for failure to file on time).

48 *See generally* Robin Feldman, *Regulatory Property: The New IP*, 40 COLUM. J. L. & ARTS 53 (2016).

49 *See id.*, at 66.

50 *See id; see also infra* text accompanying notes 72–77 (briefly describing the Orphan Drug Act and subsequent manipulations).

51 *See* Feldman, *supra* note 48, at 69, 72–73, 83–92, 103 (describing 13 regulatory exclusivities with a chart of all of them at Appendix A).

52 *See e.g.,* Feldman & Frondorf, *supra* note 2, at 102–04 (discussing so-called skinny labels).

53 An expanded version of the methodology with additional details is available, along with the data on the Inter-University Consortium for Political and Social Research (ICPSR), at www.icpsr.umich.edu/icpsrweb/ (last visited Oct. 30, 2018).

54 U.S. FOOD & DRUG ADMIN., *Orange Book Data Files*, www.fda.gov/drugs/ informationondrugs/ucm129689.htm (last visited Oct. 30, 2018).

55 On its Orange Book Frequently Asked Questions page, the FDA states that, "Over time, there will be an archive for the annuals and each year's December Cumulative Supplement." Thus it appears that the FDA plans to make prior editions of the Orange Book available at some point in the future, but those prior editions are not easily accessible online at the present. Moreover, the FDA plans to make the Cumulative Supplements from only December available, excluding the Cumulative Supplements from the other months of the year. Using the December supplement, one would be able to see all the new patents and exclusivities added that year, but one would not be able to parse out in which month the patents and exclusivities had been added prior to December. For more details on the difference between "Annual Editions" and "Cumulative Supplements," and the information contained in each, please visit the Inter-University Consortium for Political and Social Research (ICPSR), www.icpsr.umich.edu/icpsrweb/ (last visited Oct. 30, 2018).

56 *See supra* note 53.

57 Dr. Donald Kennedy, Comm'r, U.S. Food & Drug Admin., *Keynote Address at the UC Hastings Conference: Faces of Forensics* (Mar. 2008).

58 Of course, a company *could* bring a novel drug to market and not apply for any type of patent or exclusivity. It would be unlikely, however, for a company to do so, given the associated market benefits of patents and exclusivities. It could also gain approval for a new drug late in the year and, in doing so, have those patents appear in the following year's Orange Book. We could not eliminate that possibility from our data set, which

represents a limitation of our analysis. In addition, we would expect that the number of drugs falling into any year-end would be small.

59 Feldman & Frondorf, *supra* note 35, at 530. Although the FDA found the new drug bioequivalent to the old one, Delzicol is listed as a separate new drug application from Asacol in the Orange Book. *Cf. id.*, at 530.

60 As an example, see the FDA's Center for Drug Evaluation Research Exclusivity Board's memorandum on granting both orphan drug exclusivity and new chemical entity exclusivity to Teva's drug Deutetrabenazine, and noting that, "it is appropriate to grant orphan drug designation to [the drug] without a plausible theory of superiority." Kurt R. Karst, *FDA Determines that Deuterated Compounds are NCEs and Different Orphan Drugs Versus Non-deuterated Versions*, FDA LAW BLOG (2017), www.fdalawblog.net/2017/07/fda-determines-that-deuterated-compounds-are-nces-and-different-orphan-drugs-versus-non-deuterated-v/, citing CDER EXCLUSIVITY BOARD, DETERMINATION OF WHETHER SD-809 (DEUTETRABENAZINE) AND TETRABENAZINE ARE DIFFERENT ACTIVE MOIETIES (2015).

61 Some scholars have suggested tailoring the patent award to provide different strengths of protection based on different invention characteristics, such as time-to-market. *See e.g.*, Benjamin Roin, *The Case for Tailoring Patent Awards Based on Time-to-Market*, 61 UCLA L. REV. 672 (2014). This approach, however, would add significant complexity to the system and provide endless opportunities for game playing. As noted in Chapter 6, section 6.4 (on ruthless simplification), complexity breeds opportunity. Drug companies have proven quite adept at exploiting those opportunities in ways that run counter to society's interests.

62 PRESCRIRE EDITORIAL STAFF, *New Drugs and Indications 2014*, 24 PRESCRIRE INT'L 109 (2015) (table showing that 66 out of 1,032 new products and indications provided an advantage, and 532 out of 1,032 provided "nothing new").

63 As explained in section 5.2 (on the methodology), *supra* notes 53–56 and accompanying text, we first compiled the top 50 bestselling, nonbiologic drugs from each year between 2005 and 2014. There is, however, a great deal of overlap between the bestselling drugs from one year to the next. We eliminated duplicates from year to year, which is why the number of drugs from each year between 2005 and 2014 is far less than 50.

64 *Cf.* Kapczynski et al., *supra* note 2, at 5 (finding that late-filed secondary patents are more common for higher-sales drugs).

65 I-MAK, OVERPATENTED, OVERPRICED: HOW EXCESSIVE PHARMACEUTICAL PATENTING IS EXTENDING MONOPOLIES AND DRIVING UP DRUG PRICES 2, 6 (2017).

66 *See* Kapczynski et al., *supra* note 2, at 1.

67 *See supra* note 1 and accompanying text.

68 For a description of other exclusivities that increased, as well as exclusivities that decreased, such as pediatric exclusivity, see Robin C. Feldman, *May Your Drug Price Be Ever Green*, J.L. & BIOSCI. (forthcoming).

69 *See* U.S. Food & Drug Admin., *supra* note 18.
70 *See* Orphan Drug Act, Pub. L. No. 97–414, 97 H.R. 5238, 97th Cong. (1983); Drug Price Competition and Patent Term Restoration Act, Pub. L. No. 98–417, 98 Stat. 1585 (1984); *see supra* note 13.
71 *See* Feldman, *supra* note 48, at 73–80 (exploring the history and implementation of the Orphan Drug Act, as well its consequences for pharmaceutical competition, in detail).
72 *See id.*, at 74.
73 The quoted phrase is drawn from the title of an article by Matthew Herder. *See* Matthew Herder, *When Everyone Is an Orphan: Against Adopting a U.S.-Styled Orphan Drug Policy in Canada*, 20 Accountability in Res. 227, 227 (2013); Michael G. Daniel et al., *The Orphan Drug Act: Restoring the Mission to Rare Diseases*, 39 Am. J. Clinical Oncology 210, 210 (2016); Food & Drug Admin., Ctr. for Drug Eval. & Research, 2015 Annual OGD Annual Report: Ensuring Safe, Effective, and Affordable Medicines for the American Public 10 (2015). In 2015, approximately 47 percent of novel approved drugs were orphan drugs. Food & Drug Admin., Ctr. for Drug Eval. & Research, Novel Drugs 2015: Summary 5 (2016).
74 *See* Feldman, *supra* note 48, at appx A (providing a detailed chart of the key exclusivities awarded by the FDA).
75 *See* Daniel et al., *supra* note 73, at 210, citing Andreas Hadjivasilou, *Orphan Drug Report 2014*, EvaluatePharma, 8 (Oct. 2014), http://info .evaluategroup.com/rs/evaluatepharmaltd /images/2014OD.pdf.
76 *See* Feldman, *supra* note 48, at 77.
77 Most commonly, "off-label use" refers to the prescription of a currently available medication for an indication (disease or symptom) that has not received FDA approval. It can, however, also refer to the use of a medication in a patient population, dosage, or dosage form that has not received FDA approval. *See* Christopher M. Wittich et al., *Ten Common Questions (and Their Answers) about Off-Label Drug Use*, 87 Mayo Clin. Proc. 982 (2012). The practice of off-label use is common, with rates of up to 40 percent in adults and up to 90 percent in some hospitalized pediatric populations. *See* Madlen Gazarian et al., *Off-Label Use of Medicines: Consensus Recommendations for Evaluating Appropriateness*, 185 Med. J. Aust. 544 (2006). Off-label prescriptions are legal and can allow for life-saving innovation in clinical practice. *See* Randall S. Stafford, *Regulating Off-Label Drug Use: Rethinking the Role of the FDA*, 358 N. Engl. J. Med. 1427, 1427 (2008).
78 *See* Shannon Gibson & Barbara von Tigerstrom, *Orphan Drug Incentives in the Pharmacogenomic Context: Policy Responses to the US and Canada*, 2 J.L. & Biosci. 263, 263–91 (2015).
79 *See id.*
80 *See id.*

81 *See* Sarah Jane Tribble & Sydney Lupkin, *Drugmakers Manipulate Orphan Drug Rules to Create Prized Monopolies*, KAISER HEALTH NEWS (Jan. 17, 2017), https://khn.org/news/drugmakers-manipulate-orphan-drug-rules-to-create-prized-monopolies/ (Kaiser Health News is not associated with the Kaiser Permanente health maintenance organization).

82 *See* Ted M. Burns et al., *Editorial by Concerned Physicians: Unintended Effect of the Orphan Drug Act on the Potential Cost of 3,4-Diaminopyridine*, 53 MUSCLE & NERVE 165, 166–67 (2016).

83 *See id.* Through the "compassionate use" program, patients with serious or life-threatening diseases are able to gain access to drugs that are still undergoing clinical trials if there are no comparable or satisfactory therapeutic alternatives available. *See* Alexander Gaffney, *Regulatory Explainer: FDA's Expanded Access (Compassionate Use) Program*, REG. AFF. PROF. SOC´Y (Feb. 4, 2015), www.raps.org/Regulatory-Focus/News/2015/02/04/18343/ Regulatory-Explainer-FDAs-Expanded-Access-Compassionate-Use-Program/.

84 *See* Sabrina Tavernise, *Patients Fear Spike in Price of Old Drugs*, NY TIMES (Dec. 22, 2015), www.nytimes.com/2015/12/23/health/patients-fear-spike-in-price-of-old-drugs.html.

85 *See* Alison Kodjak, *FDA Approval Could Turn a Free Drug for a Rare Disease Pricey*, NPR (Dec. 23, 2015), www.npr.org/sections/health-shots/ 2015/12/23/460719043/fda-approval-could-turn-a-free-drug-for-a-rare-dis ease-pricey.

86 Our results most likely understate the explosion of orphan drug products on the market, because many orphan drugs are approved and regulated as biologics. Biologics fall outside the scope of our study. In 2001, five of the ten bestselling biologic drugs were originally approved as orphan drugs, and three others were approved for orphan indications in addition to the original indication. *See* Daniel et al., *supra* note 73, at 211. It is no surprise that so many orphan drugs fall within the biologics category, given that modern biologics are usually targeted at small, particularized patient populations of the type that would qualify a drug for orphan designation. *See* Feldman, *supra* note 48, at 76. As the biologics field grows into its own, and as more comprehensive patent and exclusivity data on biologics trickles out, orphan drug biologics will certainly be an area of interest.

87 *See* Kurt Karst, *Updated Analysis Shows Patent Use Codes Have Nearly Tripled since August 2003*, FDA LAW BLOG (July 8, 2013), http://www.fdalawblog .net/2013/07/updated-analysis-shows-patent-use-codes-have-nearly-tripled-since-august-2003/. The metric used in Karst's analysis differs from ours in that he measured the cumulative, total number of use codes listed in the Orange Book each year, while we measured the number of distinct times that a use code was added to a patent, noncumulatively, by year. Thus our figures for each year cannot be compared directly to Karst's. For instance, Karst counted 627 total use codes listed in the Orange Book as of 2005. This would

include use codes added to patents in 2005, as well as use codes that were added in previous years. Meanwhile, we counted 162 instances in 2005 in which a use code was added to a patent.

88 It should be noted that our measurement was of the number of instances in which a use code was added to a patent. This would include instances in which a patent and its associated use code were added at the same time, as well as instances in which a use code was added to a previously listed patent. Often, one use code number is added to multiple different patents under the same drug, or multiple patents are listed under two different drugs; thus this is not a measurement of unique use codes.

89 Those numbers are 115, 166, 112, 172, 144, 166, 136, 195, 319, 293, 364, respectively.

Chapter 6

1 John Norton, *Media Scrutiny of PBM Corporations Ratchets Up – Part Two*, NAT. COMM. PHARMACISTS ASSOC. BLOG – THE DOSE (Apr. 7, 2016), www.ncpanet.org/newsroom/ncpa's-blog—the-dose/ncpa's-blog—the-dose—2016/2016/04/07/media-scrutiny-of-pbm-corporations-ratchets-up-part-two (using the Kennedy quotation in the context of questioning whether PBMs are good financial stewards of prescription drug plans).

2 *See* Tracy Staton, *AbbVie Chief Joins the 10% Price-Hike Pledge, but Other CEOs Aren't Buying It*, FIERCEPHARMA (Jan. 12, 2017), www.fiercepharma.com/pharma/abbvie-chief-adds-his-company-to-10-price-hike-pledge-but-other-ceos-aren-t-buying-it.

3 *See* Bob Herman, *AbbVie Believes Political Risks of Drug Pricing Are "Waning,"* AXIOS (Sept. 22, 2017), www.axios.com/abbvie-believes-political-risks-of-drug-pricing-are-waning-1513305689-47a42477-3a0b-432f-8e82-87c4d2760482.html (stating that AbbVie executives told analysts, in the context of its 10 percent pledge, that it could "revert to more than one price increase per year").

4 MERCK, Press release, *Merck Reinforces Commitment to Responsible Pricing* (July 19, 2018), www.mrknewsroom.com/news-release/corporate-news/merck-reinforces-commitment-responsible-pricing.

5 Katie Thomas, *Merck Is Lowering Drug Prices. There's a Catch*, NY TIMES (July 19, 2018), www.nytimes.com/2018/07/19/health/merck-trump-drug-prices.html.

6 *See* Chapter 3, sections 3.2.3 and 3.3 (discussing unintended consequences of the Affordable Care Act); Chapter 4, section 4.2.1 (discussing the unintended consequences of section 340B providers).

7 Second Am. Compl., at 9–15, *In re: Brand Name Prescription Drugs Antitrust Litig.*, No. 94–897 (N.D. Ill. 1994), CM/ECF LIVE, Ver 6.2.1; *see also* Peter J. Hammer & William M. Sage, *Antitrust, Health Care Quality, and the Courts*,

102 COLUM. L. REV. 545, 603, n. 145 (2002); *see also* KENNETH
G. ELZINGA & DAVID E. MILLS, THE BRAND NAME PRESCRIPTION
DRUGS ANTITRUST LITIGATION: THE ANTITRUST REVOLUTION 301, 305
(1999).

8 *See id.*, at 10–11; *In re Brand Name Prescription Drugs Antitrust Litig.* 186
F.3d at 783 (claiming that a discriminatory pricing scheme precluded plaintiffs from competing with other pharmacies for contracts with third-party
payors and for drug sales to customers not covered by third-party insurance
plans; stating that "price discrimination implies market power" and that
"plaintiffs argue that the source of the drug manufacturers' market power
manifested in their discriminatory pricing is collusion").

9 *See* Edwin McDowell, *Judge Agrees to Settlement in Drug Case*, NY TIMES
(June 22, 1996), www.nytimes.com/1996/06/22/business/judge-agrees-to-
settlement-in-drug-case.html; Final Order Approving Settlement between
Class Plaintiffs and the Purdue Frederick Company, *In re Brand Name
Prescription Drugs Antitrust Litig.*, No. 94–897 (N.D. Ill. 1994); *see also*
Elzinga & Mills, *supra* note 7, at 319.

10 Norman R. Augustine, Guru Madhavan & Sharyl J. Nass, *Making Medicines
Affordable: A National Imperative*, NAT'L ACADEMIES OF SCI., ENG'G, AND
MED. 76 (2017) [hereinafter NAS REPORT]. *See also id.*, at 53–54; INSTI-
TUTE OF MEDICINE, FINDING WHAT WORKS IN HEALTH CARE: STANDARDS
FOR SYSTEMATIC REVIEWS 17–18 (Jill Eden et al., eds., 2011) (observing how
it is often difficult to assess the quality of systematic research reviews docu-
menting the potential harms and benefits of medical interventions); Matthew
J. Page et al., *Bias Due to Selective Inclusion and Reporting of Outcomes and
Analyses in Systematic Reviews of Randomized Trials of Healthcare Interventions*, COCHRANE DATABASE SYST. REV. (2014) (exploring how the choice of
which outcomes to report in systematic reviews of healthcare interventions
may result in biased or inaccurate value assessments); INSTITUTE OF MEDI-
CINE, SHARING CLINICAL TRIAL DATA: MAXIMIZING BENEFITS, MINIMIZING
RISKS 17 (2015) (discussing challenges to determining intervention efficacy
from clinical trials research, including "lengthy time frame, high cost, and
often limited relevance of the research it produces").

11 *See id.*, at 56–57 (extensively describing how different health organizations deter-
mine value or what would constitute evidence of value). *See also* Jeffrey L.
Anderson et al., *ACC/AHA Statement on Cost/Value Methodology in Clinical
Practice Guidelines and Performance Measures: A Report of the American College of
Cardiology/American Heart Association Task Force on Performance Measures and
Task Force on Practice Guidelines*, 63 J. AM. COLL. CARDIOL. 2304 (2014) (the
ACC–AHA uses a cost-effectiveness framework that measures the treatment's
dollar value per quality-adjusted life-year, or QALY, while factoring in the quality
of evidence that treatment is beneficial); Lowell E. Schnipper, *American Society of
Clinical Oncology Statement: A Conceptual Framework to Assess the Value of Cancer
Treatment Options*, 33 J. CLIN. ONCOL. 2563 (2015) (ASCO uses a point-based

framework that considers clinical benefit, toxicity, palliation, and increased time off all treatment. The framework does not integrate the drug's score with cost); INST. FOR CLIN. & ECON. REV., OVERVIEW OF THE ICER VALUE ASSESSMENT FRAMEWORK AND UPDATE FOR 2017–2019 (2017) (the ICER value framework considers cost-effectiveness, clinical effectiveness, various contextual considerations such as ethical/legal issues, and overall budget impact on GDP); MEMORIAL SLOAN KETTERING CANCER CTR., *Drug-Abacus Methods*, https://drugpricinglab.org/tools/drug-abacus/methods/ (last visited Oct. 30, 2018) (value framework considers survival, toxicity, novelty, cost of research and development, rarity of the treated disease, and the burden of the disease on the U.S. population); NAT´L COMPR. CANCER NETWORK, *NCCN Clinical Practice Guidelines in Oncology (NCCN Guidelines) with NCCN Evidence Blocks*, www.nccn.org/evidenceblocks/ (last visited Oct. 30, 2018) (stakeholders judge value based on overall impression of efficacy, safety, evidence quality and consistency, and affordability).

12 *See* NAS REPORT, *supra* note 10, at 59; *see also* Jeanne S. Mandelblatt et al., *Evaluating Frameworks that Provide Value Measures for Health Care Interventions*, 20 VALUE IN HEALTH 186, 189–90 (2017) (proposing and applying criteria for evaluation of value frameworks to assess healthcare treatments); Stephen Barlas, *Health Plans and Drug Companies Dip Their Toes into Value-Based Pricing: The Pressure is on P&T Committees to Monitor Utilization*, 41 PHARMACY AND THERAPEUTICS 39, 39–41, 53 (2016) (describing that Amgen agreed to provide two "pay-for-performance" rebates if its drugs failed to obtain certain results, and citing performance-based agreements between drug manufacturers and insurers); Alan M. Garber & Mark B. McClellan, *Satisfaction Guaranteed: "Payment by Results" for Biologic Agents*, 357 N. ENG. J. MED. 1575, 1575–76 (2007) (noting an extreme instance in which Johnson & Johnson offered to waive charges for consumers who did not obtain desired results for one of its drugs).

13 NOVARTIS, Press release, *Novartis Receives First Ever FDA Approval for a CAR-T Cell Therapy, Kymriah(TM) (CTL019), for Children and Young Adults with B-Cell ALL that is Refractory or Has Relapsed at Least Twice* (Aug. 30, 2017), www.novartis.com/news/media-releases/novartis-receives-first-ever-fda-approval-car-t-cell-therapy-kymriahtm-ctl019.

14 *See e.g.,* Paul Melmeyer, *Comment on HHS Notice: HHS Blueprint to Lower Drug Prices and Reduce Out-of-Pocket Costs*, NATIONAL ORGANIZATION FOR RARE DISORDERS (July 16, 2018), https://rarediseases.org/wp-content/uploads/2018/07/NORD-2018-Comments-on-HHS-Blueprint.pdf. *See also* Alaric Dearment, *CVS Move Points to Growing Interest in Value-Based Drug Pricing*, MEDCITYNEWS (Aug. 22, 2018), https://medcitynews.com/2018/08/cvs-move-points-to-growing-interest-in-value-based-drug-pricing/.

15 TAKE CARE STAFF, *Drug Pricing Experiment Offers Oklahoma Rebate if Drugs Don't Work*, WRVO (Aug. 19, 2018), www.wrvo.org/post/drug-pricing-experiment-offers-oklahoma-rebate-if-drugs-dont-work.

16 Dylan Scott, *Drug Makers and Insurers, Longtime Rivals, Eye an Alliance on Prices*, STAT (2015), www.statnews.com/2015/11/24/drug-prices-health-insurers/; *see also* Eric Sagonowsky, *Lilly CEO: With Pharma Friends in High Places, It's "Time for Action" to Ease Drug Costs*, FIERCEPHARMA (2018), www.fiercepharma.com/pharma/lilly-ceo-says-pharma-hasn-t-done-enough-pricing-but-now-time (quoting Lilly CEO praising value-based pricing).

17 For example, one recent study concluded that Novartis' new Car-T drug Kymriah is overpriced, even including enough profit to underwrite both research and development successes and failures for the company. *See* Paul Kleutgen et al., *Drugs Don't Work if People Can't Afford Them: The High Price of Tisagenlecleucel*, HEALTH AFF. (Feb. 8, 2018), www.healthaffairs.org/do/10.1377/hblog20180205.292531/full/. Including these assumptions, the study estimated that the cost of the drug should be $160,000 for the one-time infusion, rather than the $475,000 planned by Novartis. *See id.*

18 *See* Laura Lorenzetti, *Is It Time for the FDA to Consider Cost When it Comes to New Drugs?*, FORTUNE (Feb. 4, 2015), http://fortune.com/2015/02/04/is-it-time-for-the-fda-to-consider-cost-when-it-comes-to-new-drugs/.

19 Paige Kelton, *Some Pharmacists Barred from Helping Patients Save Money*, ACTION NEWS JAX (Feb. 22, 2018), www.actionnewsjax.com/news/local/some-pharmacists-barred-from-helping-patients-save-money/705277162 (explaining that "[t]he key question is not: What's it worth to save a child's life... If that was the question, the polio (vaccine) they gave me when I was 6 years old would have cost a million dollars. The right question is: What is the price that will maximize accessibility and affordability, while maintaining a robust R&D pipeline").

20 *See e.g.,* PATIENTS FOR AFFORDABLE DRUGS, *Let's Negotiate*, YOUTUBE (July 26, 2018), www.youtube.com/watch?v=vzFXLIofASw&feature=youtu.be; Bernie Sanders, US Senator for Vermont, Press release, *Sanders Statement on Trump Drug Prices Address* (May 11, 2018), www.sanders.senate.gov/newsroom/press-releases/sanders-statement-on-trump-drug-prices-address; Anna Edney, *Trump Forces Pharma to Face More Medicare Drug-Price Negotiation*, BLOOMBERG (Aug. 7, 2018), www.bloomberg.com/news/articles/2018-08-07/trump-forces-pharma-to-face-more-medicare-drug-price-negotiation. *See also* Ed Silverman, *To Lower Drug Costs, CMS Wants Medicare Part D Plans to Loosen Formularies*, STAT (Aug. 30, 2018), www.statnews.com/pharmalot/2018/08/30/drug-costs-cms-medicare-formularies/ (describing an indirect move by the Administration, which will give Medicare drug plans the power to carry only certain versions of a medication on their formularies in the hopes that this will encourage greater negotiations between the plans and drug companies).

21 Juliette Cubanski & Tricia Neuman, *Searching for Savings in Medicare Drug Price Negotiations*, KAISER FAMILY FOUNDATION (Apr. 26, 2018), www.kff.org/

medicare/issue-brief/searching-for-savings-in-medicare-drug-price-negoti ations/; 149 Cong. Rec., S15671–2, 15736, 15760–1 (daily ed., Nov. 24, 2003) (Senator Frist arguing in support of a competitive market of private plans, which was ultimately included as policy in the Medicare Modernization Act of 2003); see also Medicare Prescription Drug, Improvement, and Modernization Act, Pub. L. 108–73.

22 42 U.S.C. § 1395w–111(i)

23 See Cubanski & Neuman, *supra* note 21. Additionally, Medicaid rebates are set by the federal government, although states can negotiate lower rebates. *See* Trish Riley, *Lower Drug Costs: The Next Frontier for State Flexibility*, HEALTH AFF. (Feb. 16, 2018), www.healthaffairs.org/do/10.1377/ hblog20180214.827973/full/.

24 See Letter from Douglas Holtz-Eakin, Director, Congressional Budget Office, to Sen. William H. Frist (Jan. 23, 2004), www.cbo.gov/sites/default/ files/108th-congress-2003-2004/reports/fristletter.pdf; CONGRESSIONAL BUDGET OFFICE, A DETAILED DESCRIPTION OF CBO'S COST ESTIMATE FOR THE MEDICARE PRESCRIPTION DRUG BENEFIT (2004), www.cbo.gov/ sites/default/files/108th-congress-2003-2004/reports/07-21-medicare.pdf.

25 Thomas Greaney, *The New Health Care Merger Wave: Does the "Vertical, Good" Maxim Apply?*, J.L. & MED. ETHICS (forthcoming); Erin E. Trish & Bradley J. Herring, *How Do Health Insurance Market Concentration and Bargaining Power with Hospitals Affect Health Insurance Premiums?*, 42 J. OF HEALTH ECON. 104 (2015); *see also* Anna Wilde Mathews, *Behind Your Rising Health-Care Bills: Secret Hospital Deals that Squelch Competition: Contracts with Insurers Allow Hospitals to Hide Prices from Consumers, Add Fees, and Discourage Use of Less-Expensive Rivals*, WALL ST. J. (Sept. 18, 2018), www.wsj.com/articles/behind-your-rising-health-care-bills-secret-hos pital-deals-that-squelch-competition-1537281963?mod=hp_lead_pos5.

26 15 U.S.C. §§ 1011–15.

27 15 U.S.C. § 1012(b).

28 See e.g., H.R. 1081, 110th Cong. (2007) (example of a bill seeking to amend McCarran-Ferguson that ultimately stalled in session); *see also* Charles D. Weller, *The McCarran-Ferguson Act's Antitrust Exemption for Insurance: Language, History, and Policy*, 2 DUKE L.J. 588 (1978) (describing the history of support for reform or repeal of the McCarran-Ferguson Act prior to 1978).

29 For examples of the ability of the pharmaceutical industry to extract benefits when faced with unpalatable legislation, *see* Robin Feldman, *Regulatory Property: The New IP*, 40 COLUM. J.L. & ARTS 53 (2016).

30 The Eighth Circuit, in 2018, overturned an Iowa transparency law, finding that the federal ERISA legislation pre-empts the state law. From this perspective, a different reading of ERISA could open the door to state legislation on transparency, as well as other issues. *See Pharmaceutical Care Management Ass'n v. Gerhart*, 852 F.3d 722 (8th Cir. 2018) (holding that ERISA

pre-empts an Iowa law that required PBMs to disclose how they priced pharmaceuticals to the state insurance commissioner from applying to PBMs that served ERISA plans).

31	Food and Drug Act of 1906, Pub. L. No. 59–384, 34 Stat. 768 (1907); Physicians Payments Sunshine Act of 2010, Pub. L. No. 111–48, 124 Stat. 689 (2010); Employee Retirement Income Security Act of 1974, Pub. L. No. 93–406, 88 Stat. 829 (1974). *See also* Laura Karas et al., Pharmaceutical Industry Funding to Patient-advocacy Organizations: A Cross-national Comparison of Disclosure Codes and Regulation, SANTA CLARA LAW REVIEW (forthcoming).

32	*See* ROBIN FELDMAN, VIRAL LICENSING (forthcoming).

33	Although a discussion of federalism and a state's power is well beyond the scope of this book, for an analysis of these issues in the context of state drug legislation, *see generally* Robin Feldman et al., *States' Rights: A Patent Law Analysis of NASHP Rate-Setting Model Act*, NAT'L ACAD. FOR STATE HEALTH POL'Y (2018), https://nashp.org/wp-content/uploads/2018/03/White-Paper-2018.pdf.

34	NAT'L ACAD. FOR STATE HEALTH POL'Y, *State Legislative Action to Lower Pharmaceutical Costs*, https://nashp.org/state-legislative-action-on-pharmaceutical-prices/ (last visited Oct. 30, 2018); *see also* Richard Cauchi, *LegisBrief: State Remedies for Costly Prescription Drugs*, NAT'L CONF. OF ST. LEGIS (2018), www.ncsl.org/research/health/state-remedies-for-costly-prescription-drugs.aspx.

35	EXPRESS SCRIPTS, VALUE BEYOND: DELIVERING MORE THAN MEDICINE: ANNUAL REPORT 4, 30–31 (2016), https://expressscriptsholdingco.gcs-web .com/static-files/777166b9-6d1a-4b3f-b979-f798b856955c [hereinafter EXPRESS SCRIPTS 2016 ANNUAL REPORT] (listing courts that have turned down their First Amendment requests); Jay Hancock & Shefali Luthra, *As States Target High Drug Prices, Pharma Targets State Lawmakers*, KAISER HEALTH NEWS (Feb. 1, 2018), https://khn.org/news/as-states-target-high-drug-prices-pharma-targets-state-lawmakers/; *see also* EXPRESS SCRIPTS 2016 ANNUAL REPORT, at 31–32, citing *Jerry Beeman & Pharm., et al. v. Caremark Inc., et al.*, No. 02–1327 (C.D. Cal. 2011) (noting that, upon remand, district courts denied defendants' motion to dismiss the case on First Amendment constitutionality grounds of a California law requiring the disclosure of retail drug prices to clients); *cf.* Initial Decision, *In the Matter of 1–800 Contacts, Inc.*, No. 9372 (Office of A.L.J. 2017) (denying defense to horizontal antitrust agreements that the parties were merely protecting their intellectual property). A recent decision from a California court, rejecting pharmacists' First Amendment protection claims against price transparency, may provide some indication of how future analogous laws and regulation will be treated. *See Beeman v. Anthem Prescription Mgmt. Inc.*, 2007 U.S. Dist. LEXIS 103220 (C.D. Cal. 2007).

36	*Pharm. Research & Mfrs. of Am. v. Brown*, 2018 U.S. Dist. LEXIS 148499 (E.D. Cal., filed Aug. 30, 2018) (federal suit in which Pharmaceutical Research and Manufacturers of America sued the state of California over a law requiring pharmaceutical companies to alert insurers of price increases above a certain threshold and of reasoning for the increase at least 60 days before the planned increase); *Pharm. Research & Mfrs. of Am. v. Sandoval,* 2017 U.S. Dist. LEXIS 149468 (D. Nev., filed Sept. 14, 207) (federal suit in which Pharmaceutical Research and Manufacturers of America and the Biotechnology Innovation Organization sued the state of Nevada over an insulin pricing-transparency law on basis of trade-secret protection); *Ass'n for Accessible Meds. v. Frosh,* 887 F.3d 664 (4th Circ. 2018) (federal suit in which the Association for Accessible Medicines sued the state of Maryland over a law that would allow the attorney general to monitor drug price changes and seek orders to reverse increases or issue fines); *Pharm. Care Mgmt. Ass'n v. Tufte,* 297 F. Supp. 3d 964 (D.N.D. filed Nov. 7, 2017) (federal suit in which the Pharmaceutical Care Management Association sued the state of North Dakota over a law that would ban gag orders on the basis of trade-secret protection).

37 *See* Letter from Marina Lao, Deborah L. Feinstein & Francine Lafontaine, Fed. Trade Comm'n Staff to Congressman Joe Hoppe & Congresswoman Melissa Hortman 4–5 (June 29, 2015), www.ftc.gov/system/files/documents/advocacy_documents/ftc-staff-comment-regarding-amendments-minnesota-government-data-practices-act-regarding-health-care/150702minnhealthcare.pdf (suggesting that requirements for public health plans to publicly disclose pricing and cost information may facilitate collusion); U.S. Dep't. of Justice & Fed. Trade Comm'n, Statements of Antitrust Enforcement Policy in Health Care 49–51 (1996) (describing an antitrust "safety zone" and stating that, without adequate safeguards, an exchange of price or cost data among healthcare providers can lead to collusion and increased prices); Fiona Scott Morton & Lysle T. Boller, *Enabling Competition in the Pharmaceutical Markets,* Working Paper 30, Hutchins Ctr. on Fiscal & Monetary Pol'y at Brookings 22–23 (May 2017), www.brookings.edu/wp-content/uploads/2017/05/wp30_scottmorton_competitioninpharma1.pdf; Leemore Dafny, Northwestern Univ. Professor, *Competitive Effects of Price Transparency* at 6 (on file with author); Joanna Shepherd, *Is More Information Always Better? Mandatory Disclosure Regulations in the Prescription Drug Market,* 99 Cornell L. Rev. Online 1, 1–2, 18–20 (2013) (stating that if pharmaceutical manufacturers know details of their competitors' rebate arrangements or price discounts, "tacit collusion among them becomes possible"); NAS Report, *supra* note 10, at 63–65 (advocating for true transparency in pricing information and citing arguments in opposition to transparency).

38 *See* Shepherd, *supra* note 37, at 19, n. 96; Dafny, *supra* note 37, at 7, citing Svend Albaek, Peter Møllgaard & Per B. Overgaard, *Government-Assisted Oligopoly Coordination? A Concrete Case,* 45 J. of Ind. Econ. 429 (1997); *cf.* David Besanko, David Dranove & Craig Garthwaite, *Insurance and the High Prices of Pharmaceuticals,* Working Paper No. 22353, Nat'l Bureau of

Econ. Res. (2016), www.nber.org/papers/w22353.pdf (noting that the economic demand model provides a rationale for drug companies to set prices above value and suggests that problems are worse with smaller drug firms, which cannot externalize as much of the costs, than larger ones).

39 *See* Ania Thiemann, *Serial Offenders: Why Some Industries Seem Prone to Endemic Collusion*, Org. for Econ. Coop. & Dev. 11, 30–31, 53 (2015) (stating that the cement and concrete industry frequently has been investigated for collusive behavior, with some serial offenders having been investigated or sanctioned more than ten times each); *see also* Joseph E. Harrington Jr. et al., *The Discontent Cartel Member and Cartel Collapse: The German Cement Cartel*, Discussion Paper No. 14–084, Ctr. for European Econ. Research, 7–8 (2014) (noting that cartel formation in cement markets is common because of economic and market factors that make collusive agreements profitable and stable, and describing a cartel among six large German cement companies in 1991 that lasted several years).

40 Fed. Bureau of Inv., *History: Al Capone*, www.fbi.gov/history/famous-cases/al-capone (last visited Oct. 30, 2018).

41 Letter from Eric R. Slusser, Exec. VP & CFO, Express Scripts Holding Co., to U.S. Sec. & Exch. Comm'n, Div. of Corp. Fin. (June 26, 2017); Letter from Joel Parker, Senior Assistant Chief Accountant, Office of Beverages, Apparel & Mining, U.S. Sec. & Exch. Comm'n, Div. of Corp. Fin., to Eric R. Slusser, Exec. VP & CFO, Express Scripts Holding Co. (Aug. 2, 2017); Letter from Bradley Phillips, VP, Controller & Chief Accounting Officer, Express Scripts Holding Co., to U.S. Sec. & Exch. Comm'n, Div. of Corp. Fin. (Aug. 30, 2017); Letter from Joel Parker, Senior Assistant Chief Accountant, Office of Beverages, Apparel & Mining, U.S. Sec. & Exch. Comm'n, to Eric R. Slusser, Exec. VP & CFO, Express Scripts Holding Co. (Sept. 29, 2017); Letter from Bradley Phillips, VP, Controller & Chief Accounting Officer, Express Scripts Holding Co., to U.S. Sec. & Exch. Comm'n, Div. of Corp. Fin. (Oct. 12, 2017).

42 Letter from U.S. Sec. & Exch. Comm'n to Express Scripts Holding Co. (Sept. 29, 2017), *supra* note 41.

43 Letter from Express Scripts Holding Co. to U.S. Sec. & Exchange Comm'n (Oct. 12, 2017), *supra* note 41.

44 *See* Linette Lopez, *The Feds Just Asked a Huge Healthcare Company Who Their Real Clients Are and the Answer Is Totally Unsatisfying*, Bus. Insider (Dec. 7, 2017), www.akleg.gov/basis/get_documents.asp?session=30&docid=42823 (citing accounting Professor Ed Ketz' comment that "at 40% [of receivables] we can start thinking of the pharmaceutical companies as customers. They're not just bystanders in this equation").

45 Express Scripts, Annual Report 2017 93 (2017), https://expressscriptsholdingco.gcs-web.com/static-files/76a9c03e-2e6b-4f6b-80de-fe80d4ebc826 (see esp. n. 13, 'Segment information'). That line item would also

include management fees that Express Scripts received for administering networks that are reported on a net revenue basis. *See* Letter from Express Scripts Holding Co. to U.S. Sec. & Exch. Comm'n (Aug. 30, 2017), *supra* note 41.

46 *See e.g., Chi. Dist. Council of Carpenters Welfare Fund v. Caremark, Inc.*, 474 F.3d 463, 477 (7th Cir. 2007); *In re Express Scripts, Inc., Pharmacy Benefits Mgmt. Litig.*, No. 1672, 2006 U.S. Dist. LEXIS 65168, at 18 (E.D. Mo., Sept. 13, 2006); *Mulder v. PCS Health Sys., Inc.*, 432 F. Supp. 2d 450, 456–59 (D.N.J. 2006); *N.Y. State Teamsters Council Health & Hosp. Fund v. Centrus Pharmacy Solutions*, 235 F. Supp. 2d 123, 128 (N.D.N.Y. 2002). For a discussion of these cases, along with the perspective that PBMs should *not* be held to a fiduciary duty under ERISA, see Thomas P. O'Donell & Mark K. Fendler, *Prescription or Proscription? The General Failure of Attempts to Litigate and Legislate Against PBMs as "Fiduciaries," and the Role of Market Forces Allowing PMBs to Contain Private-Sector Prescription Drug Prices*, 40 J. HEALTH L. 2 (2007). *Cf. supra* note 30 (describing an Eighth Circuit decision holding that ERISA pre-empts Iowa transparency law). For a general description of ERISA, see U.S. DEP'T. OF LABOR, *Health Plans and Benefits: ERISA*, www.dol.gov/general/topic/health-plans/erisa (last visited Oct. 30, 2018).

47 *See* Federal Acquisition Circular 2005–73, 79 Fed. Reg. 24191 (May 29, 2014); 41 U.S.C. §§ 3501–09.

48 41 U.S.C. § 3503.

49 For another potential, indirect approach to a portion of the problem, see text accompanying Chapter 4, note 68 (commentator suggesting that co-pay coupons from drug companies actually constitute unregulated insurance).

50 *See* Greaney, *supra* note 25. *See also* Chapter 2, note 78 and accompanying text; Murray Aitken et al., *Has the Era of Slow Growth for Prescription Drug Spending Ended?*, 35 HEALTH AFF. 1595 (2016); Ernst R. Berndt, Rena M. Conti & Stephen J. Murphy, *The Generic Drug User Fee Amendments: An Economic Perspective*, NAT'L BUREAU OF ECON. RESEARCH (2017); Ernst R. Berndt, Rena M. Conti & Stephen J. Murphy, *The Landscape of US Generic Prescription Drug Markets*, Working Paper No. 23642, NAT'L BUREAU OF ECON. RESEARCH (2017); Mark Duggan, Patrick Healy & Fiona Scott Morton, *Providing Prescription Drug Coverage to the Elderly: America's Experiment with Medicare Part D*, 22 J. OF ECON. PERSPECTIVES 69 (2011); Norton, *supra* note 1 (noting that pharmacy CVS owns PBM Caremark; that pharmacy Rite Aid, of which Walgreens announced its purchase in 2016, owns PBM EnvisionRx; that PBM Express Scripts owns specialty pharmacies; and that several PBMs own smaller pharmacies); see also Thomas L. Greaney, *Coping with Concentration*, 36 HEALTH AFF. 1564, 1565 (2017); see also Lisa Ellis, *Snapshot of the American Pharmaceutical Industry*, HARV. SCH. OF PUB. HEALTH, www.hsph.harvard.edu/ecpe/snapshot-of-the-american-pharmaceutical-industry/ (last visited Oct. 30, 2018) (noting that a few

companies hold the majority of market share in the drug wholesale market in the United States).

51 This is particularly important now that PBMs are merging or being acquired by health insurers. *See* Barak Richman & Kevin Schulman, *Mergers Between Health Insurers and Pharmacy Benefit Managers Could be Bad for Your Health*, STAT (June 1, 2018), www.statnews.com/2018/06/01/mergers-health-insurers-pharmacy-benefit-managers/ (outlining how these mergers could lead to increased drug prices and health insurance premiums).

52 On the practice of anticompetitive tying, *see Suburban Mobile Homes v. AMFAC Communities*, 101 Cal. App. 3d 532, 544 (1980) ("we emphasize that the power over the tying product (here, home sites) can be sufficient even though the power falls short of dominance and even though the power exists only with respect to some buyers in the market"); *cf. Jefferson Parish Hospital District No. 2 v. Hyde*, 466 U.S. 2, 27 (1984) (the court holding that an entity controlling 30 percent of a market does "not generate the kind of market power that justifies condemnation of tying").

53 *See* Fed. Trade Comm'n Act, 15 U.S.C. § 45(a)(1) (stating that, "in defining relevant market to be used in determining whether monopolization is present, Commission is not bound to follow antitrust standards as strictly as courts must under Sherman and Clayton Acts; ultimate objective of any criteria used is to delineate markets which conform to areas of effective competition and to realities of competitive practice").

54 *United States v. Microsoft Corp.*, 253 F3d. 34, 79 (D.C. Cir. 2001) (stating that anticompetitive conduct may be inferred when exclusionary conduct is aimed at producers of both nascent and established competitive technologies).

55 *See United States v. Microsoft Corp.*, 253 F3d. 34, 109–10 (D.C. Cir. 2001) (claiming that "it would be inimical to the purpose of the Sherman Act to allow monopolists free reign to squash nascent, albeit unproven, competitors at will – particularly in industries marked by rapid technological advance and frequent paradigm shifts"); *see also* Findings of Fact, *United States v. Microsoft Corp.*, No. 98–1232, 97 F. Supp. 2d 59, ¶60 (D.D.C. 2000) (noting that Microsoft recognizes nascent paradigms that could oust its position as a primary platform for applications development and user interface, especially in a market characterized by rapid and dynamic shifts).

56 *See* Robin Cooper Feldman, *Intellectual Property Wrongs*, 18 STANFORD J.L. BUS. & FIN. 250, 304–05 (2013) (describing the way in which parties could raise prices or limit supply in a particular product market, without holding monopoly power over that market, based on a portfolio of patents across multiple markets).

57 *See* PHILLIP E. AREEDA & HERBERT HOVENKAMP, ANTITRUST LAW VI ¶ 1402c (3rd ed., 2010) (describing hub-and-spoke conspiracies); *see also U.S.*

v. Apple, Inc., et al., 791 F.3d 290 (2d. Cir. 2015) (recent win against Apple and e-book publishers, in which publishers served as a hub).

58 *See e.g.*, Terrell McSweeny & Brian O'Dea, *The Implications of Algorithmic Pricing for Coordinated Effects Analysis and Price Discrimination Markets in Antitrust Enforcement*, 32 ANTITRUST 75, 76 (2017) (noting that "the potential that pricing algorithms will facilitate tacit collusion beyond the reach of Section 1 of the Sherman Act is far from fanciful"); *cf.* Plea Agreement at 3–4, *United States v. David Topkins*, No. 3:15-cr-00201-WHO (N.D. Cal., Apr. 30, 2015) (in which defendants used a pricing algorithm to implement a previously agreed-upon conspiracy).

59 *See* Zachary Tracer, *Amazon–Berkshire–JPMorgan Health Venture Takes Aim at Middlemen*, BLOOMBERG (June 24, 2018), www.bloomberg.com/news/art icles/2018-06-24/amazon-berkshire-jpmorgan-health-venture-takes-aim-at-middlemen. *See also* Reed Abelson & Tiffany Hsu, *Amazon, Berkshire Hathaway and JPMorgan Name C.E.O. for Health Initiative*, NY TIMES (June 20, 2018), www.nytimes.com/2018/06/20/health/amazon-berkshire-hathaway-jpmorgan-atul-gawande.html.

60 21 U.S.C. § 355(j)(2)(A)(vii)(IV).

61 *See e.g.*, *In re: Janssen BioTech, Inc.*, 88 F.3d 1315 (Fed. Cir. 2018).

62 *See id.*; *see also* Dennis Crouch, *Patent Games Cannot Save Blockbuster Remicade Patent*, PATENTLY-O (Jan. 23, 2018), https://patentlyo.com/patent/2018/01/patent-blockbuster-remicade.html (briefly describing the *Remicade* case and certain pre-GATT uses of the doctrine).

63 *Cf. Mayo Collaborative Services v. Prometheus Laboratories, Inc.*, 566 U.S. 66 (2012); *see also Alice Corp. Pty. Ltd. v. CLS Bank Int'l*, 134 S. Ct. 2347 (2014).

64 *See Alice*, 134 S. Ct. 2347, 2355, citing life science case *Mayo v. Prometheus.*

65 *See* Robin Feldman, *Coming of Age for the Federal Circuit*, 18 GREEN BAG 27 (2014) (describing the history of struggles between the Federal Circuit and the Supreme Court). For modern Federal Circuit resistance against the *Alice/Mayo* two-part test for patentable subject matter, *see e.g.*, *Amdocs (Isr.) Ltd. v. Openet Telecom, Inc.*, 56 F. Supp. 3d 813 (E.D. Va., 2014) (opining that there is no workable definition of an abstract idea); *Enfish, LLC v. Microsoft Corp.*, 822 F.3d 1327 (Fed. Cir. 2016) (admonishing that courts must be careful not to apply too high a level of abstraction and moving certain inquiries from the second part of the test into the first, so that the second part of the test is never reached).

66 *See* Adam Mossoff, *Patents as Constitutional Private Property: The Historical Protection of Patents under the Takings Clause*, 87 B.U.L. REV. 689, 691 (2007).

67 *See id.* (criticizing Supreme Court decisions from 1886 onward by referencing earlier Supreme Court and lower courts cases from the 1870s, as well as by arguing against those who view passage of sovereign immunity legislation in 1887 as mooting the earlier cases). *See id.*, at 701–10, 711–15.

68 *See Oil States Energy Servs, LLC. v. Greene's Energy Group LLC.*, 584 U.S. ____, slip op., at 16–17 (2018).

69 *See id.*, at 16.

70 *See* Robin Feldman, Rethinking Patent Law (2012).

71 *See* Donald S. Chisum, 5 Chisum on Patents § 16.02 (2010), citing *Cantrell v. Wallick*, 117 U.S. 694 (1886).

72 U.S. Const. art. I, § 8, cl. 8.

73 *Teva Pharm. USA, Inc., v. Sandoz, Inc.*, 135 S.Ct. 831, 848, n. 2 (2015) (Thomas, J. dissenting) (citations omitted), quoting Caleb Nelson, *Adjudication in the Political Branches*, 107 Colum. L. Rev. 559, 567 (2007).

74 *See id.*, at 847.

75 *Cf.* 37 CFR 1.131 (prohibition of double patenting by the same party).

76 See Feldman, *supra* note 70, at 160.

77 *See e.g.*, Robin Feldman & Evan Frondorf, Drug Wars: How Big Pharma Raises Prices and Keeps Generics off the Market 31 (2017) (describing the Paragraph IV first-filer exclusivity that encourages generic companies to enter the market swiftly to challenge brand name drugs), citing 21 U.S.C. § 355(j)(5)(B)(iv); *see also id.*, at 143 (noting that the brand name companies cannot receive more than one 30-month stay period on potential generic competitors); *see id.*, at 65 (noting that new legislation "requires that citizen petitions with the potential to affect generic approval... be considered within 150 days"), citing 21 U.S.C. § 355(q)(1)(F); *see id.*, at 49–65 (describing examples of the complex second generation of pay-for-delay settlements, taking place even after courts try to shut down pay-for-delay settlements of the first generation).

78 *See* Chapter 5. *See* Feldman & Frondorf, *supra* note 77, at 34–66.

79 *See* C. Scott Hemphill, *An Aggregate Approach to Antitrust: Using New Data and Rulemaking to Preserve Drug Competition*, 109 Colum. L. Rev. 629, 686–88 (2009), https://ssrn.com/abstract=1356530 (advancing the proposal and arguing that the law should require firms to actually earn their exclusivity).

80 *See* Feldman & Frondorf, *supra* note 77, at 144 (describing the step-transaction doctrine to advocate for more liberal use of standards-based approaches in the pharmaceutical field).

81 Food and Drug Administration Safety and Innovation Act, Pub. L. No. 112–44, 126 Stat. 993 (2012) (codified in 21 U.S.C. § 355(q)(1)(F)).

82 *See* Feldman & Frondorf, *supra* note 77, at 144.

83 21 U.S.C. § 355(q)(1)(E).

84 *See* Feldman & Frondorf, *supra* note 77, at 144 (proving "purpose," as required in the citizen petition context, is a tricky affair; any time intent is involved, the government stands at a disadvantage; the accused party can always counter that it had a perfectly legitimate idea in mind; thus concepts such as "primary effect" could be more useful).

85 *See* Robin Feldman et al., *Empirical Evidence of Drug Pricing Games: A Citizen's Pathway Gone Astray*, 20 STAN. TECH. L. REV. 39, 44 (2017).

86 *See* Michael Carrier & Carl Minniti, *Citizen Petitions: Long, Late-Filed, and At-Last Denied*, 66 AM. U. L. REV. 305, 332–33, tab. 4 (2016) (finding that 92 percent of citizen petitions filed by competitors against drug companies between 2011 and 2015 were denied by the FDA); Michael Carrier & Daryl Wander, *Citizen Petitions: An Empirical Study*, 34 CARDOZO L. REV. 249 (2012) (noting that 81 percent of citizen petitions filed by competitors against drug companies between 2001 and 2010 were denied by the FDA).

87 *See* Feldman & Frondorf, *supra* note 77, at 47 (describing the Provigil cases).

88 *See id.*

89 *See* 17 C.F.R. § 201.102(e); *see also* Robin Feldman, *Comment on the FDA Notice: Administering the Hatch-Waxman Amendments: Ensuring a Balance between Innovation Access; Public Meeting*, REGULATIONS.GOV (Sept. 19, 2017), www.regulations.gov/document?D=FDA-2017-N-3615-0071 (advocating using the SEC approach as a model for the FDA).

90 *See e.g.*, Brent Saunders, *Reverse Patent Trolls are Harming Drug Innovation – and Patients*, WALL ST. J. (Oct. 8, 2017), www.wsj.com/articles/reverse-patent-trolls-are-harming-drug-innovationand-patients-1507487600 (op-ed by CEO of Allergan, arguing that the 2011 patent reforms, which created a more effective post-grant review process at the Patent and Trial Appeal Board, left them with no choice but to transfer their patents to Indian tribes to avoid having their patents reviewed).

91 The price is a reference to list price for the anti-anxiety medication Latuda. *See Latuda Prices, Coupons and Patient Assistance Program*, DRUGS.COM, www.drugs.com/price-guide/latuda (last visited Oct. 30, 2018). For the inspiration for this sentence, *see* Jeff Mosenkis, *IPA's Weekly Links*, CHRIS BLATTMAN BLOG (Sept. 14, 2017), https://chrisblattman.com/2017/07/14/ipas-weekly-links-121/.

INDEX